CONCRETE AND COUNTRYSIDE

ILLUMINATIONS:
CULTURAL FORMATIONS OF THE AMERICAS
John Beverley and Sara Castro-Klarén, Editors

CONCRETE
AND
COUNTRYSIDE

Articulations of the Urban
and the Rural in 1950s
Puerto Rican Cultural Production

CARMELO ESTERRICH

University of Pittsburgh Press

Published by the University of Pittsburgh Press, Pittsburgh, Pa., 15260
Copyright © 2018, University of Pittsburgh Press
All rights reserved
Manufactured in the United States of America
Printed on acid-free paper
10 9 8 7 6 5 4 3 2 1

Cataloging-in-Publication data is available from the Library of Congress

ISBN 13: 978-0-8229-6539-8

Cover art by Carlos Aponte
Cover design by Jordan Wannemacher

To my mother, who lived the 1950s in a way I will never be able to write about.
To my husband—my ship and my anchor.
To Gregorio Ramos, in memoriam.

It would be interesting to study concretely the forms of cultural organization which keep the ideological world in movement within a given country, and to examine how they function in practice.

Antonio Gramsci, Notes for an Introduction and an Approach to the Study of Philosophy and the History of Culture, from *Prison Notebooks*

El estudio de la cultura precisa de un enfoque interdisciplinario que presente sus procesos y contenidos evadiendo las trampas del catálogo y la generalización al asumir que toda interpretación se expone al riesgo de creer en su propia voluntad de verdad y de dar forma definitiva y límites a aquello que es incompleto y maleable por su propia naturaleza: el horizonte pasado, presente y futuro de una cultura, múltiple en sus diversas texturas, lenguajes y simultaneidades de tiempo, espacio, sujetos y eventos.

The study of culture requires an interdisciplinary focus that sets forth its processes and contents, avoiding the traps of the catalog and the generalization, as it understands that every interpretation is open to the risk of believing in its own will to truth and of providing a definitive form and boundary to that which is incomplete and malleable by its very nature: the past, present, and future horizon of a culture, multiple in its diverse textures, languages, and simultaneities of time, space, subjects, and events.

Malena Rodríguez Castro,
"Piedra y palabra: Los debates intelectuales en Puerto Rico"

CONTENTS

Acknowledgments

UN MILLÓN DE GRACIAS

THERE IS AN APPARENT tendency in the academy to think of scholarship and publication as a competitive sport: who publishes first, who becomes canonical, who debunks most thoroughly. I don't see it that way.

I think of scholarly endeavors as an extended, multifarious conversation. I see my scholarly vocation as a gift—to other scholars, to students, to whomever is interested in what I write. At the same time, I cherish what other scholars have said and done, and I rely on their wisdom, expertise, and experience to build my thoughts and ideas before I put them in writing. So saying thanks, *dar las gracias*, is absolutely essential to me.

This book was an archival journey. Today a lot of the material I needed is available online; even most of the films are on YouTube now. But when I started the research for this book, everything was in archives and libraries in Puerto Rico and the United States. Archives can be tricky places, because one depends on the knowledge and professionalism of the archivists who work there. Even when bureaucracy and process sometimes drove me to distraction, I was lucky to work with generous, friendly, and helpful teams of librarians and archivists. In the early stages of research, I received wonderful assistance at Indiana University's Archives of Traditional Music, Columbia College Chicago's Center for Black Music Research, and Hunter College's Center for Puerto Rican Studies in New York. In Puerto Rico, at the Archivo de Imágenes en Movimiento, part of the Archivo General de Puerto Rico in San Juan, Marisel Flores Patton and Delfín Rodríguez were instrumental in giving me access to the film collection and papers of the División de Educación de la Comunidad (Division of Community Education), along with many other materials that I am using in this book. At the Puerto Rican Collection in the University of Puerto Rico Library in Río Piedras, Miguel Vega never tired of my asking for still more books and magazines, and, at the Fundación Luis Muñoz Marín, Julio Quirós was a model archivist. I also want to thank Chakira Santiago García of the Museo de Historia, Antropología y Arte at the UPR, for providing access to the museum's collection of the Centro de Arte Puertorriqueño (Center for Puerto Rican Art) graphic portfolios, and the staff at the University of Illinois Archives in Urbana, for all their help in combing through the Oscar and Ruth Lewis Papers.

What would scholars do without librarians? Tracy Leonard, Columbia College Chicago's interlibrary loan librarian, was the Wizard of Loans; she seemed to find everything. Copyright librarian Maryam Fakouri was my guiding light in a world of murky regulations and laws.

There are three Puerto Rican scholars who have formed and informed my argument in this book: the historian Silvia Álvarez Curbelo, the sociologist of music Ángel Quintero-Rivera, and the cultural studies scholar Catherine Marsh Kennerly. This book is what it is because of their scholarship. Thank you for thinking so beautifully and for sharing your ideas in books and conversation.

Friends and colleagues are amazing sounding boards. The idea of this book started decades ago in conversations with my dear friend Angel Santiago about the awesomeness of Cortijo y su combo, and many of those notions made it into the book. Early conversations with scholars Juan Gelpí, Frances Aparicio, Silvia Álvarez Curbelo, and Cati Marsh helped me figure out which way to go, but this book really found its shape as I chatted with Eugenio Ballou, Wilfredo Hernández, Gregorio Ramos, Carlos Aponte, Edna Acosta, Bernardita Llanos, Eric Miranda, and Reynaldo Román. My colleagues in the Department of Humanities, History, and Social Sciences at Columbia College Chicago were quite influential, especially Zack Furness, Rob Watkins, Sean Andrews, Teresa Prados-Torreira, Lisa Brock, Ann Gunkel, Jaafar Aksikas, and Andrew Causey. And then there's the love, support, and encouragement of my husband, Joseph Myers, and the many dear friends, especially Gregory Colombe, who were always certain I would finish this darn thing.

I remain very grateful for the support of three deans at Columbia College Chicago: Cheryl Johnson-Odim, Deborah Holdstein, and Steve Corey; their guidance and encouragement were helpful in surviving the long, perilous process of writing and putting a book together.

And, of course, students. I wrote this book while periodically teaching a course called Puerto Rican Culture: Negotiation and Resistance, and all of the conversations I had with my students there really shaped not only my ideas about culture and the arts in Puerto Rico but also the way to write a book that a wider audience could read and enjoy. My students kept my objectives real.

I don't know if this is common practice, but I actually want to thank the two anonymous readers who reviewed my manuscript: whoever you are, you were careful, amazing readers, and your meticulous comments have made *Concrete and Countryside* a better book. I appreciated your knowledge of Puerto Rico and its scholarship, and I was excited by your active engagement with my arguments and my perspectives. Of course, this means that I must thank my thoughtful editor Josh Shanholtzer and the University of Pittsburgh Press for choosing such good readers! And, also, John Beverly and Sara Castro-Klarén, the editors of the series in which this book is being published, for including my work among such excellent monographs. And to Alex Wolfe and Maureen Creamer Bemko, whose meticulous editing made me believe in fairy godmothers, as well as Maria Ortiz Myers, for joining me in the obsessive-compulsive world of indexing.

Unless specified, the prose translations are all mine, with the help of my husband's Anglo-linguistic prowess. But when it comes to songs and poetry, Joseph, with his typical generosity and his love for language (and my help with Spanish), translated them all. My eternal thanks for his talent and his love.

The research for this book was supported, in part, through two Columbia College Chicago Faculty Development Grants, plus the magic of sabbatical leaves.

I am grateful that, even though I don't teach in a publish-or-perish school, the college had these opportunities for developing my scholarly objectives.

I also want to thank all those who have helped with the process of copyright permissions and image preparation—Sergio Mundo, Carlos Aponte, Edna Acosta, Dominic Rossetti, Aaron "The Wiz" Green, Jovani Narváez and María V. Rivera from the Compañía de Turismo de Puerto Rico, and Marnie Pérez Moliere at the Museo de Arte de Puerto Rico—and a big thanks to the owners of copyright who allowed me to reproduce the gorgeous art, photographs, and song lyrics in this book, especially Pablo Tufiño and Marc Bauman.

And lastly, I want to thank my mother, Nilda Bermúdez Monserrate, a woman who grew up in the 1950s that I wrote about here and who was a living encyclopedia and a lovely listener throughout my research and my writing. *Te debo, literalmente, la vida.*

I am honored and excited to have Carlos Aponte as the artist who provided an illustration for the amazing cover of this book. Thank you for making such beautiful art!

Prologue

PRELIMINARY WORDS AND ACADEMIC ELUCIDATIONS

CONCRETE AND COUNTRYSIDE IS a multidisciplinary inquiry into the official, popular, literary, and media maneuverings in mid-twentieth-century Puerto Rico around a plethora of spaces and languages, rhythms and velocities, as well as practices and registers that have been historically, and somewhat problematically, summarized as the binary of the urban and the rural. The small farm, the "slums," and the sugarcane plantation; the public housing projects, the small country hut, and the shack on the outskirts of the city; the mountains, the highways, the rivers, and the cement bridges; the rural men and women and the new urbanites— all these, places that were deliberately transformed into metaphors and emblems; words that, with clashing cymbals, took on a nationalistic resonance; subjects who, many times disconnected from their surroundings and their historical subjectivities, were inserted into a national project of culture and identity.

Globally speaking, the multiple ways of imagining what is thought to constitute the rural and the urban, since at least the late eighteenth century, have been connected to the complicated accomplishments of the processes of modernization. Whether the discussion focuses on Argentina in the 1920s, Malaysia or Senegal in the 1960s, Egypt or Venezuela in the 1950s, or even England or France in the 1800s, the ways of thinking and representing urban and rural practices, spaces, and subjects are better understood within the context of that profound transformation. In Puerto Rico, as in many other nations of the Caribbean, the twentieth century was laden with the talk of modernization. But on this island, rapid and unprecedented industrialization and urbanization occurred under some unique situations: as a territory of the United States while the rest of the world was starting a process of decolonization; under bombardment by the promise of progress that economic development discourses were promulgating during these confrontational years of the Cold War; and under a charismatic governor, the first Puerto Rican elected to the post, who in the rise of leftist political revolutions in Latin America led the creation of a government that claimed a form of sovereignty through cultural nationalism without the need for political independence.

That centrality of culture is another reason why the midcentury is so foundational to Puerto Rico. Along with modernization, these years remain indispensable for making sense of that which wants to be named Puerto Rican culture today. This is when the newly formed government began to create a series of official spaces that directly or indirectly aided in establishing a national culture through the arts and when a cadre of visual artists and writers, filmmakers and composers obtained jobs that allowed them to work in this endeavor. Of course, this was a very particular notion of culture, one in which a certain version of rurality was paramount to its construction, and things urban never truly formed part of it. To be sure, this proto-official, national cultural project had its supporters—in academia, in some sectors of the media, in the general population—but it was not blindly embraced by everyone, not even by those same artists who were working for the government to foment it. And so a veritable explosion in the arts, albeit sometimes with radically different projects, began to tweak and question this national program, from inside those government offices, and also from outside, in art collectives, in literature and drama, even in popular dance music. Some did so by reconfiguring the rural constructed in that version of national culture, others by inserting elements of the urban into it, and in a few cases by responding with representations of a culture that summarily dismissed the rural/urban dichotomy. This book aims to explore those cultural negotiations in the arts produced during the middle years of the twentieth century as they maneuvered the momentous transformation of modernization and faced the deliberate materialization of a national culture on the island.

Concrete and Countryside would probably not exist if my teaching had not informed my scholarship the way it has. Like many who circulate around the colossal Modern Language Association and work on Latin America, I had my doctoral training in a Spanish department, where literature and language were the core of my courses and my expectations. In a typical academic conundrum, at the time of looking for a job I was expected to teach not only literature and language but also "culture," something graduate programs, at least in the late 1980s and early 1990s, simply did not have in their curricula. Theory was quite present— from Freud to Derrida, from Gramsci to Barthes—but no Mexican muralism, no Cuban cinema, no Chilean *arpilleras*, no Puerto Rican graphic arts, no Colombian punk. The early years of my first academic position I spent catching up with Latin American culture (popular and otherwise) to teach it in my classes every day, every semester. But it was there, in the classroom, that I soon discovered the necessity of multiple cultural texts to gauge and understand, to analyze and read culture in its complex configuration. It was there that I realized the importance of working through the arts, as well as making the arts dialogue with each other.

Indeed, this focus on the arts belies the unashamedly humanities orientation of this book, but I believe it is one that considers the boundaries of the humanities productively porous. Perhaps the most direct interdisciplinarity in *Concrete and Countryside* is the dialogue—and tension—that it maintains with that formidable antidiscipline called cultural studies. Something that has always attracted me about cultural studies—particularly as someone trained in the humanities—is its decidedly postaesthetic positioning. Regardless of the kind of cultural studies that one might practice—whether located within the Birmingham school or forged by scholarship produced in other regions of the world, whether housed in film and media studies, in qualitatively based analyses in anthropology or sociology, or in more textually based literature programs—the aim of cultural studies, paradoxically and wonderfully, moves beyond formal analyses but without forgetting form, and definitely beyond evaluative conversations about the good or bad quality of an artistic or cultural text. This permitted a different gaze: texts, practices,

and subjectivities could be studied and explored as symptomatic of the naturalized implications of that specific culture or as interventions that critiqued aspects
of that culture or unveiled its contradictions—in many cases the analysis could
even potentially include both gestures, depending on the query posed about
the cultural aspect in question. These ways of reading, in addition to the radical
importance of context (social, political, cultural, historical, etc.), the inherent
fluidity of culture, and the political gesture of the entire discipline—notions not
unique to cultural studies but fundamental to its project—have informed the way
I have approached Puerto Rico and its cultural production in this book.

But I don't embrace the project of cultural studies wholesale, at least in some
of the ways it has developed. For instance, there has been a tendency to approach
culture mostly through the wide spectrum of popular culture. The rationale
for this has been clear since its inception in the 1950s: the discipline in Britain
emerged from an urgent need to include other forms of cultural production
that had been dismissed and in some cases vilified by the academy. This is utterly
commendable. Still, I believe there is also a need to use the tools and methods of
cultural studies with artistic forms that are not usually considered popular: easel
painting or classical music, just to mention two examples. Indeed, some work
has been done in these areas, but it has been minimal compared to the focus on
popular forms of art. I hope that some parts of this book point toward ways of
achieving this.

Another tendency in cultural studies is to investigate and intervene in issues
of the "now"; the institute in Birmingham was, after all, called the Center for
Contemporary Cultural Studies. Perhaps this is an effect brought about by the
foundational idea of the structure of feeling, formulated by Raymond Williams in
the early 1960s in *The Long Revolution*, with its concomitant notion that we have
no real access to what it meant to live in the past. This inclination to remain in
the contemporary moment is no doubt a politically savvy position that recognizes
the trappings of tradition—of the selective tradition, Williams would have said—
but it has resulted in a lot of cultural studies work being reluctant to move away
from the most recent phenomena. This book develops from the belief that what
the field of cultural studies does can be equally useful in investigating previous
historical and cultural moments.

By now, some might be starting to wonder if this book is too obsessively grounded in the Birmingham school of cultural studies. Obviously, echoes of Raymond Williams and Larry Grossberg will be heard throughout the book, but also heard will be Arcadio Díaz Quiñones and Ángel Rama, Jesús Martín-Barbero and Graciela Montaldo, Frances Aparicio and Jorge Duany—Latin American scholars who have been examining questions of culture and politics, sometimes but not always in response to those "founding fathers" of the Birmingham school of cultural studies. Sophia McClennen is right in warning us about the beatification of those early scholars, but this should not mean their dismissal. There is a lot in there that is still quite suggestive today.

One more thing, if slightly marginal. Oscar Wilde said more than 120 years ago that "the highest as the lowest form of criticism is a mode of autobiography" (3). This book is not far from that very interesting notion.

CONCRETE AND COUNTRYSIDE

Part 1

THE MOMENTOUS 1950s
Bootstrapping Puerto Rican Culture

Aserrín aserrán
los maderos de San Juan
los de alante comen queso
los de atrás se quedarán.

Sawing off, sawing on
On the ramparts of San Juan
Those in front get cheese to eat and
Those in back get left behind.
Traditional children's rhyme

Todo parecía posible, nuevo, una frontera. Nos vacunaron, nos educaron, nos mudaron.
El pasado era la miseria, otro mundo, otro siglo, otro planeta.

Everything seemed possible, new, a frontier. They vaccinated us, they educated us,
they relocated us. The past was misery, another world, another century, another planet.
Arcadio Díaz Quiñones, "La vida inclemente"

CEMENTING MODERNIZATION

Soy el Desarrollo en carne viva
un dicurso político sin saliva.

I am Development in the flesh,
a political discourse gone dry.

Calle 13

Rápidamente y bien
no puede ser
no puede ser sin redes
entre la fábrica y el hambre.

Rapidly and well
Cannot be,
Cannot be, without ties
Between the factory and hunger.

Rafael Acevedo, "Quién" (Who?)

AS A CLEAR INDICATION that the Commonwealth of Puerto Rico had
achieved a level of development worth bragging about, on January 17, 1961,
the American biweekly magazine *Look* published a cover story about the island.
Entitled "Surprising Puerto Rico," this twenty-three-page spread assured Cold
War American readers that, for the most part, all was well in this territory of the
United States.

Look was a popular large-format magazine that attracted a very general audience and, like *Life*, its main competitor, consisted of striking color and black-and-
white photographs accompanied by short articles. The feature about the island
focused on its recent modernization and the dramatic transformation that had
been occurring under the recently established commonwealth and the administration of Luis Muñoz Marín, the first Puerto Rican governor elected by Puerto
Ricans themselves. He was by then in his fourth term of office.

"Surprising Puerto Rico" displayed for its readers some very telling images of
the island. Not surprisingly, the main focus was on tourism: the enticing cover
showed a young, light-skinned woman on the beach at Luquillo, on the northeastern coast of the island. She is looking up, with her eyes closed, and smiling,
clearly enjoying the bright and warm sunlight that bathed her face (a sight that
would have appealed to northern readers of that January issue). Similarly, the
first photos inside showed images of newly constructed hotels, swimming pools
with "local" girls, government-controlled gambling, and even a shot of Americans
hiking through the rainforest.

Look's choice of hotels was particularly interesting: all of them were done
in high modernist architectural style. In fact, the first page of the article was a
photograph of the thoroughly modernist La Concha Hotel, a building that had
just opened in the tourist area of El Condado. The photograph, which covers the
entire page, is stunning: it shows the façade of the hotel's main building, cropped
to show (and show off) its impressive *brise-soleil*—an exterior wall that allowed
sunlight to partially penetrate into the hallways of the hotel without having direct
sun heat up the area. This feature decorated the building with repetitive shapes of
partially cut-out diamonds. To scale the massive detail, the top of the photograph
had a proportionately minuscule couple, smartly dressed, enjoying the view from
the hotel. This was tourism with an ultramodern touch.

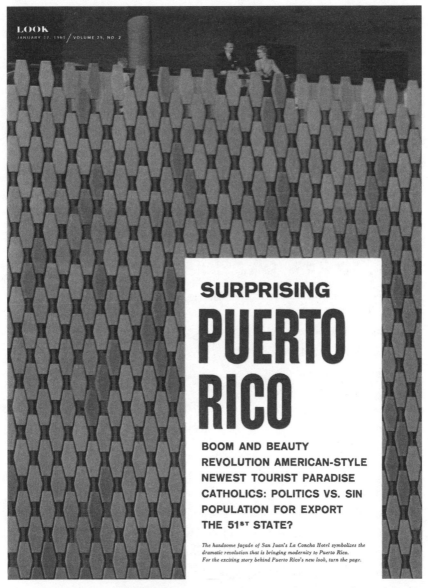

First page of *Look* magazine's cover story, featuring the La Concha Hotel in San Juan. Photograph by Frank Bauman, courtesy of Marc Bauman.

But the feature mixed these appealing and touristy photos with images of
another Puerto Rico: a helicopter putting the finishing touches on a power line
in the mountainous interior of the island; a former US Marine, now an engineer,
working at an oil refinery on the southern coast; a cement plant; new, sturdy,
low-income housing made out of concrete; an air-conditioned factory full of
diligently working Puerto Ricans. This was not only a tropical paradise but an
industrialized, modernized, urbanized Puerto Rico. And this is, in part, what
makes this *Look* issue so intriguing: it synthesized a number of key "looks" that
were prevalent during the 1950s and early 1960s, those years of furious development in the island. This imagery presented Puerto Rico as a desirable tourist
destination, as an appealing site for American economic investment, and as a
modernized space that deserved a second look.

The various texts that accompanied these photographs did not stray from
these "looks," but they did add some important dimensions to the image of the
island. The series of subtitles right under the title at the beginning of the piece
summarized, in a neat list, the desires and fears, the aspirations and expectations
of the United States for its territory:

> Boom and Beauty
>
> Revolution American-Style
>
> Newest Tourist Paradise
>
> Catholics: Politics vs. Sin
>
> Population for Export
>
> The 51st State? (21)

Here was a modernizing island that was revolutionizing itself without resorting
to "communist" ideologies, a place that marketed itself as the latest tourist haven,
with a booming economy to boot. But the list also pointed to issues that were
continuing to disquiet some sectors of the United States: the incessant migration
of Puerto Ricans to the mainland, the predominance of Roman Catholics on
the island (John F. Kennedy had just been elected US president), along with the
possibility of the island becoming the next state of the Union (Hawai'i and Alaska
had become states just a couple of years earlier).

Still, the first sentence that introduced the feature story gave the reader a sense of the uncontainable optimism—almost a sheer exhilaration—about Puerto Rico: "The long-time 'poorhouse of the Caribbean' is today a booming island in the sun. After 400 years as an under-the-heel colony, lovely, green Puerto Rico is attracting American factories and tourists and leaping into the modern world" (22). The sentence intimates many of the assumptions that had persisted in the United States' view of the island, some of them since its incorporation in 1898. The colonial oppression referred to here was that of Spain, which had had control of the island from the time Columbus landed on it in 1493 until it was ceded to the United States after the Spanish-American War. The United States' official rhetoric, since its military occupation, had historically contrasted Spain's "despotic" rule with its own, which was always presented as benevolent and humane; as a matter of fact, in the official rhetoric the colonial rubric was always applied to Spanish domination, never to American rule. *Look* continued this gesture of presenting "lovely, green Puerto Rico" as an undoubtedly decolonized island, one where poverty was in the process of being eradicated and industrialization was well under way.

The cover story also signaled a dramatic change in the way Puerto Rico had been portrayed in American mass media. In fact, *Look*'s piece should be seen in contrast to an issue *Life* magazine had published about the island in the early 1940s. There, the island was portrayed as a lost case, overpopulated, filthy, and crammed with slums in its urban areas. This article is headed by a photograph of El Fanguito, an infamous slum that First Lady Eleanor Roosevelt had visited in the early 1930s and that had grown quite a bit by the time the *Life* photographer arrived on the island at the beginning of 1943. The article's tone is the polar opposite from the feel of *Look*'s first sentence, quoted above: "The picture above and those on the following pages are a shocking disgrace to the U.S. They portray conditions in our island possession of Puerto Rico. . . . The face of Puerto Rico has always been dirty and its belly empty. There are few places in the world with slimier slums, more acute poverty, or a denser population" ("Puerto Rico: Senate Committee" 23). *Life* insisted on the embarrassment of possessing an island in such squalid conditions and saw no immediate way to solve its problems; *Look*, in contrast, persisted in an optimism that was willing to erase any problematic side effect of modernization. For instance, if, as mentioned above, one of the subtitles on the first page of the feature story in *Look* revealed a certain anxiety toward Puerto Rican migration to the mainland, this might simply have been a journalistic ploy to lure the reader in, since the articles themselves presented the new residents as a welcome addition to the working-class population of the United States. *Look* even predicted that in the next fifteen years, the mayor of New York would be Puerto Rican ("Surprising Puerto Rico" 44).

It would be accurate to say that this optimism was partly due to the island government's progressive policies; the magazine included a two-page spread on Gov. Luis Muñoz Marín and a section on Felisa Rincón de Gautier, the energetic woman who served as mayor of San Juan. But what actually seemed to be driving the exhilaration of *Look*'s rhetoric was the commonwealth's embracing of the post–World War II reigning discourses of development: capitalist-driven industrialization, infrastructure-based modernization, and American-inspired social progress and urbanization. To be sure, Henry Luce, publisher of *Life*, always found every opportunity to criticize Pres. Franklin D. Roosevelt's administration—and the 1943 article was no exception—but the almost two decades that separated the two articles had witnessed a transformation in world politics: *Look*'s optimism toward Puerto Rico was fed by the ideological scaffolding of the Cold War.

This optimistic view is clearest in the way *Look* frequently contrasted Puerto Rico with the island of Cuba, which had just ousted dictator Fulgencio Batista and where a group of young rebels, led by Fidel Castro, were making radical changes in Cuban society, including the nationalizing of several American companies.[1] Even though Castro had not yet declared himself a Marxist-Leninist at the time of the *Look* issue, the US government had already enacted a partial economic embargo against the island, and it regarded Castro's government as dangerously close to practicing communism.

The near hysterics of the Cold War were plainly evident in some of *Look*'s captions—for example, "Pro-Castro propaganda is hidden in second-grade readers sold for use by pupils in Puerto Rican schools" ("Surprising Puerto Rico" 33)—but it is perhaps the use of the word *revolution* that most persuasively communicated the magazine's eagerness to push for the commonwealth's professed radical changes in the context of American anxieties toward left-wing social transformations. The island's development and modernization were frequently labeled "the Puerto Rican revolution," and the section on Muñoz Marín was titled "The Practical Revolutionist" (30); elsewhere, the director of the economic development office, Teodoro Moscoso, was described as "the general of the revolution" (36). Even the dramatic image of the La Concha Hotel that opens the feature was captioned as symbolizing "the dramatic revolution that is bringing modernity to Puerto Rico" (21).[2] Needless to say, the magazine presented the island's "[r]evolution American-[s]tyle" (22) as an alternative to communist revolution because it seemed, from the perspective of the Puerto Rican government and the United States, that the "poorhouse" was no more.

Inadvertently, though, a different and intriguing issue becomes evident as one goes through the photographs and the brief articles that compose *Look*'s feature story: the conundrum of the urban and the rural. In the typical gesture of mid-twentieth-century development, the focus on industrialized, modernized Puerto Rico implicitly called for the ineluctable urbanization of the island. When the rural was presented, it was because it had just been filled with newly built concrete homes. Nonurbanized spaces were presented as recreational spaces— like the spot where those American tourists were trekking the rainforest, for example, or even the beach on the magazine's cover. The agricultural was, not surprisingly, absent, though it was indirectly referred to in a breathtaking full-page photograph of a warehouse owned by the Serrallés family (a prestigious rum producer) showing a veritable mountain of sugar sacks about to be shipped to the United States. Clearly, as far as *Look* was concerned, Puerto Rico was a once-upon-a-time rural society, a status that authenticated the success of the modernization process. In Muñoz Marín's Puerto Rico—that modern "island in the sun" that the local government dubbed the "Showcase of the Caribbean"—it seemed that the countryside had decidedly yielded to all things urban.

FROM PEASANTS TO URBANITES

It would not be an exaggeration to say that Puerto Rico went from being a principally rural society to becoming an unavoidably urban one in a matter of fifteen years. Someone who was living in the countryside in 1948 could very possibly have been living in some sort of urban space by 1964: either in a town or in the capital of San Juan, if they were not in a large city in the United States, in the Mid-Atlantic region, or in the Midwest. This brisk transformation from the late 1940s to the early 1960s is plainly evident in three speeches given by Luis Muñoz Marín throughout his sixteen years as governor of the island. These speeches not only document this transition but also reveal how the rural and the urban were perceived during these years and how that perception was enmeshed in the discourses of the time.

On February 23, 1949, in his inaugural speech as the first elected Puerto Rican governor of the island, Muñoz Marín envisioned the need for a certain balance toward the improvement of life: "La batalla para la vida buena no ha de tener todo su énfasis en la industrialización. Una parte ha de estar en la agricultura" (The battle for the good life can't have all its emphasis in industrialization. A part of it has to be in agriculture) ("Mensaje" 439). The sentence is curious, because Muñoz Marín presented the island as a space of factories and fields, not one of cities and countryside. His language was thus unmistakably and irrevocably aligned with economics and development—the notion of the urban being somewhat superseded by industrialization, while the countryside was transfigured as agricultural. It was indeed the agricultural that ruled supreme as metaphor in this speech, as he spoke of the new era about to begin in Puerto Rico: "Me parece que podemos hacer una regla tan simple como la semilla y tan honda como el futuro que lleva dentro: que todas nuestras decisiones sean tomadas a base de conciencia, y de conciencia que busque siempre estar informada" (It seems to me that we can make a rule as simple as the seed and as deep as the future that it carries inside: may all our decisions be made based on insight, and on an insight that always aims to be informed) ("Mensaje" 436). With this image of the seed, the governor reaffirmed a connection with the rural population, as the island embarked on its rapid modernization.

By the inaugural speech of his second term, however, delivered on January 2, 1953, Muñoz Marín had little choice but to face the increasingly urban quality of the island. Still somewhat unwilling to let go of the countryside, he pointedly called for a certain rurality to deal with the seemingly inevitable urbanization of Puerto Rico: "Estamos inexorablemente disminuyendo el campo y agrandando las ciudades. . . . No se puede preservar la manera rural en la vida urbana, pero será noble el esfuerzo de buscar en nuestra educación, en nuestro sentido de nosotros mismos, una manera de adaptar en alguna forma válida el buen saber del campo a la vida de nuestra industrialización en marcha. Veo éste como un objetivo digno en nuestro ideal cultural" (We are inexorably diminishing the countryside and enlarging the cities. . . . Rural ways cannot be preserved in urban living, but it is worth the attempt of searching for, in our education, in the sense of ourselves, a way of adopting in some valid way the good rural wisdom for our life under industrialization. I see this as a worthy objective in our cultural ideal) (qtd. in Sepúlveda Rivera 70). Since the rural space was now literally disappearing, Muñoz Marín could only resort to a call for the "good rural wisdom" as a sort of antidote to urban ways, as a way to preserve a "sense of ourselves." Although industrialization is still referred to here, the economic development platform has now yielded to urban concerns, with a marked sense of loss for rural ways and the assumption that something positive, something "noble," had been lost in the process.

By Muñoz Marín's last address as governor, on February 11, 1964, the countryside was not part of his language anymore. As an image, it was totally gone: "Debemos derivar lo más aproximadamente posible la ciudad que le sirva al espíritu de Puerto Rico, ciudad de iniciativas arquitectónicas, de vecindarios que faciliten la buena relación humana, de rica producción industrial, de excelentes servicios de educación, cultura, reposo, comercio, vida social, actividad cívica y religiosa" (We should develop, as much as we possibly can, a city that can serve the spirit of Puerto Rico, a city of architectural initiatives, of neighborhoods that furnish good human relations, of rich industrial production, of excellent services in education, culture, leisure, commerce, social life, civic and religious action) (qtd. in Sepúlveda Rivera 70). At the end of his administration, Muñoz Marín continued to be concerned with quality of life, but it was now the quality of urban life. As Aníbal Sepúlveda Rivera accurately points out in his remarkable four-volume work *Puerto Rico urbano*, the governor who became the leader of Puerto Rico in 1948 by connecting with the peasantry was in 1964 not addressing that population anymore (77): his audience, the peoples of Puerto Rico, were now urbanites.[3] And the so-called "spirit of Puerto Rico"—affected, absorbed, and transformed by the materiality of modernization—had ceased to be rural.

URBAN AND RURAL TENSIONS, FLOWS, ASSEMBLAGES

These transformational middle years of the twentieth century were without a doubt momentous for Puerto Rico. And to a certain extent what made this point in time so important (and the Muñoz Marín speeches are clear indicators of this importance) was its intricate connection to the semiotic power of the city and the countryside, the cultural and political appropriations of country folk and urbanites, and the transculturation of social practices linked to living, working, and playing in cities and towns and away from them.

To be sure, because of its focus on contextualized representational effects, this book limits itself to questions of the country and the city as images—indeed, as socially and culturally constructed images. But this constructedness does not mean (and should never mean) that these images are simply arbitrarily "made up." As Nestor García Canclini and Rebecca Biron stress frequently in their work on urban imaginaries, the city is not simply an imagined place; it is also a material, real place, inserted into historical and social conditions. García Canclini asserts, "We should think about the city as simultaneously a place to inhabit and a place to be imagined. Cities are made of houses and parks, streets, highways, and traffic signals. But they are also made of images. These images include the maps that invent and give order to the city. But novels, songs, films, print media, radio, and television also imagine the sense of urban life" (43). There is, then, a rich materiality in both the city imagined and the city corporeal; as Biron clearly surmises, "the urban imaginary is both a real and a made-up projection" ("Introduction" 8), with effects on and consequences for how the city represents and is represented. The same argument on materiality, of course, can be made for the countryside and things rural.

But what exactly is regarded as urban or rural, what ideas are implicit in these concepts, what desires are inscribed in them, what effects these notions produce by being installed as a binary—even what to call their relationship—are issues complex and paradoxical, and fraught with unreliable foundational assumptions. These issues have occupied writers, artists, and scholars from multiple disciplines for quite some time—not only because the issues are not at all recent in

Western thought (we could go as far back as Virgil, Horace, and Theocritus, if not back to the epic of Gilgamesh), not only because they vary due to historical, geographical, and cultural specificities but also, and especially, because myriad modernization strategies and narratives have drastically transformed the geopolitical landscape of the globe.

I am not particularly interested in definitions that are grounded on the measurable material space of the rural and the urban, those classifications that take into account geographical area covered or population data, including the policy-friendly and intensely simplistic rural-urban continuum, which constructs a shades-of-gray scale while still maintaining a rigid, quantitatively based narrative about what constitutes the urban and the rural. But neither do I want to rely on those lingering notions that persist even today in establishing the urban and the rural as an essentializing binary: the city of progress and cosmopolitanism versus the backward, even retrograde rural; the immoral, polluted, alienating space of the urban versus the purifying, communal nature of the rural; even the urban as the place to escape the rural and vice versa.[4] Counteracting this tendency to think of the two notions as Manichaean opposites, I am interested in the productive effect of interrogating and destabilizing this dichotomy.[5]

As many have pointed out, picturing the relation between the urban and the rural as a "divide" presupposes a neat demarcation line that, at least since the early twentieth century in Latin America, has unquestionably deteriorated—if it ever existed at all. In his studies of Mexico City, García Canclini has unpacked some of the assumptions that have been made about this divide. Not only does a clear demarcation between the two produce insufficient definitions, but "the distinction is limited to superficial traits" because it does not take into consideration "the structural differences [or] the similarities that sometimes arise between what happens in the city and what happens in the countryside or in small towns" (38). More specifically, the binary fails to account for the fact that the boundaries between the rural and the urban are unbelievably porous; as García Canclini correctly admits, "we often describe our Latin American cities as having been invaded by the countryside" (38).

Indeed, this permeable character partly derives from an incontrovertible issue of flow. One of the principal reasons (if not the only reason) for the difficulty of fixing notions of the urban and the rural is that the phenomenon of migration—be it nomadic, permanent, diasporic, or circular—has persistently undermined such attempts, especially in those cases where urbanization and industrialization accelerated the phenomenon. Migration is an effect of modernization, but it is the effect of an image as well: the paradigmatic flow toward the city has frequently been the consequence of a certain representation of what the city depicts and signifies for those who do not live in it. Thus, the flow of migration ultimately does away with the possibility of a veritable "divide" between what is rural and what is urban because, many times, the countryside is already in the city.

The binary sometimes assumes a curious chronology: the rural is sequentially placed before the urban—even Raymond Williams's required reading on the topic, *The Country and the City*, does not avoid this in its title. Some might object to what I am implying, but it seems to me that a faulty narrative has crystallized here, by granting the rural an originary place in regard to the urban, a relation that is irresolute at best, since (as it will be clear in this book) many ideas and images about the rural in fact originate in the urban space. But more importantly, the gesture pushes the rural dangerously close to a notion of the natural: if the urban has been represented and historicized as artificial and "built"—literally, human made—then to designate the rural as natural belies its historical and cultural configurations. The images of the rural must never be portrayed as natural: in more ways than one, the rural is also, like the urban, human made.

I am not advocating here for simply abandoning the terms. While it is crucial to destabilize them, it is also important not to dismiss them. If they have somewhat disappeared from recent scholarship in the humanities—possibly due to the clearly problematic nature of defining the rural and the urban usefully—the rural and the urban are too encroached culturally in many historical moments to simply set them aside, not only in Latin America and the Caribbean but globally speaking as well. Indeed, these are incredibly stubborn concepts, and the binary is still active today, replicating itself incessantly, from advertising to food labels, from environmental movements to movies, and it was very much alive in twentieth-century Latin America, when modernization strategies used and abused it. It is true that defining the city as what the countryside is not conveys some fundamental problems; however, it is undeniable that there are material and social imaginary elements that have been, historically and culturally, attached to things urban and things rural. The danger is to ignore their contextual character and carelessly naturalize those features.

Arguably, one way to begin rethinking this relation is, following Biron, to reconfigure it as a tension, one that pushes and pulls at the naturalized notions historically mapped within the urban and the rural ("Marvel" 119). I remain quite compelled by this. Still, perhaps something more drastic needs to take place: a dismantling of sorts, a conceptual implosion that might potentially liquefy the persistent dichotomy.

A way to trigger this is to finally acknowledge that these two concepts are not exactly a binary. They are and always have been pure heterogeneity. The farm and the isolated hut, the forest and the ocean shore, the plantation and the forest preserve, the resort and the manicured state park relentlessly complicate the conception of the rural. A similar list could, of course, be summoned for the multiplicities of the urban. In addition, the supposed binary has privileged certain meanings over others for each category. The urban is almost always connected to the large city but seldom to the small town. The most common assumption of the rural is to think it agricultural, deemphasizing and almost thinking inconceivable the rurality, for example, of a beach or a rainforest.[6]

It seems to me much more fertile—if I may be allowed a traditionally rural metaphor!—not only to take up this multiplicity of rurals and urbans but to confront them in order to force the units to resist and elude clear and "useful" definitions, dismantling their essentialized boundaries and limiting equivalences. One suggestive way of reconfiguring these multiplicities could be to rethink them and partly reimagine them with a gesture drawn from the theoretical work of Gilles Deleuze and Félix Guattari: to potentially conceive the rural and the urban as assemblages.

The assemblage, central to Deleuze and Guattari's work in the monumentally difficult and infinitely thought-provoking *A Thousand Plateaus*, strikes at the core of the Western notion of a binary: instead of conceiving in twos, the French thinkers propose the notion of conceptualizing from a system of multiplicities. The assemblage is in fact composed of different fields of content—desires, enunciations, apparatuses—and these fields perennially intersect and interact. In an

assemblage, not simply "lines" but complexes of lines draw up and map out organizations that simultaneously fix and disperse, stratify and decodify, construct
and dismantle (Patton 42). To use their well-known terminology, an assemblage
reterritorializes and deterritorializes. In addition, as Teresa Rizzo explains, the
assemblage needs to be imagined as a radically open system, "made up of connections between different bodies, discourses and institutions." This open quality,
she continues, suggests an incessant transformation that is intrinsic to it: "[a]n
assemblage is never fixed because a change in the relationship between any of
these bodies, discourses and institutions reverberates throughout the whole
assemblage, and in so doing changes the nature of that assemblage" (8). To be
sure, this seems to point to a potentially precarious instability in an assemblage,
but this is ultimately advantageous, enabling even, because under this pressure
the assemblage remains dynamic, susceptible, fluid, loose.

I do not intend with this theoretical appropriation to simply strip the case
of Puerto Rico of specificity, contextuality, historicity. But conceptualizng the
urban and the rural as Deleuzo-Guattarian assemblages would bring to the fore
the multivalent, paradoxical, and historically intricate uses of these terms in the
context of Puerto Rico and twentieth-century Latin America. Since the middle
years of the last century, which is the scope of this book, seem to have articulated the conundrum of the urban and the rural at the peak of its complexity and
contradiction, the notion of the assemblage would facilitate the laying bare of the
intricacies of these concepts as they were appropriated and capitalized through
the transformative narrative of modernization on the island. Taking a close look
at the historical context of these years is therefore necessary, for it will ground
the notions of the rural and the urban within the material, social, economic, and
political transformations of Puerto Rico.

IN THE AMERICAN CENTURY

Admittedly, the profound transformation of the island was hardly an isolated
phenomenon; it has been the modernizing gesture the world over for the last
two centuries. But if modernization in midcentury Puerto Rico—with its rapid

pace, fervent industrialization, far-reaching urbanization, and massive migrations to cities—was not, globally speaking, rare, the geopolitical situation of the island from the late 1940s to the early 1960s makes it a particularly rich and layered case study. Modernization occurred there, shaped by the reigning economic development discourses of the time, which were bolstered by the expansive, international economic boom that followed World War II. Developmentalism defined this era in Latin America and was, as Ramón Grosfoguel affirms, "a crucial constitutive element in the hegemony of the West" (329), especially of the United States. The universalist assumptions of development, in its attempt to materialize a notion of inevitable stages of progress to economically transform traditional societies into modern ones, were useful tools in the years of the Cold War, both to counteract so-called communist regimes and to establish the internationalization of capitalism (319). Puerto Rico was, without a doubt, part of that project, helping to fulfill the United States' ideological messages of these years. Add to this the fact that the island was an unincorporated territory of the United States, lest we forget, right at the moment of African, Asian, and Caribbean decolonization.

In their history of Puerto Rico, César J. Ayala and Rafael Bernabe very accurately labeled the twentieth century in Puerto Rico the "American Century."[7] The island, which had been a Spanish colony for more than four centuries, was "acquired" by the United States during the Spanish-American War of 1898. Puerto Rico was, with the Philippines and Cuba, the United States' first colonial venture—if we discount the expansion to the West as a colonial gesture—and in many ways it would define the relations of the North American nation with Latin America, as well as with Asia. Although it is sometimes slightly overstated, becoming an "unincorporated possession" of the United States radically changed for Puerto Rico the political, economic, and cultural debates throughout the twentieth century.[8]

After a short, strictly military administration, the Foraker Act of 1900 enacted some timid progress toward allowing Puerto Ricans to have some say, albeit incredibly limited, in government affairs: it allowed, for example, the creation of a legislative branch in which some of the members were required to have been born on the island (Scarano, *Puerto Rico* 656). In 1917 the Jones Act gave a bit more political power to Puerto Ricans within the government structure; more importantly, it extended American citizenship to all Puerto Ricans (some would say it imposed citizenship on them). Citizenship complicated matters: here were nationals who, in their own island-territory, had little political power locally and none federally. And if there was any possibility of achieving independence from the United States, citizenship now made it close to impossible, at least through legal means. On paper, these might have looked like efforts toward that democracy on which the United States had built its global reputation—a democracy that initially excited some sectors of the island at the time of the invasion—but they were, in fact, nothing but minuscule, counterproductive gestures that further evinced the colonial nature of their relationship. The string of island governors during the first half of the century—a series of North Americans never elected but rather appointed by the president of the United States, some simply inefficient despite their good intentions, others catastrophically inept, a few honestly brutish—reinforced this imperial character.

The political status of the island became a central question, and the parties that were formed partly based their agendas on what they believed should be the proper and most advantageous relationship with the United States: either total annexation to the Union (becoming a state), total separation (becoming politically independent), or remaining in association with the States but in a way that would afford Puerto Ricans more egalitarian participation in matters of government, economics, and social justice. Many Puerto Ricans and a few political parties advocated for independence from the United States. The Nationalist Party, founded in 1922 and led by the charismatic Pedro Albizu Campos from 1930 on, was perhaps the loudest voice calling for total separation—but there were sizable groups advocating for the two other possibilities as well.

The success in the late 1930s of a newly formed party, the Partido Popular Democrático (PPD, or Popular Democratic Party), and the rise to power of its leader, Luis Muñoz Marín—first as senator and later as the first elected governor—would secure in 1952 what is to this day the official relationship with the United States: the so-called Estado Libre Asociado, literally, the Free Associated State. Originally Muñoz Marín and his party had independence as part of their platform, but they gradually moved away from this idea to advocate for a sort of

US-controlled sovereignty. The fact that Muñoz Marín remained as governor for four consecutive terms, between 1948 and 1964, assured the system's permanency.

It is important to point out that Muñoz Marín's government project benefited greatly from the historical moment in which it developed. Amid widespread global decolonization after World War II, the United States found itself in the rather awkward situation of being in possession of what could clearly be labeled a colony. Although American administrations at the time never used that word, both the federal government and the island's government were aware of the potential validity of the claim. The official translation into English of "Estado Libre Asociado de Puerto Rico" as the "Commonwealth of Puerto Rico" let slip the desire to conceal that colonial relationship.

Indeed, this form of government gave more political agency to Puerto Ricans on the island through democratic means. The commonwealth was backed by a constitution (approved by Congress though first drafted by Puerto Ricans themselves) that created a tripartite system, with elected officials, almost identical to the one in the United States. But the power of the US federal government over the island remained unchallenged: issues of "citizenship, immigration, coastwise shipping, commercial treaties and foreign relations, and all matters related to military activity, currency, and tariff policy" (Ayala and Bernabe 163) were not to be altered by the new government of the island. Congress and the federal courts still had unquestionable power. The colonial relation remained in place, regardless of the organizational changes in politics.[9]

To counter this conundrum, Muñoz Marín and his intelligentsia felt the need to find a way to forge a feeling of sovereignty within this clearly nonautonomous political status. Their strategic solution was to adopt a notion of cultural nationalism: the idea that Puerto Rican cultural identity was sufficient for creating a sense of independence from the United States. The strategy permitted, officially at least, sidestepping discussions of political nationalism, which would obviously have led to questions of sovereignty. To this day, cultural nationalism continues to be, in many ways, the reigning discourse of Puerto Ricans on the island and in the diaspora.[10]

But Puerto Rico's calling card during the middle years of the twentieth century was the unprecedented plunge into a gigantic process of modernization.

Under the leadership and encouragement of Muñoz Marín, a group of legislators, engineers, academics, business executives, and media practitioners embraced a project of development, urbanization, and industrialization that set into motion far-reaching changes in the island. These were the years of vast concrete construction, of Levittownesque subdivisions, of frequent and well-publicized factory openings, of road and highway construction, of televised culture. It is true that the 1940s had ushered in a series of government agencies established to manage and monitor the infrastructure of the island: a bus transport authority, a water distribution and sewage administration, a state-run power company offering hydroelectric energy, a communications bureau.[11] But with the consolidation of the commonwealth in the early 1950s, the rhetoric of progress became an all-too-real, day-to-day experience for Puerto Ricans.

Arcadio Díaz Quiñones, one of the most important thinkers concerned with the cultural effects of the commonwealth structure, paints a very accurate rendition of these times vis-à-vis modernization: "Todo parecía posible, nuevo, una frontera. Nos vacunaron, nos educaron, nos mudaron. El pasado era la miseria, otro mundo, otro siglo, otro planeta" (Everything seemed possible, new, a frontier. They vaccinated us, they educated us, they relocated us. The past was misery, another world, another century, another planet) ("La vida inclemente" 33). Change, newness, progress brought forth an ebullient optimism bordering on euphoria.

Not unlike the *Look* magazine issue discussed at the beginning of this chapter, there were numerous magazine and newspaper articles, newsreels, brochures, and posters, both in Spanish and in English, that disseminated and praised the "wonders" of the commonwealth. In fact, these were the years when Puerto Rico was displayed to the world as the "Showcase of the Caribbean," a label that was used ad nauseam by government offices and commonwealth supporters to present the island as a successful, capitalist example of a developing nation in the Caribbean basin. With the flare characteristic of Cold War rhetoric, Muñoz Marín boasted in a 1956 speech, "[W]e have insisted in making Puerto Rico a training center for technical assistance, a laboratory for visitors from the New World and even Africa and Asia, so that they may see for themselves our unrelenting and peaceful war on colonialism, poverty, disease, ignorance, and hopelessness—carried out in terms of a deep sense of friendship, of brotherhood with the U.S." ("America to Serve the World"). The voyeuristic ecstasy of capitalism transformed the island into a desirable political object to be gazed at; it was the Showcase of Development. And Muñoz's language laid bare the contradictions of colonialism and capitalism in the face of modernization. Emilio Pantojas-García, in his work on the political economy of the island during the midcentury period, expresses it quite well: "The island was presented to the colonial and underdeveloped world as a successful example of a 'pacific revolution,' living proof of the 'virtues' and 'benefits' of capitalist development in close cooperation with the imperialist metropolises under new forms of colonial and neocolonial arrangements" (88).

But Díaz Quiñones's quote astutely points to the discursive contradictions of progress as well: misery and illiteracy, hunger and illness were expediently erased from the present (though empirical evidence proved otherwise) and relegated to a newly constituted past, seemingly remote and incontrovertibly gone. The enthusiasm in the present existed to make the future possible, and the past was recalled to demonstrate the extraordinary present. The citizens of the commonwealth were necessarily educated, healthy, and clean. Never mind the critical housing problems in the city due to the rapid migration of rural subjects and the social disruption of urban communities that were massively displaced; never mind the social effects of the euphoria for factories and tourism; never mind the lack of efficient mass transit (the assumption being that all Puerto Rico needs is cars). This would be, fundamentally, the paradox of the commonwealth years: modernization, come hell or high water.

There was, of course, more to these years: the modernization paradox was made all the more complex by the relationship that the commonwealth, its supporters, and even some of its critics had with some elements of Puerto Rican rurality. This was particularly pertinent in the eventual consolidation of the rural as the location of a Puerto Ricanness that would become useful for the strategies surrounding cultural nationalism. Those first dozen years of the commonwealth could be summarized thus: concrete and countryside.

SIGNS OF THE TIMES

It could be argued that the navigations and contradictions of the period were neatly packaged in two ubiquitous official images, two branding visual icons, two veritable logos: on the one hand, the silhouetted profile of a *jíbaro*—the name for a rural peasant on the island—wearing the traditional hat as the emblem for Muñoz Marín's Popular Democratic Party; on the other, the image of a shirtless factory worker used by the Oficina de Fomento Económico, the commonwealth's Industry and Economic Development Office. These images encompassed some of the official, government gestures: the adoption of the rural peasant to represent the national subject (and to speak on behalf of the island as a whole) and of the urban factory worker to represent industrialization and development. These emblems also illustrated the complexity of the rural and the urban—in its many configurations—during Puerto Rico's process of modernization.

La pava, the original emblem of the Partido Popular Democrático.

Resembling an old fashioned cut-out, the silhouetted jíbaro was synecdoch-
ically called *la pava*, after the light-colored straw hat with upturned edges that
once upon a time was worn by male peasants in many parts of the island. The
image was adopted by Muñoz Marín's party for campaign purposes at the end of
the 1930s, and it became the iconic identity card of the party—so much so that
it was common to call it *el partido de la pava* (the party of the pava). As Nathaniel I. Córdova has explained, the choice was a stroke of genius: using a visual
representation of the common peasant, of the "simple man" from the countryside, the Popular Democratic Party visually gave agency—electoral and political
agency—to the rural subject through its emblem (175).

The emblem, of course, also reinforced the party's populist agenda. As the
historian Silvia Álvarez Curbelo has explained, twentieth-century populism
emerged in Latin America as a response to a series of crises: a political crisis
connected to the oligarchy, an economic crisis of capitalism (especially between
the world wars), and a social crisis stemming from a call for agency in the working classes and the peasantry (14). Populism, through a series of consolidating
narratives, tried, and in some cases managed, to dismantle politico-economic
and social contradictions to create a new symbolic and discursive order, one that
would create an effective and galvanizing, albeit problematic, national project
(16, 18). The character of populism in Puerto Rico had additional particularities,
though, especially because of its colonial status. To sidestep more problematic
terms like "nation" or "state," the Popular Democratic Party's preferred phrase
at the time was *el pueblo de Puerto Rico* (the people of Puerto Rico). Implying in
Spanish both nation and people, the word *pueblo* was quite the magical word,
the balm that helped the party soothingly sweep away questions of sovereignty
while mythographically integrating the island's amalgam of race and class into
a populist community.[12] And that pueblo, in party rhetoric, was unmistakably
jíbaro. But, as many scholars have pointed out, the jíbaro had been recuperated
by certain scholars and by the cultural elite of the island as a symbol of authenticity in the face of the American cultural influence that had been increasing since
1898; thus, by appropriating the jíbaro, Muñoz Marín's party managed with one
masterful stroke to unite the disenfranchised peasantry with those elite subjects
who had felt economically displaced by American corporations.[13]

Muñoz Marín's political appropriation of the rural subject did not end with
the emblem of the party. In a deliberate act of rhetorical and performative
cross-dressing, he presented himself as a jíbaro. A campaign postcard the party
printed up in the 1940s (Córdova 170) shows Muñoz Marín leaning against a
palm tree while pensively looking off into the distance; in the upper left corner
of the card, curiously resembling a religious ex-voto, there is a ghostlike image
of a jíbaro wearing the pava and leaning on his horse. The card's composition is
such that it implicitly suggests that the politician is thinking of the rural subject.
But what is curious here is that one seems to be the replica of the other: the body
pose of Muñoz Marín and the jíbaro are almost exactly alike.

This transfiguration did not limit itself to the visual realm. Perhaps the most
effective way in which Muñoz Marín achieved it was through his speeches and
conversations with the people of the island—in straightforward, simple language.
The jíbaro Taso Zayas, the ethnographic subject in Sidney Mintz's influential book
Worker in the Cane, explains the stark contrast of Muñoz Marín's language with
that of other politicians of the time:

> Before, at political meetings the leaders would hold forth, and it was truly elo-
> quent oratory, truly lovely. But what we heard we did not understand—orations
> about the mists, the seas, the fishes, and great things. Then, when Muñoz Marín
> came, he didn't come speaking that way. He came speaking of the rural worker,
> of the cane, and of things that were easier to understand. And the people could
> go along with him, understanding and changing. And so they learned to trade the
> mists and the sea for the plantain trees and for the land they were going to get if
> they gave the Popular party their votes. (187)[14]

If perhaps Muñoz Marín's appropriation was not precisely a "jíbaro masquerade,"
as the historian Francisco Scarano described politicians on the island during the
early 1800s, there was perhaps a sense in all this that the traditional politician
had, snakelike, shed his skin.[15]

The emblem of the party was usually accompanied by the post-*zapatista* slogan
"Pan, Tierra, Libertad" (bread, land, liberty).[16] Bookended by the eradication of
hunger and the promise of freedom, the slogan suggested that the land did indeed

have a central focus in the project of the PPD, especially in its first years—there had been attempts at limiting landownership by large corporations, especially American sugar companies, albeit with meager success. The party's emblem was thus invested in the rural subject and the rural space: the land in the slogan, needless to say, never referred to the urbanite, who didn't need it, but to the men (and only by extension, women) of the countryside. Nevertheless, with the wave of industrialization and the installation of the commonwealth in the 1940s and 1950s, the concept became more of a symbolic gesture attached to the jíbaro and less a project in itself.[17]

HANDS ON THE WHEELS OF PROGRESS

The modernization frenzy that defined the 1940s and 1950s had one important visual tag: all around the island, billboards were posted marking the site of yet another industrial or construction feat by the government's economic and industrial development agency, the Compañía de Fomento Industrial. These billboards always prominently displayed Fomento's logo: a shirtless man, with powerful, muscled back and arms, wearing pants and boots and turning a gigantic cogwheel with his bare hands. If the silhouetted pava was designed as a static portrait (and a slightly antiquated one), the "man from Fomento," as he was generally called, was active, agile, strong, and mega masculine; if the jíbaro of the party's emblem was only a head in profile, a man passively posing, here we had a full-bodied man in action. The body posture resembled a bas-relief, but he was strategically facing away, no doubt to portray him as an everyman and to exempt him from any sign connected to race or ethnicity; he was squarely portrayed as a universalized, modern, albeit male, working citizen.[18]

The Compañía de Fomento Industrial was the agency that would take charge of Muñoz Marín's industrialization project. Created in 1942, it immediately began to open government-funded factories, such as bottle factories and cement plants, though these were not very successful (Picó 262). Soon after World War II, Fomento was totally reorganized: the state factories were sold to the private sector and the agency's principal goal became to attract foreign (read, US)

Emblem of the Compañía de Fomento Industrial

corporations to establish manufacturing plants that would produce material for export (Pantojas-García 62). The postwar global economic expansion made this strategy quite successful, and the industrialization of the island took off at an unprecedented rate.

It is important to point out that Fomento's industrialization project was contingent on the island's relationship to the United States: Muñoz Marín and his cadre believed "access to the North American market was the key for Puerto Rico's future development" (Ayala and Bernabe 189). Industrial investment in a colonial space was, needless to say, quite advantageous to the United States:

A common currency (the U.S. dollar) and the absence of federal taxes; the availability of abundant cheap labor with a low degree of unionization (or with unions controlled by the government or U.S. unions); the free trade between Puerto Rico and the United States that made the island an ideal location for companies interested in producing for the U.S. market; and "political stability," which meant

that the presence of U.S. military bases in Puerto Rico and the very fact that the
only army in Puerto Rico was the U.S. Army was the ultimate guarantee against
any political upheavals that might threaten U.S. interests. (Pantojas-García 72)

Fomento was also the principal driver of the development discourses that were
taking hold in the United States' relations with Latin America, a strategy in
which modernization necessarily meant that economic growth could succeed
only through industrialization. The "man from Fomento" became the persistent
visual reminder of the government's development project: to push the island
away from its "third-worldness," or as Grosfoguel has described it, "the solution
to backwardness . . . is to develop, to catch up with the West" (330). And the
man behind Fomento, Teodoro Moscoso, its first director, was soon regarded in
the United States as a masterful spokeperson for development: his stature was
confirmed in 1961, when President Kennedy hired him to lead the newly created
Alliance for Progress.

Moscoso, an integral member of Muñoz Marín's intelligentsia, was acutely
aware of how industrialization would be a major factor in changing the image of
Puerto Rico in the world. The logo was only the tip of his iceberg. As A. W. Maldonado has stressed in his monograph on Moscoso, during his tenure with Fomento
the director was responsible for the favorable nine-page spread on the island that
Life magazine published in 1949; it prominently featured the agency. In the mid-
1950s, Moscoso actually hired David Ogilvy—considered by many the father
of modern advertising in the United States—to develop an image campaign for
Puerto Rico. Moscoso even tried to change the lyrics of *West Side Story*'s "America"—especially the line "Puerto Rico, you ugly island" (Maldonado, *Teodoro Moscoso* 103). Under Moscoso, "public relations, media relations, image-building . . .
moved to the heart of the Fomento program" (106). Fomento was an industrialization agency whose approach was decidedly focused on marketing.

This orientation is best exemplified in Moscoso's involvement in the strength-
ening of the tourism industry, an economy that depended on a positive, inviting,
and attractive image of Puerto Rico. Right after the end of World War II, Fomento
became intimately involved in the establishment of the first Hilton hotel outside
the continental United States (Bolívar Fresneda 74). The Caribe Hilton opened

its doors in 1949 with great fanfare, as a symbol of a new chapter in the island's tourism push.[19] Tourism, as Dennis Merrill has meticulously demonstrated, was also an integral part of the development project in Puerto Rico. "Scratch a tourist," Moscoso liked to say, "and you'll find an investor underneath" (qtd. in Merrill 191). In a very real way, the development and tourism gazes, which I would argue guided and steered many actions of the commonwealth in its first years, were ideologically the same, and Fomento officials were intensely aware of this.

If one examines the two icons as a pair, the pava and the man from Fomento sum up the double gesture of the commonwealth: a conscious effort to uphold tradition through the appropriation of the rural subject as the citizen of the new government configuration, as well as the embrace of progress based on the American model of modernization embodied in development strategies. The official discourses, then, imagined a new Puerto Rico through a *homo ruralis* (the jíbaro) and a *homo economicus* of sorts (the Fomento man), though not, curiously enough, through a *homo urbanus*. Not suprisingly, they were both exclusively male subjects. But as different as they were, one located in the countryside, the other emblematically housed in the factory, these two signs of the times—in a sleight of hand typical of modernization—ultimately referred to one and the same citizen: the commonwealth's inherent narrative was to persuade that peasant wearing the pava to migrate to the cities to become a worker helping to turn that cog in one of the newly established factories. Thus, what could make this brand-spanking-new Puerto Rico was, simply and unequivocally, migration. Human flow would become essential to the machinations of the commonwealth.

A MATTER OF OPERATIONS

Puerto Rico's midcentury transformation had a bit more marketing attached to it. In line with the rhetoric of modernization, and with a touch of militaristic language—these were, after all, the first years of the Cold War—Muñoz Marín and his administration promoted and sponsored their programs under the rubric of three "operations": Operation Bootstrap, Operation Commonwealth, and Operation Serenity.

Operation Bootstrap was the call for the island's industrialization and, with it, the development of an infrastructure that would make it possible. Fomento, needless to say, was the office that principally spearheaded this operation. Its name uncovers a strategic move: while "bootstrapping" in English implies a self-sustaining effort, the name of this industrialization effort in Spanish, Operación Manos a la Obra (literally, "hands to work"), had a slightly more cooperative sense to it, almost approaching community building. Thus, for the English-speaking audience the program comfortably allied itself with a very American work ethic; in Spanish, the operation referred to a more populist sensibility. Subtle differences aside, Operation Bootstrap had one objective: "to abolish poverty and rapidly increase the existing standard of life" (Moscoso 163), as Moscoso unilaterally declared in a speech from the 1960s. They were words that smack of the developmentalist agenda of the time.

Muñoz Marín's administration correctly realized that there needed to be, in tandem with industrialization, a political and legislative transformation in the island's government that would tweak the relationship with the United States without severing those ties. This was the objective of Operation Common-wealth—in Spanish, Operación Estado Libre Asociado—and the 1952 constitution legitimized those changes. The refurbished government could then present itself as wiping the slate clean in regard to US relations and then legislating locally for the transformation of the island.

If the industrial and political "operations" were to be expected under development discourses, the launching of something like Operation Serenity was, truth be told, quite remarkable. Here was an official recognition that with moderniza-tion—intense modernization—drastic social changes were bound to happen and would thus transform and even unsettle the members of that society, along with the spaces they inhabited. Operation Serenity was the attempt to manage and adjust the "spirit" of the times to acclimate island citizens to the changes that were occurring all around them. In short, Operation Serenity aimed for the formation of a national personality that would protect and safeguard Puerto Ricans from the unavoidable metamorphoses of the island.

In speeches and letters throughout the 1950s and 1960s, Luis Muñoz Marín incessantly promoted and refined this idea of a "serene" transformation. (It is

even evident in his speeches quoted at the beginning of this chapter.) The idea
was officially introduced in his commencement speech at Harvard University on
June 16, 1955. From the inception of Operation Serenity, Muñoz Marín recognized that it was intimately connected to the economic changes that were happening at the time: "We might say that [Operation Serenity] aims to give some
kind of effective command to the human spirit over the economic process" (5).
This is key: Muñoz Marín included this operation in an attempt to assure the
predominance of citizens over economics. What would this look like? If I may
use Muñoz Marín's favored word, what kind of "civilization" would it be? The
governor ventures an image in that same speech at Harvard: "a society in which
Operation Serenity had been successful would use its economic power increasingly for the extension of freedom, of knowledge, and of the understanding [sic]
imagination rather than for a rapid multiplication of goods, in hot pursuit of a still
more vertiginous multiplication of wants" (5).

Indeed, Serenity was opposed to rampant consumerism and the unruly and
excessive accumulation of wealth (A. Dávila, *Sponsored Identities* 41), but the
operation also seemed to position itself away from radical notions of change. The
name itself promulgated a sense of an unruffled and centered attitude toward
modernization: serenity rather than violence, reform rather than revolution.
With the nationalist uprising of 1950 and the several violent acts committed
in Puerto Rico and the United States by the Nationalist Party overshadowing
his administration and projects, Muñoz Marín's Operation Serenity summoned
Puerto Ricans to face modernization without the use of impatient force, to adjust
to changes, and to reject militant behavior. Indeed, this operation could be seen
as one clear, strategic way in which the commonwealth distanced itself from the
Nationalist Party.

Ultimately, what Governor Muñoz Marín and Operation Serenity were proposing was a transformation beyond the political and the economic: a transformation, in fact, in the realm of culture in order to prepare the island's citizens for
the bright, modernized future ahead. But there was more, much more to it than
that. Culture would be a fundamental issue for Puerto Rico and Puerto Ricans,
for the government, and for those who had issues with it, and it was the battle-

ground for several heated debates throughout the development, installation, and governing of the commonwealth. Culture was the word.

CEMENTING CULTURE

As mentioned earlier, Muñoz Marín's party and government embraced a discourse of cultural nationalism to skirt questions of sovereignty. First and foremost, he needed to step away from the sticky notion of nation, which for many contained in its core ideas the status of an independent state; he achieved this sidestepping strategy in part by addressing the island as *el pueblo de Puerto Rico*. But the people of this pueblo required the consolidation of a generalized culture, a national culture, to make cultural nationalism work. In countless ways, what we now call Puerto Rican culture, what Puerto Ricans both in the United States and on the island today regard and boast as national culture, began to solidify and crystallize during this period.

These were years of beginnings and inaugurations. After finally putting an end to having English as the official language of instruction in 1948, the school system would become one of the most important venues for the teaching and learning of Puerto Rican culture. There was also unprecedented legislation for the creation of government spaces directly involved in the promotion and sponsorship of culture. In 1949, Luis Muñoz Marín himself created the División de Educación de la Comunidad (Division of Community Education); although fundamentally an adult education program to create civically engaged citizens who would be informed about the possibilities of transformation in a modernizing state, the division—through dozens of films, booklets, and posters—elusively filmed and printed an entire arsenal of Puerto Rican images and sounds, effectively inscribing a national culture for viewers and readers. In 1955, under the leadership of the anthropologist Ricardo Alegría, the Institute of Puerto Rican Culture was established; its charge was, in the words of the law that created it, "to conserve, promote, enrich and disseminate the cultural values of the *pueblo de Puerto Rico* and bring about their broadest and most profound knowledge and appreciation" (qtd. in A. Dávila, *Sponsored Identities* 39). The institute organized exhibitions, concerts, workshops, conferences, festivals, and competitions; it was in charge of "the study and restoration of the historic, architectural, and cultural patrimony of Puerto Rico . . . and was made responsible for conducting archaelogical, folkloric, and historical research" (61). (The Institute of Puerto Rican Culture is still active today.) Along with these more official changes, there was also the arrival of television in 1954, which would quickly mediate culture through music and comedy programming, just as radio had done since its arrival on the island in the 1920s. Also, and no less important, a group of writers and visual artists, from inside and outside the government, would respond in a variety of ways to the establishment of that national culture.

Of course, the various important attempts by the commonwealth to cement a shared set of practices, symbols, subjectivities, texts, histories, and the like were aiming for a particular Puerto Rican culture. And herein lies part of the distinctive conundrum of the island: in a period in which several configurations of the rural were rapidly yielding to the modernizing urban, the scaffolding for the development of national culture was based on a simplified and idealized—I would even say dehistoricized—notion of the rural.

That cultural configuration was not something originally imagined and brought forth by Muñoz Marín and his intelligentsia.[20] As many scholars have noted, the commonwealth's ideological gesture toward national culture took shape during the culturalist debates of the 1930s. To counter what seemed like the inevitable Americanization of the island, intellectual leaders of the period, some of them academics working at the University of Puerto Rico, began to forge a cultural identity for Puerto Ricans from what they considered the most salient features of their culture. Their slightly homogenized concoction placed the Spanish language at the core, undoubtedly to challenge the United States' cultural invasion but also because of these intellectuals' class and racial alignment with Hispanic (read, Spanish) culture. One of the consequences of this position was the tendency, as Jorge Duany encapsulates it, "to idealize the preindustrial rural past under Spanish rule and to demonize U.S. industrial capitalism in the twentieth century" (19). Thus, rurality gradually became a defining space for Puerto Rican culture, and the jíbaros, with all their paraphernalia, including the land itself, were reappropriated as iconic national cultural signs.

Highly influenced by this template, the Muñoz Marín government and some academic circles proceeded to put forward a more official narrative of the island's culture. The Hispanic heritage continued to be a prominent source, though Alegría and the Institute of Puerto Rican Culture, recognizing the multicultural nature of the island, promoted what the *reggaetón* artist Tego Calderón would later call the "racial trilogy" ("Loíza"): the argument that a composite of Spanish, African, and indigenous elements constituted the historical foundation of contemporary Puerto Rican culture. These elements had already been slowly acknowledged and validated by artists and writers, in poetry, painting, fiction, music, essay, drama, and dance, throughout the first half of the twentieth century. In the culturalist discussions of the 1930s, this hybridity had been perceived, with few exceptions, as a cause for alarm: a prominent figure like Antonio S. Pedreira, hispanophilic and negrophobic, believed this racial mixture was responsible for the supposedly vacillating and insecure character of Puerto Ricans (Duany 22). His attitude was not taken up by the Institute of Puerto Rican Culture, but the institute's officializing task, as might have been expected, involved a serious prioritization job in which cultural features were ranked, underscored, or disregarded, achieving what Arlene Dávila has described as "the unequal valorization of . . . racial components under the trope of racial mixture" (69). For instance, the Catholic tradition of the Spaniards was deemed essential, while any African elements of religiosity were summarily discarded as not authentically Puerto Rican. The African heritage—almost always described generically as such, without a recognition of the staggering cultural diversity of that continent—was limited, for the most part, to its connections to colonial slavery and (sometimes reluctantly) the music tradition. The indigenous element was specifically identified as Taíno; officially regarded as extinct, Taínos were useful due to their "symbolic malleability," meaning that they could safely become the ancestral Puerto Ricans, the community that connected contemporary subjects to the island itself (70). The jíbaro, though paradoxically rendered as the alleged product of this naturalized ancestry, was refurbished—whitened and de-Africanized, permanently locked in rurality, claimed as the bedrock of true folklore—to become the proof of the predominant Hispanic heritage of the island (72–73). The overhauled jíbaro could now be appropriated as the central figure of this national culture.

The "racial" triad, and the prominence of the jíbaro as quintessentially Puerto Rican, albeit with some tweaking through the decades, has been incredibly resilient and remains today a key discourse, not only in official spaces, like the public school system and cultural centers, but in the popular social imaginary of the island as well, in advertising and on television programming, on and off the island. Even so, it has been hotly debated. Indeed, the Institute of Puerto Rican Culture quickly became a de facto cultural gatekeeper on the island in the 1950s, but various artistic, literary, and media figures and organizations were quick to challenge, critique, or altogether reject the establishment and dissemination of this version of national culture.

Because of these struggles about culture under a ferocious regimen of modernization and within a neocolonial experience, I would venture to say that the middle years of the twentieth century in Puerto Rico were not only foundational, as I hope I have demonstrated in this introduction, but conjunctural. I borrow that term from the work of Lawrence Grossberg, who is taking it up from an extensive bibliography in cultural studies. "A conjuncture," he writes, "is a description of a social formation as fractured and conflictual, along multiple axes, planes, and scales, constantly in search of temporary balances or structural stabilities through a variety of practices and processes of struggle and negotiation" (40–41). This is precisely what occurred in the curious case of Puerto Rico from the 1940s to the early 1960s around the negotiations of culture and the machinations of cultural nationalism: a multilayered tug-of-war. Grossberg thinks of the conjuncture as a moment of crisis and risk, of possibility and transformation as well, of regulation and of contestation, all characterized by "a condensation of contradictions" (40). These contradictions in Puerto Rico, I want to argue, were entangled in the dilemmas and paradoxes of the rural and the urban. The imagery, the practices, the identities attached to the diverse configurations of culture during these years revealed the tensions triggered by the discourses and representations surrounding the city and the countryside with all their political, economic, social, and cultural implications in a modernizing state. This book is an intervention into this fascinating conjuncture.

1

FABRICATIONS, CONFABULATIONS, CONTESTATIONS

Fashioning and Negotiating Puerto Rican Culture in the Arts

IT HAS ALWAYS SEEMED difficult for me to think of the cultural amalgam of Puerto Rico without taking into account the possible dialogues and clashes among diverse and sometimes disparate artistic manifestations. I wonder what possible conversations could result from the relations and tensions between, for instance, the transnational musical output of the composer Rafael Hernández in the 1930s and 1940s and the adult lullabies of electro-acoustic bands Balún and Superaquello from the first decade of the 2000s; the paintings and prints of Myrna Báez and the street stencil art of Rafael Trelles; the seemingly appropriate poems of Luis Lloréns Torres and the apparently inappropriate lyrics of the hip-hop band Calle 13; the vernacular in the body language of the *performeros* Javier Cardona and Viveca Vázquez, the frenzied shimmy of the vedette Iris Chacón, and the flamboyantly gay entrances of Guille in the 1980s TV show *Entrando por la cocina* (Coming in through the kitchen); the folkloric Christmas specials sponsored by Banco Popular and the postmemorial pieces of Nuyorican collage artist Juan Sánchez; the photographic portraiture of Ukrainian-born Jack Delano and those "portraits" of the painter Arnaldo Roche Rabell imprinted with organic material; the "homosexual" horses of Charles Juhasz-Alvarado's sculpture and the gay, Old Testament plays of René Marqués. The questions and observations that arise from these kinds of intellectual confrontations across the arts potentially gesture toward a relocation of cultural production both as a mode of critique and as a complex sign of its epochality.[1] Also, they generate connections beyond issues of genre and form but without disregarding what genres and formal structures can produce culturally and aesthetically.

Perhaps more importantly, culture—especially "national" culture—never emerges from a single sphere. Its development can be understood only if we delve into the negotiations and disputes of myriad voices, spaces, and discourses: the official and the folkloric; the popular, the populist, and the commercial; the literary, the filmic, the musical, and the televisual. The absences, the voids, the repressed in one art form or discourse are many times made present, made visible or audible, in another form. It is in the maneuverings within and among these fields of production and circulation that the always tricky notion of culture is actually consolidated. And this is why a multiplicity of vantage points seemed absolutely indispensable in a book of this nature.

To be sure, *Concrete and Countryside* is interested in these negotiations within and across the arts, though the focus here is historically limited to the middle years of the twentieth century, when both the commonwealth's project of modernization and the establishing of a particular notion of national culture defined the period. Intrigued by Antonio Gramsci's notion that opened this book, I wish to focus on the artistic and cultural production actually created during the four terms of Luis Muñoz Marín (1948–64), rather than including later texts that dialogue with this period, either by setting the narratives, images, and sounds in the 1950s—Esmeralda Santiago's *When I Was Puerto Rican* immediately comes to mind—or by positioning their interventions as reconfigurations or critiques of that historical moment, like a lot of the work of the visual artist Antonio Martorell.

The dynamics of these years present a special circumstance: how different artists and artistic forms contemporarily faced, appropriated, dismissed, attacked, and negotiated the transformations of the island and the solidification of a certain national culture. Moreover, the situation unveils the paradoxes and fluctuations in the relationship that Puerto Rico and Puerto Ricans had (and, I would argue, still have today) with the rural and the urban, and with the cultural configurations that spring from them.

Even though throughout *Concrete and Countryside* I refer and look into many art forms and spaces of cultural production, the book focuses on three distinct cultural interventions: the cinematic output of the commonwealth's División de Educación de la Comunidad (DIVEDCO, or the Division of Community Education), the popular dance music recordings of Cortijo y su combo, and the literary texts of a group of writers who began to publish their work during this period, especially René Marqués and José Luis González. These choices might at first seem disparate and perhaps even arbitrary, but these specific interventions actually cover a number of crucial spaces that allow for a minute and extensive navigation of the negotiations of culture in the arts: the governmental and educational character of DIVEDCO, along with its particular interest in documentary and fiction film; the semiotic power of Rafael Cortijo's band in regard to class and race, in addition to his group's incursion into early television; and the historically important contributions of González's short fiction and Marqués's theater in the 1950s and early 1960s, important on the one hand because they were foundational for the literary endeavors of the time and, on the other, because they persistently critiqued the contemporary transformations of the commonwealth years from very different perspectives. And, of course, all of these interventions were intensely and inevitably involved in the multiple, paradoxical notions of the urban and the rural of these years. This chapter introduces and discusses in detail these interventions in the context of Puerto Rico's modernization process and its cultural negotiations.

FOR THE CINEMATIC TUTELAGE OF THE CITIZEN

Up against an image sometimes overshadowed by the Hollywood film industry, the act of cinematic self-representation in Latin America has always been, culturally and politically, a powerful and moving experience. Especially during the emergence of a local/national film production, be it industrial or artisanal, what occurs is a process both mesmerizing and valuable: cinema becomes not merely spectacle but spectacular, not simply entertainment but a kind of transformative, visual, and aural documentation in which the traditional appears remarkable and the new, striking.[2] Puerto Ricans seeing Puerto Ricans on-screen, recognizing landscapes and buildings, music and lyrics, witnessing ordinary social practices—making coffee, riding a horse, taking a bus—must have had an exciting and empowering feel. Of course, the citizens' recognition of their world on the cinema screen has been one of the most effective ways of instilling the national. And what better way to register modernization and the alleged marvels of progress than with cinema, the art of the twentieth century?

In the case of Puerto Rico, the emergence of a film tradition did not occur in commercial filmmaking. Cinema had been present on the island more or less since its invention—there is, as a matter of fact, some cinematic documentation of the 1898 invasion—and a number of feature films, documentaries, and quite a few newsreels had been produced during the first half of the twentieth century.[3] However, it was not until the late 1940s that a small but steady production of films began. The job of producing them fell, most tellingly, to a government institution: the Division of Community Education. It would not be an exaggeration to say that the division was, in fact, the first full-fledged film industry in Puerto Rico.

The Division of Community Education was very possibly the government project most directly linked to the objectives and ideals of Operation Serenity (see the introduction). By engaging citizens with issues of health and medicine, literacy, infrastructure (electricity, running water, bridges, roads), political opportunism, and social prejudice, even consumerism, DIVEDCO strove to educate adults about how to make the best use of the advantages of modernization, while also preparing them for the sea change that usually accompanied it.

The law that created the office—written by Luis Muñoz Marín himself— clearly spelled out its charge: "to provide the good hand of our popular culture with the tool of a basic education" (Law 372). The statement, first and foremost, called for the use of the available culture for instructing and informing, equipping and preparing communities to tackle local problems. As Muñoz Marín wrote elsewhere in the law, "[t]he community should not be civically unemployed." But the document also pointed to some very pivotal gestures. Muñoz Marín's phrase "our popular culture," especially because of its possessive pronoun, seemed to allude to a shared Puerto Rican culture, in song and music, tradition and beliefs, language and symbols, that could aid in the process. The sentence is preceded by another stating that this adult education "will be imparted through moving pictures, radio, books, pamphlets and posters, phonograph records, lectures and group discussion" (Law 372). So it seems, then, that "our popular culture" was also referring to the then already common experience of media—cinema, radio, print, recorded music—and that the division's charge was to exploit these forms of communication for educational purposes. The ambiguity of the phrase widened the apparatus of DIVEDCO: Muñoz Marín's office was to appropriate both national culture and mass media in order to reach the population of the island. It is important to point out that the "basic education" he referred to in the law was not curricular in nature. As Muñoz Marín stated in a November 1948 letter to Fred Wale, who would become the first director of the division, "As you may recall[,] the kind of adult education we are thinking of is not putting adults in school to study what they did not have a chance to learn as children or adolescents, but rather to develop the people's wisdom through community study, community organization and action."

Housed under the Department of Public Instruction, DIVEDCO was responsible for the production of more than a hundred shorts and half-features.[4] They consisted of documentaries and docudramas, melodramas, and even comedies, along with the printing of educational and promotional posters and booklets designed by the most creative artists and writers of the time. The writers René Marqués, Pedro Juan Soto, José Luis Vivas Maldonado, and Emilio Díaz Valcárcel; the visual artists Rafael Tufiño, Lorenzo Homar, and Carlos Raquel Rivera; the composers Amaury Veray and Hector Campos Parsi—all of them important figures in the 1950s—worked at some point in their careers for the division. Lorenzo Homar rightly called the division "a Puerto Rican Bauhaus" (qtd. in Marsh Kennerly, *Negociaciones* 73).

The audiovisual materials were produced for community meetings, which were organized and conducted by division employees who were specifically hired and trained for this purpose.[5] The meetings were held in the communities themselves, no matter how far they were from San Juan.[6] A couple of weeks before those meetings, the division would deliver posters promoting the films to be shown (in many cases a pair of films, one of them a short), along with booklets that explored a topic related to the films through essays, short fiction, and illustrations. The screenings and meetings more often than not were preceded by an all-out party: the people in the community would bring food, play music, and sing songs (*Community Education Program* 7); in film footage shot by the RCA Corporation for *The Schoolhouse on the Screen*, a documentary about the division that was never completed, we can see the extent of the celebrations that preceded the screenings. After the film screening, the division leaders would gather together the audience—men and women, young and old—to discuss the dilemmas and issues presented in the films. These meetings were at the heart of DIVEDCO's objectives: it was here that the commonwealth's ideals of democracy and participation were put into action and that the community became "civically employed." In fact, the seating arrangment for the discussions was almost always what the office called a "democratic circle," in an attempt to engage everyone in the community and break down possible social hierarchies among the members of the audience. This circle as an image was repeatedly exploited in photographs and booklets promoting DIVEDCO.

As many scholars, especially Catherine Marsh Kennerly, have pointed out, the Division of Community Education was in many ways a continuation of the ideas and ideals of Franklin Delano Roosevelt's New Deal and the politico-cultural use of the arts that pervaded the Works Progress Administration (WPA) and its several offices (Marsh Kennerly, *Negociaciones* 23). Luis Muñoz Marín was profoundly inspired by Roosevelt's programs, and many New Dealers were highly influential in Puerto Rico, including the last American governor, Rexford Tugwell. No less important, the Americans who were hired to create and organize DIVEDCO had come with New Deal experience: Jack Delano, who would be in charge of cinema, had worked as a photographer for the Farm Security Administration (FSA); his wife, Irene Delano, who would lead the Graphics Division, had done some work for the WPA in the late 1930s and came with lots of experience in graphic arts, especially silkscreen, having designed posters and booklets for the war effort in the 1940s; Edwin Rosskam, another member of the original team who did some work writing booklets and designing posters, also worked for the FSA; and the division's first director, Fred Wale, a sociologist quite experienced in community education, had been a New Dealer as well. With the exception of Wale, these Americans worked in the division only during the first few years, instructing and training a number of Puerto Ricans in silkscreen technique and film production; by the mid-1950s, the office was mostly being run by Puerto Rican writers, visual artists, and newly trained filmmakers.

Not wanting to wait until a long process of legislation would approve the creation of a community education office, Muñoz Marín, then president of the Puerto Rican Senate, formed in 1946 the Taller de Cinema y Gráfica (Cinema and Graphics Workshop) as part of an already existing Parks and Recreation Commission (Delano 20; Tió, *El cartel* 43). In a very real way, this workshop was a dry run for what would become the Division of Community Education a few years later. The handful of films that the Taller managed to make had more the feel of traditional newsreels, but the educational project was already very much imprinted in them. The short film *Una gota de agua* (A drop of water), for instance, gave audiences access to the invisible life in water through the modern technology of the microscope; this was life that could be potentially dangerous to the viewers' health. *Jesús T. Piñero*, a documentary that celebrates the recent inauguration of the first Puerto Rican governor of the island (albeit one still appointed by the president of the United States), takes advantage of the event to inform audiences about the modernizing advancements of the island in industry and education, in hydroelectric power and new housing.[7] Alongside these, the majority of the striking and colorful posters produced by this preliminary office, all of them silkscreens, were educational in nature, focusing on voting rights, health issues, and housing—though a few were promotional posters for the films produced, and some were decidedly propagandistic, providing information about the changes initiated by the government.

After the Division of Community Education was established in 1949, some of this type of material of course continued to be produced, though it became an effort more focused on education and community development. DIVEDCO was meticulously organized: the Production Section had a graphic arts unit in charge of producing posters (in most cases, promotional pieces for the films to be screened) and the illustrations for the informational *Libros del pueblo* booklets; an editorial unit penned a lot of the fiction and nonfiction pieces for those booklets, in addition to overseeing the writing of film plot developments and scripts; and a cinema unit ran the entire production of the films. Besides these, the division included the Field and Training Section, in charge of selecting the communities for the screenings and discussion meetings and of supervising the personnel who would lead the postscreening conversations. There was also the Analysis Section, in charge of assessing the effect of the division's programming on the communities themselves.

I have decided to focus on the film productions of DIVEDCO because, it seems to me, cinema quite quickly became the cornerstone of the project. If this was perhaps not necessarily the case in the early years of the institution, eventually the booklets began to be designed and produced as a way of prefacing the issues to be presented in the films, and the posters came to be the principal advertising tools for promoting the films and their screenings. This is not to say that all of the booklets and posters served only this purpose or that they lacked any representational, artistic, or cultural value (far from the truth, as is evident in the excellent work done by Marsh Kennerly and Colón Pizarro), but the films acquired, in the development of the division, a leading role.[8]

From very short films to feature length, mostly in black and white, working in fiction and nonfiction, with a palpable influence of neorealism, drawing from several schools of documentary—a bit of Pare Lorentz, a lot of John Grierson— and blending the form with fictional narratives from different genres, the filmic output of the division tackled a wide variety of topics and situations. While a few films exalted Puerto Rican culture and tradition or were simply informational, the great majority were structured as "problem" films, that is, motion pictures that presented a dilemma in order to prompt discussion after the screening. Some films would provide a solution, while others were a bit more open-ended to allow a discussion with the community about the possible solutions to the issue at hand; in all of them the community was an active participant and an influential agent. No doubt to heighten the impact on audiences, many of the stories were based on actual events, and amateur actors—in fact, members of the communities themselves—were widely used in the films. These were not films with fancy production values, but they were exceptionally effective.

To be sure, the films addressed some of the expected issues in a modernizing state: the suspicion of rural subjects toward Western medicine was featured in *Doña Julia* (Skip Faust, 1955), the beneficial uses of science in small-scale agriculture in *Pedacito de tierra* (Small plot of land) (Benjamin Doniger, 1952), and the power of technology and engineering over nature in *El puente* (The bridge) (Amílcar Tirado, 1954). The importance of adult literacy was the central theme in *Una voz en la montaña* (A voice in the mountain) (Amílcar Tirado, 1952). Of course the need for community involvement was a common theme in many films, and some made it their primary focus, like *Los peloteros* (The baseball team) (Jack Delano, 1951) and *Ignacio* (Ángel F. Rivera, 1956).

But DIVEDCO didn't stay with the safe topics of technology and literacy, medicine and science: there were films like *La casa de un amigo* (A friend's house) (Amílcar Tirado, 1963) that tackled the issue of housing—one of the most difficult problems of these years (see chapter 2). A few films, like *Modesta* (Benjamin Doniger, 1956), the short *¿Qué opina la mujer?* (What do women think?) (Oscar Torres, 1957), and *Geña la de Blas* (Luis A. Maisonet, 1964), even attempted to spark a discussion about the integration of women as full-fledged citizens of the commonwealth (see chapters 2 and 3). Some films, like *El cacique* (The local boss) (Benjamin Doniger, 1957) and *El de los cabos blancos* (The one with the four white hooves) (Willard Van Dyke, 1957), even dealt with authoritarianism, although they contained this issue by limiting themselves to local bosses—the *caciques*, as they were called. And the exceptional films *Juan sin seso* (Witless Juan) (Luis A. Maisonet, 1959) and *El gallo pelón* (The featherless rooster) (Amílcar Tirado, 1961) even educated Puerto Ricans about rampant consumerism and the devious tactics used in marketing and advertising, practices that were already quite present in Puerto Rican life by the 1950s.

Indeed, it would be quite fitting to talk about this cinematic output as an idealizing gesture, a "developmentalist utopia," as Antonio Lauria-Perricelli has called it (94), one in which the community and the citizen on film inhabited a space full of potentiality and promise. This is not suprising in an educational project that was part of a process of modernization. But the creation of a government office dedicated to adult education inevitably triggered a certain tutelage of the citizens. The division skillfully led a project to ease the transition of Puerto Ricans facing the changes that were promoted and conducted by the newly established commonwealth, but it also became an official space that instilled the ideological foundations of the ruling party: fundamentally neocolonial, decidedly antirevolutionary, and politically pro—United States. As the scholar Félix Jiménez has accurately stated, DIVEDCO "sirvió a las 'necesidades especiales' que no eran particularlmente las de la comunidad social, sino las de la comunidad política que sujetaba el nuevo ordenamiento gubernamental" (served the "special needs" that were not particularly the ones of the social community, but rather the ones of the political community that held on to the new government order) (72).

This is quite evident in the essay-documentary *Las manos del hombre* (The hands of man) (Jack Delano, 1952), in which industrialization and economic development were framed by a propagandistic discourse of productivity. Already the film's title directly referred to Muñoz Marín's political agenda, as his Operation Bootstrap was a loose translation of the Spanish Operación Manos a la Obra (literally, hands to work). And, in fact, this twenty-five-minute film is composed of close-ups of hands, all sorts of hands, being active in various ways—applying for jobs, working at factories and hospitals, building roads, houses, schools. But the film ultimately pushed the productivity of these hands toward the tenets of the United States' Cold War. With quasi-religious choral music as background, the film ends not with hands but with a series of shots of the monumental stone walls of El Morro, the colonial Spanish military fort that sits at the northwest corner of Old San Juan, as the voice-over narration exclaims, "Estas murallas del Morro están todavía con nosotros. Las manos del pasado construyeron para las necesidades de su tiempo. Y las manos de hoy construyen y se afanan y se quiebran y encallecen para darnos más progreso, un mundo mejor y una paz duradera. Las manos del hombre laborando siempre por el bienestar de la humanidad" (These walls of El Morro are still with us. The hands of the past built for the needs of their time. And today's hands build and endeavor, broken and calloused, to give us greater progress, a better world, and a lasting peace. The hands of man always working for the welfare of humanity). This is an abrupt shift in the film, since the talk now is of security and "lasting peace," as we watch shots, alas, of a military fortress. So the synechdochical hands don't seem to be working anymore for the improvement of social and economic conditions in Puerto Rico; rather, their productivity helps in the fight for the defense of this US territory in the Caribbean.

Las manos del hombre was a very early film in the production history of the division. It was also an oddity: films like this one were not made again, once the educational objectives of the office were in full force. But the commonwealth's Cold War mentality still pervaded the films, especially because the first years of the division coincided with the pro-independence Nationalist Party uprising, an event in October 1950 that prompted a series of government measures to quell any anti-American rhetoric and revolutionary action on the island. Thus, character and community decisions in the films' plots were never made by a radical social transformation but by discussion, negotiation, and consensus, and co-op associations were frequently presented as the preferred solution for workers rather than, for instance, unions—the way it happens in *El yugo* (The yoke) (Oscar Torres, 1959), set in a community of fisher folk, in the eastern town of Fajardo, trying to free themselves from the exploitative behavior of a middleman.

Still, dismissing DIVEDCO as merely a propaganda tool would be a gross error. The true, unashamedly propagandistic midcentury cinematic tool in Puerto Rico was not the division but the private company Viguié Films, a prolific newsreel producer that incessantly and euphorically documented the latest marvels of urbanization and industrialization on the island.[9] The creators of the division films were quite aware of the problems and paradoxes of modernization—some of them, as I discuss later, were even very critical of the process—and they attempted to cautiously, albeit idealistically, depict the ways in which Puerto Ricans could take advantage of the changes while making them aware of potential pitfalls. DIVEDCO's most telling contradictions resided elsewhere.

Even though the law that established the division didn't require it, the office ended up focusing its community education work on Puerto Rico's rural areas. The films reflected this choice, setting almost all their stories away from urban spaces of any type. In the few instances urban spaces appeared in films, they did so fleetingly; some very early films used the city and the industrial space as the expected image of modernization, but by the mid-1950s these had all but disappeared. Only one film, *Un día cualquiera* (A day like any other) (Ángel F. Rivera, 1954/1993), tackled the urban head on by setting its story and community dilemmas in the one space that the commonwealth preferred not to include in its visual construction of the island: the slums of San Juan. Not surprisingly, the film was never completed under division auspices (see chapter 3).

It was the rural that persisted in DIVEDCO output. And the countryside the films tended to depict was profoundly idyllic, full of picturesque landscapes, with *jíbaras* and *jíbaros* as part of that landscape. It was also a landscape in which traces of urbanization and industrialization had been positively erased (see chapter 2). Although the division neorealistically recruited dozens of jíbaros to act in the films, in several pictures the rural citizens were portrayed by radio, theater, and television actors who added an affected, slightly melodramatic style to the films and gave a glamorized touch to the scenes. The division's depiction of the rural was even puritanical: the film director Amílcar Tirado, in a memorandum discovered by Catherine Marsh Kennerly, pointed out the surprise the jíbaro actors expressed when the film crew was about to shoot a party scene in the countryside in which no one was going to be drinking alcohol (Marsh Kennerly, *Negociaciones* 105). In fact, many rural audiences perceived the films anachronistically: the Analysis Section of the division was dismayed to discover that the jíbaros were assuming the films they were watching were set in the past and not in contemporary times, because of the way rural life was portrayed (R. Muñoz 44).

By privileging the rural, and by emphasizing this specific configuration of the rural in film after film, the division's cinematic corpus aligned itself with the establishment's notion of the rural as the seat of national culture, and it thus effectively located "authentic" Puerto Rican culture away from urban spaces (see the introduction). To be sure, the division was not specifically in charge of the dissemination of culture per se, but, as Marsh Kennerly convincingly argues, the Division of Community Education, even more than organizations like the Institute of Puerto Rican Culture and precisely because of its educational objectives, more efficiently became an instrument of consolidation and dissemination of the establishment's national cultural project.

Contrasting how different national cinemas help in assembling national cultures, Félix Jiménez has juxtaposed the massive production of Mexican cinema with DIVEDCO's film production in Puerto Rico: "En términos estratégicos, el cine mexicano enfrentó al país *imaginándolo*, mientras que el cine puertorriqueño evocaba al país imaginario *instruyéndolo*" (In strategic terms, Mexican cinema confronted the nation *imagining* it, while Puerto Rican cinema evoked the imaginary nation *instructing* it) (73; original emphasis). The educational aspect of DIVEDCO is undeniable, but it is hard for me to conceive this cinema without its imagining and imagistic power. DIVEDCO both instructed and imagined Puerto Rico and Puerto Ricans, even if in the process it ended up with a number of problematic contradictions.

A TRANSFORMATIVE ECONOMY OF JUBILATION

As irrefutable evidence that by the early 1930s radio (which had begun transmitting in 1922) was already established as a ubiquitous element in the island's urban lifestyles, a 1933 newspaper article by the poet and journalist Luis Lloréns Torres quoted this classified ad: "Se alquila hermosa residencia en la calle de la Salud; no hay radio en toda la calle, ni nadie aprendiendo piano" (Beautiful residence for rent on Salud Street; there is no radio anywhere on the street, nor is there anyone learning the piano) ("Por amor" 108). Radio eased and solidified the transformation of popular and traditional music into commercial music. If, as was undoubtedly the case, much music was performed outside the realm of the recording industries (e.g., at Christmas, in religious celebrations and in family gatherings, even in strikes), by the 1950s, especially in urban areas, popular music was, for many, commercial music. And the phonograph, the radio, the jukebox, and, after 1954, television, assured its rapid dissemination.

But the midcentury project of establishing a national culture almost never included commercial music. To be sure, since its creation in 1955 the Institute of Puerto Rican Culture had tried to promote and disseminate different genres of Puerto Rican music, such as plena and bomba, although in the 1950s and early 1960s these were never as salient as the supposedly more Hispanic *danza*. These genres, however, were always thought of as traditional music, and therefore any commercially recorded versions of this music, usually considered modernized music, were dismissed as not really a part of the "authentic" musical culture of the island. It was not until the 1980s and early 1990s that there was a shift in official spaces to include commercial music as an integral element of Puerto Rican culture.

In addition, commercial music was not viewed as a platform from which one could launch an artistic critique of society. In the midcentury, two spaces of artistic production were the preferred modes for critical intervention against the commonwealth, the rapid modernization of the island, and the colonial relation Puerto Rico had with the United States. One of them was literature, which had historically been a legitimized space for social critique, not only in Puerto Rico but all over Latin America (see the section "A Writerly Scaffolding for Nation" below). The other was graphic arts, which, heavily influenced by the graphic tradition of the Mexican Revolution and the sociopolitical graphic tradition in North America, mounted a critique against the commonwealth and its intimate ties with the United States (see chapter 3). Commercial music in the 1950s, in contrast, was never considered a cultural location from which to question the radical social transformations that were occurring in Puerto Rico. Nevertheless, I would like to argue that there were interventions in commercial dance music that should be taken into account when surveying the different voices of documentation and critique that were produced during these years of modernization.

Diametrically opposed to DIVEDCO's cultural notion of the rural as the principal locus of authentic national culture, one musical group, perhaps the most influential dance band of the 1950s, kept alive the incipient urban culture of Puerto Rico and documented the social paradoxes of urbanization: Cortijo y su combo. This mostly Afro–Puerto Rican group musicalized the confrontation with modernization and with the commonwealth's faith in technology and progress, and it did so from the vantage point of working-class neighborhoods and the expanding communities in the margins of the city that were dismissively labeled as slums. In addition, the group's songs were one of the most complex musical documents of Afro–Puerto Rican urban life, something almost totally absent in official and media spaces of the time; the group's musical contributions ultimately reconfigured the national culture evoked during these years, inserting working-class, urban culture and Afro–Puerto Rican life into the social imaginary of the island. All of this, packaged within the deceptively inoffensive popular dance music of the time: in guaracha, in plena, in mambo, in bomba.

Energetic and full of swing, catchy and irresistible, fun, funny, and fabulous, Cortijo y su combo, with Ismael Rivera as its lead singer, was formed in 1954 by Rafael Cortijo Verdejo, a talented percussionist who had grown up playing in the streets of Santurce and had trained in many popular orchestras of the time. Santurce, an important section of today's metropolitan San Juan, had been established for the most part by communities of freed slaves back in the eighteenth century, and since then it has historically included sizable communities with working-class neighborhoods. As Ángel G. Quintero Rivera has recently (and exquisitely) documented, the area has had a living musical culture since its formation; it was a place where the music of the Afro–Puerto Rican plena and bomba was played regularly at parties and celebrations (*Cuerpo y cultura* 282–90). Rafael Cortijo, along with many members of the band, fed on this musical tradition of Santurce's streets. In fact, that particular sound of the street corner jam (*el rumbón de esquina*) was one of the most characteristic elements of the combo, distinguishing the group from other bands of the era, such as Lito Peña's Orquesta Panamericana and César Concepción y su orquesta—ensembles that produced a fuller, structured, orchestral sound but without the exciting, improvisational feel of the jam.

Cortijo's band started humbly enough, working in some San Juan brothels (Steward 99; Quintero Rivera, *Cuerpo y cultura* 165).[10] But soon they became popular on the radio and on television (the band was formed the same year of the first TV transmissions) and began performing all over the island, as well as in New York City for the Puerto Rican and Latino communities there. By the time the combo disbanded in 1962, the group had traveled throughout the Caribbean and had performed as far away as the West Coast in the United States. They had also become a regular feature on Puerto Rican television. While the band was active, they produced nine albums, sometimes at the rate of two per year.[11] These were filled with songs that became huge radio and nightclub hits.

Besides guaracha, a music form with Cuban origins that had been thoroughly Puerto Ricanized by the time Cortijo's band began to perform, the ensemble is known for the extensive repertoire of two important Afro–Puerto Rican musical genres: bomba and plena. Bomba, dating from at least the early 1800s, developed mostly in the sugar plantation cultures of the coast (Quintero Rivera, "El tambor camuflado" 201) but gradually spread to working-class neigborhoods and communities throughout the island's towns and cities. It was, and remains today, neo-African dance music, and it has the peculiarity of the drummers actually following the movements of the dancer, rather than the other way around.[12] The plena is a turn-of-the-twentieth-century rhythm with urban origins and diasporic influences—some English Caribbean rhythms and possibly even bomba music itself (Miller 42–43). Although both bomba and plena have a call-and-response structure in their singing, in plena the words define the genre: loaded with satiric, biting lyrics, plena lampoons and critiques and is always willing to use irony, humor, ridicule, and exaggeration. (This is part of why plena today is alive and kicking during strikes and political demonstrations in Puerto Rico.) Many scholars have pointed out that Cortijo adopted and adapted the bomba and plena for the modern combo: bomba's traditional drumming, done with a pair of large drums called *barriles*, and plena's hand drums, the *panderos*, were performed with Cuban *tumbadoras* (Flores, "¡Ecua Jei!" 65). Cortijo y su combo's performance of these two genres was about continuing the island's music tradition without the need for folkloric authenticy: the danceability of bomba and the emphasis on the word as a way to lampoon and critique in plena remained intact in Cortijo's repertoire.

While it is true that the popularity of plena in the 1950s does rely, in part, on the recordings of Cortijo y su combo, the band was not the first to commercialize plena; recordings of the genre go back to the 1920s, and orchestras like Canario y su grupo and Augusto Coen y sus boricuas made plenas popular both on the island and in US Puerto Rican communities. But Cortijo y su combo was certainly the first commercial band that produced albums in which bomba music predominated.[13] As many have noted, they took the bomba out of Santurce neighborhoods and into the recording studios. If the midcentury musicologist María Luisa Muñoz was correct in her statement about bomba starting to dwindle in the late 1940s (Álvarez and Quintero Rivera 12), perhaps Cortijo y su combo is partly responsible for the popularization of bomba in the 1950s. With Cortijo, everyone starting dancing to bomba.

The band's popularity and visibility in 1950s Puerto Rico was vitally important.[14] Cortijo y su combo took full advantage of the arrival of television, and their performances on *La taberna India* (and later on *El show del mediodía*) forged a televisual space that opened the possibility for a redefinition of Puerto Rican national culture with a more complex racial composition.[15]

To be sure, the Institute of Puerto Rican Culture's seal included a male African slave as representing one of the three essential elements for the formation of Puerto Rican culture—the other two figures in the now iconic seal were a Spanish man and an indigenous Taíno—and the founder of the institute, Ricardo Alegría, had been advocating in his writings and speeches for the incorporation of African traditions into the island's culture.[16] But the dominant gestures for national culture during these years were certainly not focusing on the African element; rather, it was the European heritage of Spain—language, religion, literature (in sum, so-called "civilization")—that predominated in the official construction of national culture. This Hispanophilic discourse had been utilized since the 1898 American invasion as a nationalist tool to counteract the potential Americanization of Puerto Rico; under the commonwealth, it became hegemonic. I would like to argue that the musical world of Cortijo y su combo, including the televisual presence of the band itself, helped in the rectification of this imbalance in the construction of national culture in the midcentury.

Their televisual appearances, however, were not without paradox. Indeed, the band was regularly on the small screen, to the delight of Puerto Ricans all over the island, but, as Yeidi Rivero has pointed out, their performances were often framed in a way that revealed the problematic racial politics of the time. In the variety show *La taberna India*, Cortijo y su combo's numbers were introduced by the white actor Paquito Cordero in the role of Reguerete, a comedic character in blackface "and . . . generally portrayed as an idiotic black male figure" (Rivero 59). Still, backup vocalist Sammy Ayala stressed in an interview how Cordero frequently prodded members of Cortijo y su combo for words and phrases that were current in working-class neighborhoods in order to maintain his character's street credibility on television. The vibrant Afro–Puerto Rican and working-class linguistic neologisms were kept alive by the band in these conversations, though, alas, broadcast by means of a white actor in blackface. Even so, the band performed song after song that, through radio and television, on record players at home and in live concerts, gave testimony of a racialized existence in the island, without forgetting distinctly articulated notions of class. If Afro–Puerto Rican audiences might have noticed the jarring contrast between Reguerete and Cortijo's band, they probably focused, as Rivero argues, on the significant fact that a mostly Afro band was regularly playing on television (Rivero 64).

Part of what is refreshing about Cortijo's music and lyrics is that they never resorted to a simplistic racial pride: here the representation of Afro–Puerto Rican daily life does not appear as a "project" but as a living experience that has been musically internalized. For example, the mega hit "El negro bembón" (The thick-lipped black man), from the album *Baile con Cortijo*, exposes the complexity of racism in Puerto Rico in the tale of a police officer who tries to hide his own thick lips as he interrogates a murderer for killing a black man because of his thick lips. Less known songs like "Madame Calalú" and "Doña Chana" (both from *Fiesta Boricua*) emphasized, sometimes humorously, sometimes not at all, daily life in a racist society.

It is not surprising that slavery appears in the group's songs; what is fascinating is the way in which it is inserted. In the plena "Déjalo que suba" (Let him get on) from *Baile con Cortijo*, dark-skinned Cachón—upset with a black man called Guliver who wants to crash his party—uses the rhetoric of a slave trader to embody his anger:

Déjalo que suba a la nave	Let him just come on shipboard,
Déjalo que ponga un pie	Let him just put one foot on—
Que van a llevar latigazos	They're going to get such a whipping,
Hasta los que están por nacer.	Even those who aren't yet born.

Cachón dares Guliver to try and crash the party and threatens him not only with lashes but his entire descendancy; to leave no doubt that his language is referring to the Atlantic trade, Cachón's threat metaphorically goads him to dare to put even one foot on the ship (thus, the title of the song). The allusion to the violence of slavery leaves no doubt about Cachón's anger. And the chorus assumes a collective memory of that experience: the trader as the violent subject par excellence. Like the *reggaetón* artist Tego Calderón today, Cortijo y su combo processed racial violence and shifted its center: instead of perpetuating it, the band revealed its repugnant aspects.

Of course, Afro–Puerto Rican culture was also embedded in the music that the combo played, especially the way in which they played it.[17] The band presented itself on television and in concerts quite differently than most orchestras of the period did, and eventually they changed the performing style of Puerto Rican dance music. While popular bands like Orquesta Panamericana and César Concepción y su orquesta performed while sitting in rows with music stands in front of them, Cortijo y su combo jammed standing up and without any music sheets. Lead singer Ismael Rivera and his backup singers danced to funkily choreographed steps—something that would become widespread in salsa ensembles later on. The band also made percussion the chief sound, instead of its merely functioning as background. In fact, while in most orchestras of the time the percussion section was relegated to the back (modeled after North American big band jazz ensembles), the percussion section in Cortijo y su combo was up front. Cortijo was on the *timbales*, along with Roberto Roena on bongos.[18] Martín Quiñones was on congas, and singers Sammy Ayala and Roy Rosario, on minor percussion instruments (*güiro*, maracas, cowbell, sticks), were always in front of the bass, played by Miguel Cruz. The piano was played by Rafael Ithier, and the brass instruments by Eddie Pérez and Héctor Santos (both on saxophones) and by Mario Cora and Kito Vélez (on trumpets) (Quintero Rivera, *Cuerpo y cultura* 291).[19] Also, to mimic the female voice in choruses, which were quite common in both traditional bomba and plena, Cortijo added a falsetto voice, performed by band member Eddie Pérez (Rodríguez Juliá, *El entierro* 34). This "female" sound was something that had been totally suppressed by other orchestras.

But it was the sound of the combo that in a way made the group stand out from all the other dance ensembles of the 1950s. Cortijo's is most literally a combo—smaller than the orchestras of the time—and with a street sound that had been cleaned out of most orchestras. That sound is what Quintero Rivera refers to as the sound of a *rumbón de esquina*, a street corner jam, full of polyrhythmic lines and improvisation. In his book *Cuerpo y cultura*, the sociologist accurately renders the achievement of Cortijo's sound: this was not a big band–style ensemble that simply incorporated bomba and plena into their repertoire but a combo of bomba and plena that incorporated the big band sounds of brass, bass, and piano, transforming the traditional genres—some would have said "modernizing"—without debilitating that "roots" or, arguably, urban sound that most of the members of the band had acquired playing bomba and plena in the streets of the working-class neighborhoods of Santurce and other areas of the capital (291).

The musical legacy of Cortijo y su combo led the way, at least in the context of Puerto Rico, to salsa music, that thoroughly urban genre that would become defining for Puerto Rican culture from the 1970s on, and some members of the band would have a leading role in its development.[20] After the band's breakup in 1962, Rafael Ithier, the combo's pianist, formed El Gran Combo de Puerto Rico, one of the leading salsa bands in Puerto Rico (it is still active today, more than fifty years later). Lead singer Ismael Rivera eventually became one of the most influential singers in salsa music.[21]

This legacy has been carefully studied in academic and nonacademic writing in both Puerto Rico and the United States. What has barely been discussed is how their music can be read as a response to the years of the commonwealth—not only to urbanization but more specifically to the prevalent rhetoric of progress and development. I would argue that Cortijo y su combo was a significant intervention that effectively critiqued the euphoria of modernization.

It is their ironic and frankly mocking posture toward the technological—be it industrial, agricultural, scientific, or medical—that places Cortijo y su combo as an undeniable site for exposing the modernizing 1950s. While the agricultural space is industrialized by the government, Cortijo amusingly suggests an alternative to the sugarcane harvest in "Pa' tumbar la caña" (To cut the cane) (from *Bueno, ¿y qué?*): a ravenous, scorpionlike creature that cuts the cane and packs it in bunches with perfect efficacy (see chapter 2). In some songs, the technological meets the personal, emphasizing the discrepancy that existed between economic strata and the improvement of life conditions: while the island witnessed medical advances, poor Culembo (in the song "El negrito Culembo," from *Cortijo en New York*), who is ecstatic at having a new set of teeth, seems unaware that he has been cheated by his dentist, who put dog teeth in his mouth. In other songs, the technological is connected to the gigantic transformation in automobility in San

Juan, as well as the old clashing with the new: in "La caleza" (The coach) (*Cortijo en New York*), a monumental traffic jam is caused by a line of cars that can't get through the street because it is blocked by a coach (*caleza*) drawn by a very old horse. Even the hysterics of the Cold War are documented in Cortijo's songs: the voice of the song "El satélite" (The satellite) (*Baile con Cortijo*) equates the Soviets' launching of Sputnik with the end of the world.

As can be detected in some of the songs already discussed, Cortijo y su combo is an outburst of pleasure—of diverse desires, really. I am not saying this just because it is popular music, dance music, and not even because it is music, but rather because part of its repertoire is dedicated to the appropriation of pleasure and joy as a legitimate act and, fundamentally, as an alternative to work. Obviously, theirs is a dance repertoire—plena, bomba, guaracha, Cuban *son*, Brazilian samba, some with arrangements coming from Dominican *merengue* and even some songs that come from the English-speaking Caribbean tradition. But, in a way, it seems to me that Cortijo y su combo responded to the modernizing, industrializing rhetoric of the commonwealth not with simple, escapist hedonism but with what I would call a transformative economy of jubilation.

One of the best-known songs of Cortijo y su combo is "Maquinolandera" (from *Invites You to Dance*). The lyrics do not relate a narrative of any sort; they are a series of gleeful tongue-twisting phrases. A chorus containing a word like *chúmalacateramaquinolandera* is, without a doubt, a genuine linguistic shindig. This completely made up word does not have a meaning in Spanish (nor, as far as I can tell, in any other language), but it seems to imply certain technological connections. The word for machine (*máquina*) is almost present in it—and the word *máquina* is actually sung during the vocal improvisations of Ismael Rivera toward the end of the song; the suffix attached to the word, *-era*, could be read as the Spanish ending for a word that implies an occupation done by a woman (like *lavandera*, a washerwoman, which "landera" could be a contraction of), perhaps mechanizing here a washerwoman. The onomatopoetic sound of the first six syllables (*chúmalacatera*) seems to re-create some sort of mechanical racket.

When the band reunited to make an album in the 1970s, they rerecorded this song (*Juntos otra vez*). Almost as proof that this mechanical meaning had been actually picked up by the band, Ismael Rivera and the backup vocalists started this new version of the song by repeatedly singing "*chúmalacatera, chúmalacatera, chúmalacatera*," a chant eerily close to the sound of a machine, like a locomotive or an engine of some sort.[22] What's more, in one of the few television performances of Cortijo y su combo that has survived, the band starts this song with a dance routine that imitates the motion of the locomotive's wheels, as they chant "*chúmalacatera*" ("Ismael Rivera: 'Maquinolandera'"). This version of the song even has at one point a long, drawn-out *yee* that is curiously similar to a factory whistle. If the song, when it does use Spanish, denotes a party scene, "Maquinolandera" can be ultimately listened to as the musicalization of industry, as the Afro–Puerto Rican transformation of mechanical noise into rhythm, of unbearable din into danceable beats.

Pleasure in Cortijo's music is never simply party time nor is it always depicted as escapist. Often it is fundamentally an economy of affirmation and resistance. Part of the combo's strategy is to locate pleasure within identity politics, as in "Cuembé" (*Cortijo en NewYork*), a catchy and ebullient bomba. The refrain repeatedly urges the listener to "speak" only *cuembé* when things don't go as well as planned; the request is somewhat odd because *cuembé* is a type of bomba rhythm and dance, not a language or even a kind of slang. The song, then, prompts us to speak a dance, to talk with music. But to do so with a music genre that possesses an Afro–Puerto Rican specificity is, for all intents and purposes, a call to embrace and appropriate that element of the island's culture. The reference toward the end of the song to Loíza, a coastal town in the northeastern part of the island that has a predominantly Afro–Puerto Rican population, reinforces this strategy of pleasure and identity housed in the black Puerto Rican experience.

One of the most interesting songs of the band is "Mofongo pelao" (Plain mofongo) (*Fiesta boricua*). Written by Rafael Cepeda Atiles, one of the most important composers of bomba and plena on the island, the song tells the story of a black woman called Marcola who is interested in losing some weight. She goes to a doctor, and he prescribes a rather limiting diet of salads and other not very appetizing foods and thus prohibits Marcola from eating basic staples like a stew made with codfish (an inexpensive and nourishing fish) and the typical *mofongo*, a concoction made out of deep-fried green plantains mashed with oil,

garlic, and pork rind. The chorus of the song is her response to the doctor's rec-
ommendations:

Yo no como mofongo pelao	I won't take my mofongo straight—
Ponle chicharrón por el la'o.	put some pork rind on my plate.

This chorus is a musical slam-on-the-brakes: Marcola's shouts categorically refuse
to accept not only a certain nutritionist rhetoric but the medical culture of diet-
ing as well, especially when it pretends to erase an entire gastronomy of Afro–
Puerto Rican cuisine: a salad will never replace mofongo (and besides, Marcola
reasons, mofongo without pork rinds is simply not mofongo). In a clever negotiation, the second half of "Mofongo pelao" focuses on what Marcola decides to do:
she asks a friend to run to the market and bring her a whole series of vegetables
typical of the island's diet to replace the bland salad that the doctor had required.
Okra, cabbage, and purple bell peppers will be her mulata diet to stay in shape.

It is quite important not to forget that the language of pleasure in Cortijo
comes out of a musical period that is dominated by another musical genre: the
bolero, a slow-tempo, lyrical type of ballad that reigned supreme as the axis of
romantic love and forbidden desire—in fact, seduction, passion, and unrequited
love become central in 1950s commercial music (and not only in Puerto Rico)
thanks to the bolero. But even though the bolero had an almost complete monopoly over love (perhaps *because* it had that monopoly), this musical genre created
certain genre frontiers: the sense of an irresistible, polyphonic musical euphoria,
a laugh-out-loud humor, a mocking, daring, dismantling of social mores—all of
these part of a certain economy of pleasure—stayed outside the boundaries of
bolero. Even a certain hilarity toward sex: boleros feel more comfortable in a
sublimated sexual act, but for the most part it refuses to mix sex with laughter.
All of this specific landscape of pleasure that seems to be beyond the orbit of the
bolero Cortijo y su combo appropriated and made their own.

Through Cortijo y su combo's take on technology, on modernity and modernization, with their focus on the urban and working-class cultures, along with
their reconfiguration of the national, I would venture to say that the recording
output of the group could be described as "an actual mechanism of semantic dis-

order: a kind of temporary blockage in the system of representation" (Hebdige 90). Even though those words, written by the British cultural studies scholar Dick Hebdige, were applied to the potential nature of subcultures, I do in fact believe Cortijo's repertoire, on the radio and on television, subtly realigned the culture evoked and sponsored by the Commonwealth of Puerto Rico by injecting working-class urban culture and the Afro–Puerto Rican life into the national imaginary. Their songs are leagues away from the jíbaro and the jíbara of the commonwealth, even from the muscular man turning the cog that appeared on those billboards of Compañía de Fomento Industrial. If in government rhetoric the slums and the poor represented threat and fear—citizens in erasure, as I discuss later—in Cortijo y su combo they were the central life of the newly urbanized Puerto Rico.

A WRITERLY SCAFFOLDING FOR NATION

It would not be totally inaccurate to think of the Division of Community Education as an official space of cultural production; the musical space of Cortijo y su combo could be said to have successfully straddled commercial music and the traditional genres of Puerto Rican and Caribbean music, but the location of literature in Puerto Rico is a lot more difficult to pinpoint. In almost all cases, writers have felt the need to distance themselves from any official positioning; the notion of a poet laureate, for example, is simply nonexistent in Puerto Rico. At the same time, many literary figures have pretty consistently felt uncomfortable inserting themselves into the realm of the popular. Literature in Puerto Rico, not unlike that of other countries in Latin America, has usually inhabited in an interstice, one that would grant the literary a certain kind of intellectual autonomy—or at least the illusion of one.

This does not mean that literature was purposefully marginal. Not at all. In the case of Puerto Rico, with its colonial and neocolonial experience, literature has been at the vanguard of nation-building; the scholar Juan Gelpí even ventures to assert that "la tradición literaria que se inicia en el siglo XIX y se consolida a lo largo del XX ha hecho las veces del Estado nacional que no existe" (the literary tradition that begins in the nineteenth century and is consolidated throughout the twentieth acted as the national State that does not exist) ("Literatura puertorriqueña" 475). For all the hyperbolic tone, his words are remarkably accurate: poetry, drama, fiction, and nonfiction have consistently created and maintained a space for Puerto Rico and Puerto Ricans to assemble and imagine themselves, though that was not their only function. In addition, and no less important, literature has been a preferred site of political, cultural, and social critique; the written word embodied a veritable project of contestation, of unpacking and dismantling, a productive negativity that revealed and denounced the fundamental contradictions of the Puerto Rican experience.

In the midcentury, although poetry doesn't exactly take a backseat, the favored modes of literary production were fiction and theater, and the processes of modernization, along with the establishment of the commonwealth, were pivotal for the emerging group of writers who would dominate Puerto Rican letters for a couple of decades. As the writer Pedro Juan Soto confessed in the 1970s, "Todos surgimos a la sombra del Estado Libre Asociado y todos nos rebelamos" (We all emerged in the shadow of the commonwealth and we all rebelled) (*A solas* 72). Indeed, the literature created by the major writers of the time—especially the work of René Marqués, José Luis González, and Pedro Juan Soto himself—was particularly anticolonial and quite wary of the enthusiastic rhetoric of development and progress that the government was employing for its projects. This is why their literary output zeroed in on urban spaces, especially on experiences that could clearly expose the paradoxes of the commonwealth: the phenomenon of migration, the liminal existence in the slums of San Juan, the arduous living in urban centers of the United States, even the onerous adoption of urban culture by rural subjects. Issues revolving around the sordid conditions of peasants in the countryside never completely went away, but many of these writers tended to address them in the context of the island's urbanization. There was also an attempt to deliberately stay away from literary traditions that depicted the countryside in a picturesque manner. In literary journals and magazines, in anthologies and books, these writers, in fact, filled in the urban and rural spaces that the cinema of DIVEDCO, with its emphasis on an idealized rural, had left out.

Perhaps attracted by its immediacy and celerity, its effective brevity, its critical punch, the short story became their preferred genre in fiction, though the novel was never abandoned. I agree with Gelpí that the most representative books of these years were three short-story collections: José Luis González's *El hombre en la calle* (Man on the street) of 1948, Pedro Juan Soto's *Spiks* of 1957, and René Marqués's *En una ciudad llamada San Juan* (In a city named San Juan) of 1960 ("Literatura puertorriqueña" 484), all books that deliberately focused on urban space and the urban life of Puerto Ricans, both on and off the island. But perhaps the book that consolidated these writers as a group, as a "generation" of sorts, was the anthology *Cuentos puertorriqueños de hoy* (Puerto Rican fiction today), published in 1959 and edited by René Marqués, who was without a doubt the leading figure of this group at the time. As the title explicitly states, the anthology positioned itself as a collection of stories that dealt with the contemporary situation of the island, rather than its past.[23] Marqués's selection of writers did, however, combine a few transitional figures with others who were key writers of the 1950s and a sprinkling of some who were emerging at the end of that decade.[24] Not surprisingly, the compilation worked as a way to establish this group in literary history. Marqués included, for example, the 1940s author Abelardo Díaz Alfaro to act as a connection with those even older writers who had mostly focused on the rural space but had a decidedly anticolonial (and, frankly, anti-American) stance in regard to the status of the island. Marqués also included the exiled writer José Luis González, who had been publishing work since the early 1940s and was welcomed into the fold as an initiator of the urban trend in fiction that Marqués and his colleagues were advocating in the late 1950s.[25] This anthology is still in print (its twelfth printing was in 2002), legitimizing these writers as the literary voices of the midcentury.

Aside from fiction, theater was the other literary form favored during these years. Drama had had a small but significant tradition in Puerto Rican letters in the second half of the nineteenth century, and competitions like the one sponsored since the late 1930s by the cultural center Ateneo Puertorriqueño sparked a keen interest in the genre among writers and audiences (Stevens 26–27). Several companies were formed in the 1940s and early 1950s, but it is with the Festival of Puerto Rican Theater, an annual event initiated in 1958 by the recently formed Institute of Puerto Rican Culture, that a solid tradition of national theater took off. The festival mixed newly written plays with revivals of older plays; not unlike the fiction of the period, the works dealt with issues of urban migration and the community of Puerto Ricans in New York City, though rural life remained a major topic in the productions. René Marqués was virtually the only fiction writer who also worked in drama.[26] In fact, he thoroughly dominated the theater of the time, and his plays *La carreta* (The oxcart) from 1953 and *Los soles truncos* (Truncated suns) from 1958 are some of the most influential dramatic works of the period. But other figures wrote some very significant plays during these years. Francisco Arriví immediately comes to mind; he successfully focused on the conflicts of a racialized Puerto Rico in *Medusas en la bahía* (Jellyfish in the bay) from 1956, one of the plays in the diptych *Bolero y plena*, and in his best-known play, *Vejigantes* (1958), named after the Afro–Puerto Rican popular masks from a celebration in the town of Loíza.

In a prologue to a brief anthology of previously unpublished stories and plays, Pedro Juan Soto acknowledged the ambitions of his literary generation: "Hacerlo todo menos aventurar con la poesía, ésa era nuestra consigna. . . . [N]os lanzamos al ensayo, a la novela, al libreto radiofónico y a otros experimentos" (Doing everything except dabbling in poetry, that was our slogan. . . . We embarked upon the essay, the novel, the radio script and other experiments) (*El huésped* 8–9). Curiously, his statement didn't point out one major contribution: quite a few of the playwrights and fiction writers of the midcentury also authored many, many film scripts and booklets for the Division of Community Education. Soto worked there from 1954 until 1966 (Soto, *A solas* 66); René Marqués started working in 1950, almost at the beginning of the division, and directed the editorial section from 1953 to 1969 (Marsh Kennerly, *Negociaciones* 80, 85); Emilio Díaz Valcárcel started in 1955, right after serving in the military during the Korean War (Marqués, *Cuentos puertorriqueños* 241), and his years there were formative for his literary vocation, as he was working daily with the most important writers of the time. If, on the one hand, having a salaried position with writing at the heart of it was quite beneficial for these writers, working at the division created a new dilemma, because the location of literary production began to slip into a more official space than in the past, a space that in many ways was supervised and sometimes censored by cultural officers and official leaders (including the governor of the island). To counter this, most writers working for DIVEDCO went for partitioning their literary project: writing plot treatments and scripts for the production of government educational cinema "during the day," while writing, outside official spaces, "literature" that unmistakably denounced the project and discourses of that same government.[27]

This parceling out was not as real as Marqués and Soto might have thought. Marsh Kennerly, looking into the literary and political maneuverings of Marqués, provides an excellent case study.[28] René Marqués consciously and persistently tried to keep his literary endeavors separate from his production at the division; in his introductory biographical notes included in *Cuentos puertorriqueños de hoy* (really autobiographical notes, since he wrote them himself), Marqués doesn't even mention his substantial work at DIVEDCO. While working at an adult education office that aided in the transition to modernization, he wrote award-winning essays that consistently criticized the government's educational programs and modernizing endeavors as chaotic and destructive. He continued to advocate for political independence, though he was employed by a government that was not interested in political sovereignty. But as Marsh Kennerly observes, Marqués's belief in the position of the intellectual as a figure of authority and scrutiny was actually possible thanks to the commonwealth's insistence on democratic processes and DIVEDCO's goals of civic and citizen engagement. In addition, his critique—often Manichaean and moralistic, always conservative and didactic—ironically had some common ground with the commonwealth's position on the national culture, especially with the notion of the rural as a site of Puerto Ricanness and authenticity, and with the overall use and defense of things Puerto Rican for the purposes of educating the people of the island. Atlhough opposed to the commonwealth, René Marqués fit nicely within the commonwealth's project of the division.[29]

Throughout this book I examine the contributions of a number of writers, but there are two prominent figures that will stand out. The first, as I assume it has become clear by now, is René Marqués. It would be impossible—I dare say, irresponsible—to delve into 1950s Puerto Rico and ignore his literary contributions; he was emblematic of these years and without a doubt a veritable icon of the cultural production of the period. Few would disagree that he was the island's leading intelletual of the midcentury. The other writer is José Luis González, who, from a decidedly Marxist vantage point, broke away from many literary traditions on the island, not by discarding them but by transforming them, I would argue, into the bedrock for the literature to come in the second half of the twentieth century. He was simultaneously central and marginal to Puerto Rican letters: central to the installation of an indispensable space from which to articulate and denounce the contemporary social and cultural transformations of Puerto Rico, marginal in his condition as a de facto exiled writer; because of his open association with the Communist Party, he was not allowed to travel to Puerto Rico for decades (he eventually became a Mexican citizen). González's marginality also extended to the fact that he was poorly represented during the midcentury years in the nationalizing of literature, especially in school curricula.

Both writers were untamable voices inimical to the commonwealth; both of them criticized the processes of modernization and urbanization, and both railed against the colonial condition of the island and favored political independence from the United States. But their similarities ended here. Beyond the fact that Marqués produced most of his work while living on the island, a lot of it while working at the Division of Community Education (Marsh Kennerly, *Negociaciones* 85), while González wrote the majority of his work abroad, in New York City, in Prague, and, after 1953, in Mexico (Irizarry 19–20), it was the nuances of their ideological positioning, their approach to denunciation, that made them radically different writers. Marqués's textual production was framed by a deep sense of mourning for a (mostly Hispanocentric) Puerto Rican culture and society threatened by the American occupation of the island and the modernization spearheaded by the commonwealth. González, by contrast, wrote without that sense of loss, because his works always framed the contemporary within the complex social, historical, and political context of the past. Marqués, an existentialist writer to the core, viewed contemporary Puerto Rico as having lost its authenticity, and he depicted the present as dystopic. González, though he couldn't be considered a utopic writer, never set aside the materialist possibilities of progressive transformation. Their textual outlook on things urban and rural—and this is why I particularly focus on these two writers—confirms their attitudes. The rurality of Marqués could not escape an idyllic aroma, and it functioned as an antithesis to the urban; the rurality of González was gritty, almost social realist, but he refused to separate it from urbanization. The urban in Marqués was irremediably hellish and even culturally inauthentic, because his national/cultural inclination was toward the countryside; González embraced the contemporariness of the urban, never discarding its incipient national/cultural possibilities, and he installed the urban as the quintessential space from which to mount the most effective critique of the present, but without idealizing that space. González and Marqués were a resonant literary juxtaposition in the middle years of the twentieth century, one that I deem quite useful to examine today.

It is important to recognize that producing literature in Puerto Rico has always had a privileged position among the arts. By saying this I do not mean to legitimize that position, but I do mean to say that literature has been perceived as privileged by many. The journalist Wilfredo Braschi, in a 1958 lecture at the Institute of Puerto Rican Culture, made the following pronouncement: "El puertorriqueño hace de su literatura una fuerza defensiva, la convierte en una bandera, en un arma" (Puerto Ricans make their literature a defensive force, turning it into a flag, into a weapon) (13). Indeed, the flag of nation, the weapon of critique. Be that as it may, as I hope this book demonstrates, other art forms have actually managed to share with literature that space of critical interrogation. My aim is not to dethrone literature but to align it with a series of dialogues and contestations across the arts and to insert it into a wider series of maneuverings and negotiations on the national culture through the tensions and paradoxes of the rural and the urban. Those are the objectives of the second part of this book.

Part 2

BEYOND THE COUNTRY AND THE CITY

Landscape, Migration, Culture

UNSUSTAINABLE EDENS
The Countryside of the City

Pero todos seamos, ante todo, netamente puertorriqueños, netamente jíbaros.

But let us all be, before anything, pure and simple, Puerto Ricans; pure and simple, jíbaros.

Luis Lloréns Torres

Oye, tú eres de la ciudad
Pero yo gozo más.

Okay, you may be from the city
But I have much more fun.

Cortijo y su combo, "Yo soy del campo" (I'm from the country)

IN PUERTO RICO, IT is quite common to say that someone is heading for *la isla* (the island) when an inhabitant from San Juan leaves the capital to visit the countryside or any of the country's smaller towns. My family, however (I'm not sure why), always said we were going to *el campo* (the countryside) every time we left the city to visit my grandparents in Gurabo, a municipality in the central mountains of the island. Their countryside was not a farm or some sort of rustic place but rather a somewhat alternative version of the rural: my maternal grandparents were not farmers but rather Puerto Ricans who had migrated to New York and then returned to the island in the 1960s to move to el campo—in their case, to a cement house with a cliff for a yard (the house was supported by concrete stilts) and abutting a paved rural road. But at least for my family and me, that was the countryside.

I grew up in the 1960s and 1970s with an odd divide between the countryside and the city: I was living in a San Juan that was sprawling quickly, absorbing every town and community that pretended to be outside its borders, and I was witnessing a countryside that was being urbanized incredibly fast. The division imprinted in that urban labeling of anything that was not San Juan as "the island"—whether or not the phrase originally dates from when the capital of Puerto Rico was the small "island" of San Juan and the "big" island was the rest of the country—intensified that confusion, because that "island" indiscriminately included both rural and urban spaces.

What I didn't see during my childhood and adolescence was the curious relationship between the urban space and el campo. I did imagine the countryside as being like the surroundings of my grandparents' house, but I also was surrounded in San Juan itself by a counstryside constructed and reconfigured from the city: in the bucolic posters designed by the Division of Community Education for display in my elementary school; in the many television shows featuring *jíbaro* music; in the Christmas rituals of roasting a pig and *parranda* singing; and in the idyllic Marlboro and Winston advertisements shown at the movies—a couple (always an urban couple) driving around the countryside and enjoying local food and culture while smoking their cigarettes. Indeed, this was—I now realize—the countryside of the city.

What I was aware of was the fact that what was presented to me as quintessential *boricua* culture was not urban but rural. What school, family, government, and media called Puerto Rican culture did not come from where I lived, in the city, but from somewhere else, away from the noisy traffic and the white fields of cement: it came from el campo. The *cuatro*, a string instrument long associated with jíbaros and usually imagined as being played in the mountains; the visual image of sugarcane and its flower, the *guajana*, blowing in the breeze; that small wooden vernacular country house that is used today in the diaspora, in cities like New York and Chicago, as the architectural icon of Puerto Rican culture: all of these functioned as tangible symbols of the existence of a Puerto Rican culture, of "our" culture. And all of them were proclaimed as originating in the country-side.

My small bewilderment before this riddle—that a kid from the city was expected to culturally identify with all this rural paraphernalia—has not really diminished now that I am not a kid anymore. There are, of course, urban elements in today's Puerto Rican culture—salsa music and *reggaetón* are undoubtedly good examples of this (though they have entered the cultural inventory through some fierce struggles)—but the rural imaginary remains the national matrix. The cuatro is undoubtedly national patrimony, but I haven't heard of any first-grade teachers trying to instill Puerto Rican culture in their students by teaching them a megahit from the 1980s boy band Menudo.

But as one delves deeper into the processes and representations that helped produce this conundrum, something becomes disquieting: the countryside—the space, its subjects, and its practices—had ultimately been stripped down to folklore, that is, flattened to an easily consumable, one-dimensional sense of the rural. This chapter centers on those simplifications of the countryside, constructions that for the most part crystallized during the urban pulse of the 1950s and unmistakably deprived the rural of its fundamental and complex historicity. It also explores several cultural spaces that resisted and reconfigured that simplification with alternative visual, aural, and textual images of el campo.

FANTASY ISLAND

In the cultural landscape that developed in the middle of the twentieth century in Puerto Rico, there was a figure that encapsulated the rhetorical mechanisms used in certain literary and cultural spaces to establish a very particular rural image of the island. The academic and writer María Teresa Babín, without producing especially innovative or original works, provides in her output a good example that sums up the dominant midcentury image of the countryside.

Although Babín published a number of monographs and essays on Spanish Peninsular literature (especially about the work of the poet and playwright Federico García Lorca), most of her writings centered on Puerto Rico, on the literary image of the jíbaro, and on the rising group of writers who shaped the fiction and theater of her time. Her thorough knowledge of the national literature led her, in the early 1970s, to edit the groundbreaking *Borinquen: An Anthology of Puerto Rican Literature*, one of the first anthologies in English of the island's literature.[1]

It must be noted that, as part of the academic and government intelligentsia and through her involvement in education, Babín was instrumental in establishing what would become canonical Puerto Rican literature. She was an important figure during the Muñoz Marín years. She became the first director of the Department of Spanish in the School of General Studies at the University of Puerto Rico (appointed by Jaime Benítez himself, the influential and controversially conservative president of the university). In the early 1960s, she directed the Spanish division in the island's Department of Education (then named the Department of Public Instruction), and during her tenure she established the first curricular list of Puerto Rican literary texts to be taught in public schools. In the 1970s, as a professor at Herbert Lehman College, part of the City University of New York system, she worked in the first Puerto Rican studies program in the United States (Doncel et al.). All of these official positions make Babín a very important figure in the consolidation of a literary canon.

In the 1950s, as the government and particular academic spaces were beginning to consolidate a certain notion of Puerto Rican culture, Babín published two texts that are, in my view, classic examples of contemporary cultural aspirations and machinations: the nostalgic *Fantasía boricua* (Puerto Rican fantasy) in 1956 and the encyclopedic and hegemonic *Panorama de la cultura puertorriqueña* (Panorama of Puerto Rican culture) in 1958.

Certainly her *Panorama* repeats and promulgates the notion of a national culture based on the Spanish, Taíno, and African heritages that the Institute of Puerto Rican Culture and its founder, Ricardo Alegría, were already establishing in multiple publications and events. But her literary endeavor *Fantasía boricua* is an intriguing book that deserves a closer look here because of its depiction of the countryside.

A very poetic and personal book, *Fantasía boricua* is composed of brief impressionistic prose texts set away from the capital. The brief book depicts the childhood and adolescence of the author without following the usual chronological structure of traditional memoirs, though in the process Babín surveys Puerto Rican traditions and landscapes: the life and routine of the small town and the sugarcane plantation, the mountains and the coffee plantation; Christmas celebrations like Three Kings Day and their traditional foods and religious ceremonies—all this surrounded by lush descriptions of land and sea, at dawn and dusk, facing hurricanes and heat.

The book had much readership on the island: there were multiple editions of the book published by several government agencies from the early 1960s all the way to the 1980s. Its dissemination, however, was limited mostly to schools, and this made the book much more than a simple, isolated output: it circulated, in fact, as a textbook. Thus, because of its educational role, I would like to position *Fantasía boricua* as a text symptomatic of the cultural negotiations of midcentury Puerto Rico.

There are several references in the text to the fact that Babín wrote the book while she was away from the island.[2] Babín recognizes the presence of a nostalgic quality in her writing, but the confession tries to dismiss this attribute: "Mi fantasía boricua . . . parece enturbiarse con un velo casi imperceptible de nostalgia" (My Boricua fantasy . . . seems to be clouded by an almost imperceptible veil of nostalgia) (8). Reading through the book, however, one finds that the nostalgic veil is never "clouded" but rather is quite transparent, almost producing a sugary aftertaste: "Isla hecha de colinas juguetonas, de cielo cambiante, límpido su azul, acogedor de nubecillas errantes; de mar tranquilo que a ratos espumea con bravura" (Island made of playful hills, of changing skies of a blue most clean, welcoming errant small clouds; of a tranquil sea that now and then foams with bravura) (154); somewhere else she remarks, "la leche espumosa acabada de ordeñar; el mugido de los becerros prestos al retozo y a la caricia" (the foamy milk recently extracted; the lowing of calves ready for romp and caresses) (47). Babín's imagery makes the island one that is calm, gentle, comfortable, agreeable, unsoiled, almost infantile. Nostalgia indeed veils this text, but it is not by any means imperceptible: we are before a vision distorted by a filtered lens that produces a dreamy and idyllic image.

It is clear from the text that Babín comes from a higher social class, one comfortable in this bucolic image of the rural. Her vantage point is thus that of an observer: the countryside here is, ultimately, landscape. And this landscape is, in a word, Edenic: "[L]a montaña es accesible y generosa, los caminos se abren al menor empeño de la mano, el sol no falta a nadie y el agua resquebraja las peñas" (The mountain is accessible and generous, the paths open up with the least effort of the hand, no one lacks sun and the water breaks open the rocks) (123). The description is uncanny: almost reminiscent of those comments in Christopher Columbus's diary during his first voyage in the Caribbean, the landscape acquires an inviting, gentle, and appealing character. The imagery of Babín, the one that alludes to the country, to the mountain (the coast, interestingly enough, almost never appears in her book, almost as if that type of landscape is not thought of as rural in her imaginary), does not allow an inhospitable space, one that might be difficult to wander into. The countryside is nice and affable. Babín's is a depiction clearly produced by a gaze that contemplates the land but has never worked it. And the island is perceived as static, perennial, almost outside time: "Un día de mi isla es otro día de mi isla" (One day of my island is another day of my island) (29).

The countryside in *Fantasía boricua* is not uninhabited—not at all. The jíbaras and jíbaros are indeed part of Babín's landscape. Still, though surrounded by this idealized space, they are not aware of her impression of the countryside. While the author hovers in a state of euphoria about her surroundings, the rural subjects are weighed down by lethargy and immobility: "El andar es pesado; la mirada no mira; el cerebro se quebranta y se adormila. Ni hablar, ni reir, ni pensar: sólo es posible rezongar en el vaho amarillento y viscoso que emana de las fauces de la tierra" (Walking is heavy; the gaze does not see; the brain is crushed and sleepy. No talking, no laughing, no thinking: only moaning is possible in the yellow and viscous vapor that emanates from the mouth of the earth) (22). This paradox—an appealing landscape inhabited by subjects that do not seem to perceive this Eden-like panorama—begins to destabilize her imagery into an unsustainable one.

Additionally, references to labor, to the countryside as a working space, and to the jíbaros as working subjects are scarce. When they do pop up, these are intensely problematic, because they are imbued with picturesque, folkloric tinges. The passage that describes payday ends with the following sentence: "Dentro de una semana justa volvería a repetirse la fiesta del pago, esperada por mí como si fuera el más pintoresco de los circos" (In exactly a week the celebration of payday would repeat, anticipated by me as if it were the most picturesque of circuses) (94). The jíbaros, "con una cara expresiva de compunción y derrota" (with a face conveying sadness and failure) (92), are simply elements of a scene that produces pleasure for the observer-author.

The portrayal of the rural inhabitants in *Fantasía boricua* turns even more problematic because they themselves become mere landscape: "La virtud primordial de la isla verde, cañera y pescadora, es la conformidad, esa forma de resignación cristiana que ha prendido en el corazón borincano desde el principio del mundo y ha de persistir por los siglos de los siglos" (The primordial virtue of the green island, island of sugarcane and fishing, is conformity, that form of Christian resignation that has latched onto the Puerto Rican heart from the beginning of the world and will persist forever and ever) (90). This is an odd but revealing sentence, for in her description of this (supposed) virtue the land absorbs the subjects: they disappear into landscape. This landscaping of the jíbaros is, in fact, a form of erasure, of dehistoricizing them into scenery. And it ultimately unveils in Babín's text a decidedly class-based positioning.[3]

As is well known, the British cultural studies scholar Raymond Williams has analyzed this phenomenon in *The Country and the City*. In the introduction to a Spanish edition of that book, the Argentine scholar Beatriz Sarlo explains it succinctly: "El paisaje, tanto en su dimensión material como en su referencia literaria, es la producción de un tipo particular de observador, sustraído del mundo del trabajo. . . . Es más: para que la intervención estética paisajística tenga lugar, es preciso su articulación con un punto de vista que, mágicamente . . . anula el trabajo y despersonaliza la fuerza de trabajo. El campo nunca es paisaje antes de la llegada de un observador ocioso que puede permitirse una distancia en relación con la naturaleza. El paisaje, entonces, antes que construcción material, es distancia social" (The landscape, both in its material dimension and in its literary reference, is the production of a particular kind of observer, removed from the world of labor. . . .

Moreover, in order for the aesthetic intervention of the landscape to take place, its articulation is necessary from a point of view that, magically . . . annuls labor and depersonalizes the workforce. The countryside is never landscape before the arrival of an idle observer that can allow himself or herself a distance in relation to nature. The landscape, then, before it is a material construction, is social distance) (19). *Fantasía boricua* fits perfectly within this tradition. It is this social distance (and not so much the exilic distance from which the text is written) that makes Babín's stance so prickly: the countryside becomes landscape, and in that rhetorical gesture the historicity of the rural withers away. It is this kind of enthrallment with the Puerto Rican countryside that connects her vision to the rural representations that were so prevalent in the cultural discourses of her time.

COUNTRYSIDE INTO LANDSCAPE

This attitude toward the rural as mere landscape, as a passive space for picturesque contemplation, is of course not original with Babín. She is the culmination of a tradition in Puerto Rican literature. In the 1930s, the essayist Antonio S. Pedreira, in his pathbreaking book *Insularismo*, had already described the island's landscape in a similar vein: "Nuestro paisaje posee un sentido mesurado y armoniza con la geografía y la etnografía. Nada de fuerza, de estruendo o de magnitud . . . es un paisaje tierno, blando, muelle, cristalino" (Our landscape possesses a measured feeling and it harmonizes with its geography and ethnography. Nothing forceful; no din, no immensity . . . it is a tender landscape, soft, pliable, clear) (161). A few years later, in 1939, in an essay that studies poetry's dialogue with the island's geography, the scholar Margot Arce de Vázquez continued this trend in "El paisaje de Puerto Rico" (The landscape of Puerto Rico): "Todo tiene en ella dimensión breve, gracia infantil" (Everything has in it a small dimension, a child's grace) (68). And almost as if to end debate on all literary and rhetorical elations, she makes the clearest prounouncement: "la isla es paisaje puro" (the island is pure landscape) (72).[4] She is correct in focusing on poetry, but it is odd that she doesn't discuss or even mention the quintessential poem of the land in Puerto Rico: Virgilio Dávila's poem "La tierruca" (The tender land):

Es el móvil Océano	Behold the pulsing Ocean,
gran espejo	Great mirror
donde luce como adorno sin igual	Wherein shines, like a matchless jewel,
el terruño borincano,	The land of the Boricua—
que es reflejo	Reflection
del perdido paraíso terrenal.	Of the lost earthly paradise.
Son de fáciles pendientes	Gently rolling
sus colinas,	Are its hills
y en sus valles de riquísimo verdor	And in its valleys of richest greenery
van cantando bellas fuentes	Lovely fountains sing
cristalinas,	Crystal clear
como flautas que bendicen al Creador.	Like flutes praising the Creator.
Primavera sus mejores	Its finest qualities
atributos	Springtime
muestra siempre generosa en Borinquen	Displays in abundance in Borinquen.
En los campos siempre hay flores,	The countryside forever in flower,
siempre hay frutos:	Forever in fruit:
¡Es Borinquen la mansión de todo bien!	Borinquen: mansion of all goodness.
(19–20)	

Perhaps because the poem idealizes the island beyond recognition, perhaps because the poem fails to link Puerto Rico to its Hispanic roots—a clear objective in her essay—Arce de Vázquez omits "La tierruca." But Dávila's green, gentle, generous island, while it didn't quite inaugurate this gesture toward the island (the nineteenth century takes credit for that), it most certainly cemented it for the twentieth century. Dávila's poem is still part of the poetic canon of twentieth-century Puerto Rican literature. Most Puerto Ricans know this poem, however, because they learned it as a song in schools around the island. At the beginning of the twentieth century, it had been set to music by the composer Braulio Dueño Colón and published in *Canciones escolares* (School songs), a collection for which Dávila and the writer Manuel Fernández Juncos collaborated with the composer ("Braulio"). (Dávila himself was a schoolteacher.) A 1954 edition of this book, introduced by the secretary of public instruction and revised by the general supervisor of music from the department, solidified its permanency in school curricula (Dueño Colón). There are several generations of Puerto Ricans who can sing this poem from memory—which gives an idea of the weight this poem has had in the social imaginary of the island.

What makes Babín distinctive from these other writers, though, and an iconic figure in the 1950s, is that her portrayal of the rural is generated while the countryide was beginning to vanish. In seeing this "disappearing," Babín launches a rescue of the rural that ends up being, almost literally, its burial in a crypt. She says in her introduction to the book, "Mucho habrá cambiado mi isla desde entonces, pero ese tiempo que me tocó a mí de ella no podrá cambiarlo nada ni nadie" (The island might have changed much since then, but those moments that I got to experience no one and nothing will be able to change them) (8). Her reconstruction of a rural past—since Babín seems to suggests that the rural is in fact past and not present—does not function as a reconfiguration or reinsertion onto a socio-historical process but rather, simply, as its mummification.

THE ETERNAL RETURN OF LANDSCAPE

Puesto que Puerto Rico no es otra cosa que un verde grito de tierra en el celeste océano.

Since Puerto Rico is nothing more than a green shout of land in the sky-blue ocean.
Cesáreo Rosa Nieves

Landscape is a natural space mediated by culture. It is both a represented and presented space . . . both a frame and what a frame contains, both a real place and a simulacrum.
W. J. T. Mitchell

This distortion of the rural was, without a doubt, not limited to the literary realm. Throughout the first half of the twentieth century, the rural indeed dominated Puerto Rican visual culture, especially in painting; the artists Ramón Frade, Oscar Colón Delgado, and Miguel Pou were possibly the most representative figures of this trend. Their rural focus has been generally perceived as a strategy to process and counteract the colonial status of the island (Torres Martinó, "El arte puertorriqueño" 79). Noel Luna, in a thought-provoking essay on the poet Luis Lloréns Torres, quotes Edward Said's *Culture and Imperialism* on what is a recognized tactic of the invaded, one that could easily apply to plastic arts in Puerto Rico right after the 1898 invasion: "'If there is anything that radically distinguishes the imagination of anti-imperialism, it is the primacy of the geographical element. . . . Because of the presence of the colonizing outsider, the land is recoverable at first only through imagination'" (53). What Frade's *El pan nuestro* (Our daily bread) (1905), Colón Delgado's *Paisaje con bohío y ropa* (Landscape with hut and clothes) (1916), and Pou's *Paisaje de montaña* (Mountainous landscape) (1923) arguably achieve is a visual appropriation and ownership of their invaded land.

Not all art historians were this sympathetic. In her writings on Puerto Rican art, Marta Traba dismissed these painters, who preferred more realist styles of painting, as anachronistic and reactionarily nostalgic. What is true is that their pictorial insistence also contained some of Babín's desire to capture a disappearing landscape; Frade himself confessed in a letter that "como todo lo puertorriqueño se lo está llevando el viento . . . en mi deseo de perpetuarlo, lo pinto" (since everything Puerto Rican is being blown by the wind . . . in my desire to perpetuate it, I paint it) (qtd. in Torres Martinó, "El arte puertorriqueño" 77). Their increasing distance from more modernist and avant-garde styles of painting seemed to reinforce this.

The rural was still found in painting through the middle of the century, though it increasingly yielded to more urban subjects and spaces during the modernization period, in addition to making a decisive turn toward more modernist styles; Fran Cervoni's *Flamboyán* (1954–55) and Carlos Osorio's *Guavate entre las nubes* (Guavate among the clouds) (1962) are good examples of this continuing tradition.[5] I would like to argue, however, that the real inheritor of this rural visual tradition in the 1950s resided not in the plastic arts but in cinema. It was in DIVEDCO's educational films where the mummified rural was best entombed.

There is a sense of perpetual déjà vu in the DIVEDCO films. Shorts and half-features, documentaries, docudramas, and fiction films, many of them begin with a similar sequence: accompanied by either jíbaro music or classical music (sometimes Stravinsky, sometimes music by the Puerto Rican composer Amaury Veray), the establishing shots were low angles of rolling mountains against monumental skies with large puffy clouds, very possibly inspired by the photography of the Mexican cinematographer Gabriel Figueroa; pleasant brooks, refreshing groves, and *flamboyan* trees in bloom swayed by a gentle breeze. In some instances the sequence included some pre-industrial element of the countryside; oxen plowing the land was the most common. If rural subjects appeared in this first sequence, they would almost always do so backlit in silhouette, which made them part of the landscape itself; here they were not filmed as individuals but rather as figures that completed the picture. This, with very minor differences, was the beginning of *El puente* (The bridge), *Desde las nubes* (From the clouds), *Una voz en la montaña* (A voice in the mountain), *La casa de un amigo* (A friend's house), *La guardarraya* (The fence), *Cuando los padres olvidan* (When parents forget), and *Doña Julia*, just to mention a few. One DIVEDCO film was composed entirely of landscape shots: the 1958 short *El contemplado isla cordillera*, using a choral version of Rafael Hernández's "Los carreteros" (The oxcart riders), placidly moves—in color!—from dawn to dusk through the island without ever venturing into a single urban space. The repetition *ad absurdum* of the rural in these sequences, if narratively and cinematographically necessary, also pointed to DIVEDCO's inclination to blur the contemporary traces of the urban, when what was disappearing was the countryside.

LOCATION SCOUT POET

There is something quite intriguing about the rural imagery in DIVEDCO's cinema: it seemed to have been the cinematic realization of certain poetry by Luis Lloréns Torres (1876–1944), especially his *décimas*, those ten-line poems that formulated an idyllic relation with the countryside and all things rural:

Ay, qué lindo es mi bohío	Oh, how pretty my hut is
y qué alegre mi palmar	And how cheerful my palm trees
y qué fresco el platanar	And how cool the plantain trees
de la orillita del río.	By the banks of the river.

("Vida criolla," *Antología* 85)

Lloréns's sentimental and truly romantic countryside is yet another countryside of the city, one "uncontaminated earthly paradise," as Arcadio Díaz Quiñones labeled it ("La isla" 56), and one that re-created the world of his lost childhood and adolescence (55).

Although most of his poetry was composed and published during the first decades of the century, Lloréns Torres was magnanimously canonized from the 1930s to the 1950s, first with celebrations and homages in theaters in San Juan—with "real" jíbaros reciting his poems (Díaz Quiñones, "La isla" 13)—and later on with the introduction of his poetry in the public school curricula of the island. The poems even appeared frequently in the almanacs and several of the *Libros del pueblo* published by DIVEDCO.[6] In the 1960s, the scholar Margot Arce de Vázquez would even insist on the startling authenticity of Lloréns's jíbaro voice in his poetry: "Las [décimas] que reproducen el habla jíbara . . . si no llevaran la firma de Lloréns, pasarían fácilmente por auténticas piezas de nuestro folklore poético" (If the [décimas] that reproduce jíbaro speech had not been signed by Lloréns, they would have easily passed for authentic pieces from our poetic folklore) (42).[7]

As I have already argued, this literary attraction to the Puerto Rican landscape is not unique to Lloréns Torres. But the launching of DIVEDCO's film production chronologically coincided with the canonization of Lloréns Torres, and their views of the rural seem two gestures of a similar nature, both of them univocally linked to the maneuverings of the national. In a very real way, DIVEDCO films were the phantasmatic projection of Lloréns's countryside, along with the jíbaro and jíbara and all their rural paraphernalia. The landscape that Lloréns waxed lyrically about in the 1920s Muñoz Marín and DIVEDCO turned into a cinematographic reality in the 1950s. With his décimas, Luis Lloréns Torres figuratively became the "location scout" for the Division of Community Education.[8]

BUILDING A FRIEND'S HOUSE

Flor de la tierra es la vivienda.

The home is the flower of the land.

Antonio S. Pedreira, *Insularismo*

Yo tengo ya la casita
que tanto te prometí . . .
Ahora seremos felices,
Ahora podemos cantar.

At last I have the little house
I've promised you so often . . .
Now we'll be happy—
Now we can sing.

Rafael Hernández, "Ahora seremos felices" (Now we'll be happy)

Now, because of the educational nature of DIVEDCO films, the notion of the rural space as mere landscape, though always there, for the most part occupied a more subsidiary or supplemental position relative to the rural subject: it was the men and women from the countryside who were the focus of these films. The division's film production was fundamentally about agency, about what the jíbaro and jíbara can/should/must do as modernization transformed their island. If at the beginning of some films the inhabitants were inserted as part of the landscape, that role soon yielded to action—or at least to a call for action—once the plot started unfolding. And yet, these DIVEDCO jíbaros were hemmed in by a paradox: in the process of being educated by these films to act and think for themselves, they were also confined to a certain subjectivity. What better way to put the jíbaros, as it were, in their place than by, for instance, building a house for them.

La casa de un amigo (A friend's house), a film completed in 1963, with a screenplay by the writer Emilio Díaz Valcárcel and directed by Amílcar Tirado, one of the most important Puerto Rican directors of DIVEDCO, is a particularly good example of the "problem" film typical of the division, in this case proposing a solution to the difficulties of housing. Filmed in San Lorenzo, a municipality in the montainous southeastern corner of the island, it tells the story of Luis and Carmen, a couple who require a house of their own in order to get married. Building it from scratch seems to them an ominous task, but Hilario, a friend who is building his own house out of wood, explains to Luis how he has been able to do it: with the cooperation of his neighbors, who provided the labor. Luis follows Hilario's advice and is able to build quite a nice house, not unlike the one promised in the famous Rafael Hernández song "Ahora seremos felices" (Now we'll be happy). The film ends with a wedding and a party in Luis and Carmen's new home.

Luis and Carmen's lovely ending is as happy as it is improbable. The first thing that stands out in this thirty-eight-minute film is how idealized the couple's circumstances seem to be. Even though the story is about an issue that will require some resources, the film conveniently evades the issue of the couple's economic circumstances. They are clearly not financially comfortable, but they seem to have no problem purchasing the materials for the construction—or going shopping in town and acquiring pots and pans for the kitchen and fabric for the drapes in the new house. Is this middle-class, consumerist rurality? The audience remains totally unaware of what Luis does for a living. Carmen, of course, does not work and spends the entire film at home, doing laundry, cooking, and making coffee for the men around her.[9]

And these jíbaros were glamorous. While many films used nonprofessional actors, there were quite a few that included well-known actors for the leading roles. In *La casa de un amigo*, two theater and television actors, Iris Martínez and Miguel Ángel Álvarez, played Carmen and Luis. Their somewhat affected performance stylized the film, thus steering clear of potentially neorealist aesthetics (quite common in many early DIVEDCO films); Martínez's over-the-top finesse, for instance, is frankly a bit incongruous, though the cinematography itself seems to stress this preference for a very stagy performance. There is a shot toward the beginning of the film that perfectly portrays this affected construction: Carmen is washing clothes in front of her parents' wooden house, her hair impeccably done; sun rays sparkle against the metal washbasin, and a flower carefully placed on the lower right corner of the frame seems to appear as a visual metaphor for Carmen's face.

La casa de un amigo was undoubtedly conceived in the context of the housing issues of the time—the making of the film coincided with the burgeoning construction of public (and private) housing developments all around the island and the government's campaign for the elimination of slums in urban areas. But the division, as it usually did, avoided the problem in the city and opted to solve the matter in the countryside, where the problem was not particularly real—migration in the 1950s and early 1960s was toward urban areas, not away from them. And it resolved the issue in a quasi-bucolic space.

However, this idealization, which connotes a certain erasure, is fraught with contradiction, and it has actually left traces of "noise" in the film, as Michel de Certeau would have called them. There is one moment that escapes the rural-utopic project: as Luis is returning from town, he walks by a construction site where there are numerous men building houses . . . out of concrete! The scene stands out from the rest of the film. While most of the film has a quiet pacing, accompanied by melodious, gentle music played on accordion and guitar, here the film's pace speeds up, with quick cuts and an extradiegetic, hasty melody on the accordion. The shots are a series of very tight frames in which the viewer witnesses with Luis hills covered with houses under construction and dozens of men passing around buckets of construction material and shouting orders. It's the commonwealth's euphoria. It's the goal of Muñoz Marín's Operations. It's the electric energy of modernization and development. It is also the urbanization of the countryside.

But the film doesn't linger here; neither does Luis linger the way he had at the beginning of the film, when he sees Hilario building his wooden house; Luis walks away from this exhilarating spectacle. The scene that immediately follows exposes the narrative trap that the film sets up for Luis and the audience. After the euphoria of concrete construction, the film cuts to a shot of Luis walking through the countryside while we hear someone sawing wood offscreen; the next shot is Hilario's house, almost finished. The camera is set at a low angle and is slowly and sweetly dollied in toward the house. The contrast with the previous scene is stark and startling. And it is precisely in this scene that Luis decides to build his house—a wooden house—with the help of his neighbors, like his friend Hilario has been doing.

Like a good division jíbaro—a Lloréns jíbaro, for sure, straight out of his décimas—Luis remains intent on building his house out of wood; the dramatic sight of concrete houses doesn't persuade him to think that one of those houses could be his. Luis seemed to incarnate a line from "Copla Lejana" (Faraway couplet), another poem by Lloréns: "Mi bohío es mi fortuna" (*Antología* 76), which means not only "my hut is my fortune" but also "my hut is my destiny." Luis is not troubled, for instance, by a series of questions: Who are these houses for? Why can't one of them be for me? Why couldn't I make mine out of concrete, to withstand hurricanes and tropical storms (like his friend Hilario had explained to him earlier in the film)?

While these concrete homes in the film undermine the division's pastoral construction—an image that temporarily dismantles the notion that the jíbaro must remain anachronistically rural—Luis is written and filmed to resist the modernization of vernacular architecture. His house must be a wooden one; to wish for it to be of concrete would complicate the Manichaean construction of the jíbaro and the idyllic stance of the narrative filmed.[10] And here lies the paradox of the Division of Community Education: a modern and progressive effort to help the peasantry with modernization, alongside a nostalgic crystallization of rural subjects and spaces. *La casa de un amigo* places Luis within the idyllic rhetoric of the DIVEDCO, while it simultaneously pushes him out of the modernizing rhetoric of the commonwealth.

JÍBARAS UNITED

Luis, as a character imbued with what we might call a certain domesticity toward the machinations of the commonwealth, is not alone in the DIVEDCO corpus. Félix Jiménez, in his thought-provoking book on Puerto Rican masculinities, *Las prácticas de la carne*, regards the jíbaro in these films as a malleable subject, almost emptied of agency: "Es el hombre anclado en la didacticidad, en el melodrama de reconocimiento que pretendía su conversión en *tabula rasa* para volver a aprender a ser" (It's the man anchored in didacticism, in a melodrama of recognition that sought his transformation into a *tabula rasa* to learn to be once more) (74). While it is difficult to argue against Jiménez's stance in regard to many of the men's compliance in the films' narratives, the role of some women in DIVEDCO's countryside clashes a bit with the fate of men like Luis. Images of women were simply not part of the government's official visual iconography of these years (see the introduction), but there were several division films produced with a female protagonist (Marsh Kennerly, *Negociaciones* 230). One of them stood out for portraying women in a decidedly empowering role: *Modesta*, a 1956 film that tackled head on the injustice of gender inequality in the rural space.

Mostly performed by the members of a community in what was then rural Guaynabo (today an urbanized municipality next to San Juan), the film tells the story of Modesta, a typical jíbara who, pregnant with a third child, is trying to keep up with all her household chores; her husband, however, is not very understanding of her situation and is constantly berating her for not having everything ready for him whenever he wants it. One day, when her husband was particularly inconsiderate, Modesta loses her cool and ends up beating him with a stick. News of her action spreads like wildfire, and it brings the women of this rural barrio to unite and form the League of Liberated Women. They eventually draft a "law" (written down by Modesta's young daughter, the only female who is able to write in the community) that establishes a series of rules, duties, and regulations for gender interaction. The men and women negotiate the law in a scene photographed and edited like a Western film's showdown, and at the end they approve the statutes, with some alterations.

The film's narrative clearly sides with the women of the community: *Modesta* begins as the families wake up, and all we hear are the men shouting for black coffee or water, complaining about unironed shirts, and ordering their women out of bed to make them breakfast. After the scene in which Modesta hits her husband with the stick, it is the men who are gossiping about the event, not the women. As the women hear about what Modesta did, they quickly decide to organize; the women's meeting is intercut with a scene of the men upset and moody at the local bar, drinking rum and beer and listening to a song that functions as their implicit thought:

Una mujer en mi vida	A woman in my life
se ha empeñado en destruirme.	is set on destroying me.
Dios le dará su castigo	God will punish her
por mala antes de morirme.	for her sins, before I die.

Still, while *Modesta* depicts the pressing need for fairness, it seems to distance itself from gender equality per se, discarding any radical reading from these women's actions in the countryside. As Catherine Marsh Kennerly has convincingly argued, the film was indeed remarkable for its portrayal of women forming an association for solidarity and support (*Negociaciones* 242), but the scholar also insists that films like *Modesta* reflect "un doble movimiento de modernización y conservadurismo" (a double movement between modernization and conservatism) (230). Indeed. The writing of the law and the subsequent negotiations reveal a less progressive project: it is presented to the men as a list of "rights as mothers and wives" instead of simply as "women," unquestionably leaving untouched the expected roles for women within a patriarchal system. The women themselves make it clear at one point during the negotiations—"We are not rebelling"—and within the parameters of 1950s Puerto Rico, they were precisely not doing that.[11] Faithful to the ideals of Operation Serenity, the film was instead a call for reform. The penultimate shot of the film reassures a nonviolent, happy conclusion: a medium frame of the ground with the couples, now reunited, stepping over the sticks that had become the symbol of resistance for the women in the community.

In addition, *Modesta*'s script keeps a temporal distance that lessens the impact of the women's rebellion and rulings about gender disparity. The male voice-over narrator at the beginning of the film states that what we are about to witness happened many years ago—that the story has come down from time immemorial to our great-great-grandparents. This is an intriguing gesture in the filmic output of the division, since the agency claimed that many of its films' plots were based on contemporary, actual events.[12] The narrator in *Modesta*, however, purposefully refuses to set this situation in the present, even when the film itself persistently contradicts this notion—the song the men hear at the bar, for example, is playing from a jukebox. That distance relegates the story to the status of myth, an elders' tale, and therefore it is expected not to be taken literally.

On the other hand, the spatial immediacy of the rural—jíbaros watching jíbaros behaving intolerantly, jíbaras watching jíbaras not tolerating that behavior—should not be underestimated. Setting the film in the countryside and, more importantly, screening it there authenticates DIVEDCO's desire to encourage changes in gender relations that move away from traditional, submissive notions of womanhood. It does advocate for a rethinking of machismo and for the recognition of rural women's rights in the private space of the home. This much is true. Be that as it may, it is impossible to forget that there is a considerable distance between the rural space represented in *Modesta* and the urban space in which these films were assembled: formal artistic decisions, political leanings, and unit committee meetings in the capital all had their role in the decisions made while shaping the film. *Modesta* was undoubtedly an attempt to spark a conversation about the way gender is enacted and perceived, but it was also an urban mythographic rendition of the rural in which women were simultaneously invited to participate in democracy while regulated and disciplined for doing so without any hint of radical adjustments (Marsh Kennerly, *Negociaciones* 219–20). For example, this ambivalence toward women as public, engaged subjects in Puerto Rican society can be explained in part by the participation of René Marqués as one of the screenwriters of the film; his advocacy for a strategic positioning of machismo as a central tenet in regard to nation and citizenship has been well documented by several scholars.[13]

Now, if *Modesta* was a partially successful, if somewhat problematic, reconfiguring of the place of contemporary women in rural Puerto Rico, other DIVEDCO films readily discarded any emancipatory project for women. Also set in the countryside, *La cucarachita Martina* (Martina, the little roach) was a short animated film based on the well-known children's story. The film, written by René Marqués, was never completed, though around 1952 the division went as far as storyboarding the entire script and filming all of the scenes; they even recorded the jíbaro music for the songs.[14]

While singing and cheerfully cleaning her house, Martina finds a penny and decides, after seeing herself in the mirror and noticing that her skin is oily, to spend her money on makeup. She is very soon courted by different animals wanting to marry her, but she decides to marry the one she has always liked: the little mouse Miguel. They live very happily except that the husband loves to eat, and one day he tries to take some cheese out of a mousetrap . . . somewhat unsuccessfully. He doesn't die, but his tail is cut off by the mousetrap. Later on, Martina asks Miguel to check on an onion soup that she is preparing, but the mouse is a bit too interested in the soup and so he falls in the pot and dies. The film ends with Martina mourning her husband.

It is true that in the story Martina is the one making the choice of a husband (and not the other way around), but the story undermines any possible transgressive element at the outset of the film. While she is cleaning her house, she sings this song (written by René Marqués):

Que gusto tan grande	What a great satisfaction
yo siento al barrer	I feel when I sweep
yo limpio la casa	I clean all the house and
y también el batey	The yard as I sing
y esto lo hago	And all this I'm doing
con mucho placer	With never a peep
porque así me ayuda	Because it will help me
a encontrar mi Rey.	To find me my King.
(La cucarachita Martina)	

Seeing herself as necessarily a future wife, Martina is portrayed within the most traditional notions of womanhood; she invested her money in beautifying herself, and this action led to courtship, which "naturally" led to marriage. In an early version of the script, there was a moment toward the end of the story when Miguel the mouse is critiqued as a husband, but the storyboard with the narration and songs—which were used for the scenes that were filmed—deleted this scene. We are clearly not in the realm of *Modesta*, where women have to call out unfair treatment in order to set parameters of conduct for their men; marriage in *La cucarachita Martina* goes back to a traditional, compulsory, and normative structure. To their credit, *Modesta* was finished and screened all over the island; postproduction on *Martina* was never finished. Although no documentation exists, perhaps the cinema unit realized a certain datedness in the story. But perhaps the film went as far as it did in production because that traditional positioning of woman was, in the context of the urban space, thought to be naturally located in the rural environment.

LINOCUT WINDOWS

Much of the literature produced during these years postitioned itself as a map that would explain the paradoxes of the commonwealth in regard to modernization and the significant geopolitical displacement of Puerto Ricans and things Puerto Rican evident in migration (see chapter 3). But it is important to remember that the rural theme in that urban literature did not simply disappear. The incipient urban fiction, and to some extent theater as well, did not ignore the intimate relationship that the city had with the countryside: the rural never went away, even in the middle of urban narratives.

A particularly interesting case is "El asedio" (The siege), a short story by Emilio Díaz Valcárcel written in 1956 and published two years later in his first collection of stories. As in much of his fiction, the protagonist is a social outsider: in this instance, it is a woman—an academic and a lesbian—who views the city and its inhabitants that surround her as aggressively alienating. At the end of the story, sitting in her apartment and staring out the window, she notices something on the wall of her room: "Miró hacia la ventana, cerca de la cual colgaba un grabado de Rafael Tufiño. Un grupo de hombres desyerbando, trazados con vigorosas líneas. Esa puede ser la felicidad, meditó; en esos brazos nudosos y en esos rostros contraídos por la miseria hay un serio compromiso con la vida, una sinceridad de propósitos que tú, la *scholar*, la humanista, nunca has tenido" (She looked toward the window, close to which a print by Rafael Tufiño was hanging. A group of men hacking weeds in a field, rendered with vigorous lines. That could be happiness, she pondered; in those hard, muscular arms and those faces creased by misery, there is a serious commitment to life, an openness of purpose, that you, the scholar, the humanist, have never had) (42). I seriously suspect that the print referred to here is Rafael Tufiño's famous linoleum print, *Cortador de caña* (Sugarcane cutter), from 1951. What stands out the most in this linocut print by

one of the most important artists of the time is that the image of the countryside
is not bucolic. It shows instead a different rural paradigm: the countryside as a
space of work, of hard work. The fact that the female character is depending on
a group of cane cutters for psychological support plainly manifests the distortion
she has made of the rural and the rural subject: happiness, for her, seems to reside
in arduous manual work and in a space away from the urban realm.[15]

Rafael Tufiño, *Cortador de caña*, linocut, 1951.
Courtesy of the estate of Rafael Tufiño.

The main character ultimately rejects the countryside as an option for her, but her thought process, revealed through the narrator's free indirect speech, uncovers the paradoxical image the character has of the rural: "No quería pensar en la honradez del campo—representada en cierto sentido, en parte, por el grabado junto a la ventana—en la honradez amatoria del campo, en las orillas de los ríos, en el cálido abandono de los bosques, en los anónimos jergones primitivos donde el amor es más puro y menos dialéctico" (She didn't want to think about the integrity of the countryside—represented in a way, partly, by the print next to the window—about good rustic love, about river shores, about the warm wilderness of the forests, about the anonymous straw mattresses in which love was purer and less dialectic) (42). With the woman in the story granting genuine pastoral significations to a print that reproduces a countryside essentially imbued with labor, we are back to the imagistic, rural vision in Lloréns Torres's poetry—rivers and all. Her gaze suppresses the social and economic conditions of the image represented, not unlike Babín's countryside in *Fantasía boricua*. These two vantage points are not identical—if the working subject in *Fantasía boricua* was framed by a Catholic rhetoric of a lost Eden, here we are before the framing of work (of hard labor, no less) as a quasi-purifying process. And yet, they both function as acts of erasure, of crossing out. In Babín, this act is only visible as an unrealized symptom; in Díaz Valcárcel's "El asedio" it is deliberately exposed as a problematic obliteration.

This critique in "El asedio" acquires an intriguing dimension with the fact that Emilio Díaz Valcárcel actually wrote the plot treatment for *La casa de un amigo* (among several other DIVEDCO films) and cowrote the script with the director; he was one of those figures in the 1950s who had to maneuver their involvement in government cultural offices while producing an artistic or literary output outside those spaces.[16] This merits a closer look.

Indeed, Díaz Valcárcel's scripts did not have the ironic standpoint, with recurring elements verging on the grotesque, that was so typical of his early short fiction. But there seems to be a revelatory correlation between his filmic and literary takes of the countryside, specifically the ways in which he, quite literally, frames the rural. W. J. T. Mitchell's notions about landscape are quite useful here:

"Landscape is a natural space mediated by culture. It is both a represented and presented space . . . both a frame and what a frame contains, both a real place and a simulacrum" (qtd. in Andrews 15). Through visual and aural cues, *La casa de un amigo* reproduces a rural that follows closely the DIVEDCO tradition, fashioning it as mere landscape; thus, the countryside is framed, that is, displayed, delimited, and contained, as an idealized space by the cinematic undertaking. By contrast, in the short story the rural is totally removed from bucolic representations, and it is made present only through the writerly description of a visual reproduction. It is quite significant that the linocut is next to a window, because the print itself becomes a window of sorts, one that allows the protagonist to view and imagine a world that contrasts with her urban existence: Tufiño's men, barefoot, with their shirtsleeves rolled up and machetes in hand, are worlds apart from what she sees through her window at the end of the story—those fancy men and women entering the city's casino, laughing and dressed to the nines, with soft necks and impossibly white teeth. So, in essence, "El asedio" provides two side-by-side frames: one that allows a (somewhat undesirable) view of the urban, another that reproduces the (spatially distant and ultimately discarded) agricultural countryside. What relations can be surmised from these cinematic, graphic, and literary frames? At one level, Díaz Valcárcel the screenwriter seems to have tolerated the Edenic constructions of the countryside in the more official cultural product, though the insertion of the concrete homes halfway through the film could be viewed as a possible strategy to unsettle that construction. But, to his credit, division films were highly collaborative: the final product of *La casa de un amigo* surely contained the decisions of the cinematographer, the editor, and the music consultant (to mention just a few technicians), all supervised by the director and the administration of the division—decisions on which a screenwriter had little or no influence. In "El asedio," the author, without hesitation, proceeded not only to dismantle these rural constructions but also to insert them within the urban quandaries associated with the countryside of the city. By framing the countryside within the reproduction of a reproduction, next to a window frame that looked out to the urban space of San Juan, Díaz Valcárcel summarily represented the complex conundrum of these years.

COUNTERPASTORAL

For the most searing gesture against midcentury constructions of the country-side, however, one must look to literature, specifically the literary output of José Luis González. His work was a disturbance, a veritable disruption against the ways in which the city had been mummifying the countryside. González con-stituted a profound writerly alteration, one that Raymond Williams would have accurately called counterpastoral. His fiction never employed the rural idealized, what González would later call *jibarismo* (González, "El país" 37), an attitude that, as María Acosta Cruz has demonstrated, has not entirely disappeared from some of today's Puerto Rican literature.[17]

Although literary critics and historians have traditionally identified José Luis González as a foundational figure in the island's urban literature, especially since the publication of *El hombre en la calle* (Man on the street) in the late 1940s, many of his stories published in that decade and the early 1950s dealt directly with the rural spaces of the island in the context of Puerto Rico's urbanization and indus-trialization. Since his very first collection of stories, *En la sombra* (In the shade), published at the beginning of the 1940s, the rural subjects and their space were neither picturesque nor glamorized. The prologue of that collection, written by the scholar Carmen Alicia Cadilla, had pointed out how far away González's countryside was from the literary depictions of the time, which were immersed in what she called a "caricatura guiñolesca de lo puertorriqueño" (a puppet show caricature of things Puerto Rican) (6). González himself was quite conscious of this; in an interview from the early 1980s he asserted, "Algo de 'novedoso' había ya [en los cuentos de *En la sombra*] en lo tocante a la visión del mundo campesino. No es un mundo idealizado, como el que presentaban muchos de los narradores *jibaristas* de las generaciones anteriores, sino un mundo en crisis, afectado ya por la urbanización acelerada del país" (There was already something "new" [in the stories from *En la sombra*] in regard to the vision of the peasant's world. It is not an idealized world, like the one many *jibarista* narrators had presented in previous generations, but rather a world in crisis, affected by the accelerated urbanization of the country) (Fernández 52). For instance, the countryside of "Encrucijada" (Crossroads), from *En la sombra*, and "La mujer" (The woman), from his second book, *Cinco cuentos de sangre* (Five tales of blood), published in 1945, was not depicted with the typical charming touches: the settings were, respectively, the construction of a dam and of an electric plant—that is, a rural space affected and transformed by modernization. Guillermo Irizarry, in his monograph on the author, has pointed this out: "Los textos simbólicamente abren el espacio campesino a influencias externas y renuncian a la nostalgia por los valores premodernos y patriarcales" (The texts symbolically open the space of the countryside to external influences and they reject the nostalgia for premodern and patriarchal values) (54). These values were intimately connected to that countryside of the city.

As in most literature of the time, urban migration of rural subjects was a recurrent theme in González. His long short story "Paisa (un relato de la emigración)" (Paisa [a tale of emigration]), published in 1950, is a remarkable text that presented the human exodus from the countryside to San Juan, and from there to the United States, through the experience of the traditional (and not the folkloric) facing the modern; the story touches on many of the issues that Marqués's *La carreta* would deal with, although with some major differences (see chapter 3). But unlike most writing of the time, González's rural went beyond the mountainous countryside so often preferred: the microstory "Cangrejeros" (Crab catchers), from *Cinco cuentos*, for example, is set in the mangroves, a marginal space that was rarely documented in midcentury literature and that was historically important for some communities on the island.

Not surprisingly, the agricultural and industrialized rural, especially the despised world of the sugarcane plantation in the coastal valleys of the island, is also present in many of González's early works. "El viento" (The wind), another story from *En la sombra*, could be read as a fascinating rewrite of Enrique Laguerre's famous novel *La llamarada* (The blaze) (1935). Without a doubt, Laguerre's text is a lacerating critique of the sugarcane workers' labor conditions during the first decades of the twentieth century, but the countryside remains bound to a distorted idealization, and the protagonist, a young agronomist fresh out of college who comes to work at the plantation, sustains a quasi-purifying relation with things rural—which for him seems closer to the "natural" than the agricultural: "¡Quiero entrar en ti, Patria, sierra, cumbres, árboles, cielo, valles, pájaros, albahaca, yerbas, prados, paisaje!" (I want to enter you, Fatherland, mountains, peaks, trees, sky, valleys, birds, basil, grasses, prairies, landscape!) (194). Toward the end of the novel, this young man, frustrated by human hatred and prejudice, throws himself into a nurturing rurality: "Todo se me metía en el alma invitándome a abandonar los trapos de la civilización. La Naturaleza quería recibirme como al hijo pródigo, con los brazos abiertos" (Everything would encroach in my soul inviting me to abandon the rags of civilization. Nature wanted to receive me like the prodigal son, with open arms) (244).

In contrast, the depiction of the same setting in González's short story never resorts to a romanticized discourse of the natural in the rural. It is instead presented as an imposing landscape; the protagonist's first encounter with the sugarcane fields has an ominous quality: "nunca había imaginado que pudiera contemplar . . . tanto verdor unánime de una sola mirada" (I would have never imagined that I could contemplate . . . so much unanimous greenness with just one look) (*Cuentos completos* 55). The word *unánime* here is an odd but terribly appropriate word: with it, the protagonist and the author refer to the transforming landscape of agricultural monocultures. This awareness continues in the following sentence: "En el medio de la llanura se levantaban los grises edificios de la central azucarera con sus altas chimeneas de las que nacían oscuros penachos de humo oloroso a melaza" (In the middle of the valley the gray buildings of the sugar refinery rose, with their tall chimneys delivering dark plumes of smoke smelling of molasses) (55). The rural is, visually and olfactorily, unmistakably industrialized.

Equally significant, the authors' critiques of that specific rural, agricultural world reveal quite different positions, even though both were very condemning of that space. *La llamarada* was smeared by a pessimism that ultimately did not allow any sort of social transformation, let alone any agency among the workers or even in the protagonist himself—the sociopolitical failure was, in fact, sublimated by the protagonist's romantic love. "El viento" also documented the failure of an educated man who genuinely wanted to make a difference in the workers' lives, but the story steps away from a purely fatalistic outcome. In a gesture that today we would label postmodern, the main character, named José Luis, like the story's author, reads out loud to the sugarcane plantation workers every night straight from the pages of *La llamarada* itself; at the end of the story, before he quits the plantation, the young man leaves his copy of the novel with the workers so someone else can finish the book for them. The insertion of the novel into the story produces a curious rearrangement: José Luis's readings rescue the novel from its pessimism by aiding the workers in recognizing their social positioning in the rural space, and it definitely plants the seed of a literary vocation in the narrator, who never resorts to an idealized notion of the rural nor a naturalized version of the natural. "El viento" uses *La llamarada* to bring with it winds of change.

But perhaps the literary rural of José Luis González could be best understood if we juxtaposed it with a figure like Abelardo Díaz Alfaro and his book *Terrazo*. González and Díaz Alfaro were viewed as the putative fathers of the new generation of writers in the 1950s. In fact, theirs were the first works in the canonical anthology *Cuentos puertorriqueños de hoy* that René Marqués had edited in 1959. Addressing the work of these two writers seems to me quite necessary.

In many ways, Abelardo Díaz Alfaro was the culmination of a literary tradition on rurality that had developed throughout the first half of the twentieth century; *Terrazo*, his collection of stories and nativist tableaux mostly set in rural Puerto Rico and published in 1947, quickly became a widely read book and was embraced by many academics and educators as a key literary text. By 1952, *Terrazo* had already become one of the required readings in Spanish classes for the ninth-grade public school curriculum (*Programa de educación secundaria* 65). González's fiction was nowhere to be found in the curriculum of those years.

The representation of the countryside in *Terrazo* does not necessarily participate in the bucolic imagery that I have been analyzing here; the title itself, a neologism, implies a violent strike of the land, or *tierra*. But there is a melancholic tone that in a certain way brings the text near the work of writers like Laguerre, and even Babín. The epigraph at the beginning of his book clearly sets the mood: "Siluetas de sangre, contra un paisaje luminoso. De los trillos, de las veredas, de los caminos reales que conducen a donde el bohío prende su ojo negro de angustia sobre los surcos abiertos al dolor y a la esperanza surgieron estos aguafuertes del terruño" (Silhouettes of blood, against a luminous landscape. From the trails, from the footpaths, from the main roads that lead to where the hut hangs its anguished eye over the furrows open to pain and to hope, did these etchings of the land originate) (7). To be sure, there is no trace of nostalgia in *Terrazo*. Rather, the rural is composed as a space of vicissitude and sorrow, a very accurate rendition of the Puerto Rican countryside of the time, and not unlike González's depictions. But as we enter the book itself, that countryside begins to show signs of staggering idealization. In the tableau "Don Rafa, caballero del machete" (Don Rafa, gentleman of the machete), Díaz Alfaro describes this man with a language engulfed by the apparent benevolence and gentleness of a "natural" countryside: "Mi amigo es del campo. La palabra le brota como al profeta Amós en metáforas de la naturaleza. Seco, rugoso, hecho al sol y sereno, parece un pensamiento de la tierra. Las lluvias del cielo y la inclemencia de los soles le abrieron surcos en el rostro. Pero su corazón es tierra virgen, tierra blanda que mana leche y miel de bondad. Ojos verdosos de donde fluye una luz tenue, suave; luz de esperanza, 'luz de domingo'" (My friend is from the countryside. Words sprout, as with Amos the prophet, in metaphors taken from nature. Dry, wrinkled, made under sun and wind, he seems a thought of the earth. The rains from the sky and the inclemency of the suns have opened furrows in his face. But his heart is virgin land, soft land that brings forth milk and honey full of goodness. Greenish eyes from where a soft and delicate light flows; light of hope, "Sunday light") (65). The description is particularly revealing: instead of personifying nature, Díaz Alfaro naturalizes the person. Almost like a mythological creation story, Don Rafa is rurality itself. The soft and generous quality of the Puerto Rican countryside—Pedreira's, Dávila's, Arce de Vázquez's—is here intensified and used to characterize, and essentialize, the rural man. We are leagues away from González's rural. A few lines below, his humble abode suffers a transformation as well: "¡Casita sencilla y rústica por fuera, como tu dueño por dentro, eres un palacio!" (Simple and rustic little house on the outside, like your owner inside, you are a palace!) (66). This rural is utterly sentimental (notice the endearing diminutive, *casita*). González, in the fiction of these same years, repeatedly and unsentimentally uses the word *rancho* to describe the country folks' dwelling, a word in Spanish that connotes the makeshift and fragile condition of the construction, very close to the terms "shack" or "hovel" in English. Díaz Alfaro recognizes the quality of the abode but can't help give it a noble quality; in that process, the house becomes palatial.

There is something else in *Terrazo* that is married to his depiction of the rural. In a number of stories, precisely the ones that have been printed and reprinted in anthologies and school textbooks, translated and disseminated away from the island as exemplary of national literature, the rural-telluric gesture of Abelardo Díaz Alfaro is fundamentally anti–United States: an attack against the English language and American culture in the short stories of the rural teacher Peyo Mercé (which close the book), and against the powerful, white, North American invasion in the now canonical story "El josco" that opens the book. But ironically, while *Terrazo* is the quintessential attack against the American colonial gestures of the first half of the century, it is an attack that does not seem (does not want?) to detect the decidedly neocolonial project of Muñoz Marín's party in its promise of modernization. And not unlike DIVEDCO's dismissal of the concrete-constructed rural community being built in *La casa de un amigo*, the urbanization of the rural space is simply set aside. This, in part, allowed Díaz Alfaro's book to become irreversibly canonical in the 1950s—because it contained an anti-imperialist critique that neglected (or perhaps more accurately, failed to consider) the consequences of modernization on the island. The telluric gesture in *Terrazo* was a direct reponse to a loss, as well as part of a mourning for the rural that was prevalent in the decade, thus making the book an authoritative text.

José Luis González, at least during the 1950s, could not be canonical in the same way that *Terrazo* was. González's fiction could not be easily appropriated, because he inserted the rural within migration discourse, because the landscape as landscape was never bucolic, because the narrating voices refused to resort to quasi-romantic notions of tradition and modernity, because González's distress was irate and not melancholic, because the jíbaros' houses were always too accurately labeled *ranchos*. The literary corpus of José Luis González was the gaze that dismantled the commonwealth's notion of progress, and this early work was squarely at odds with the rural depictions of the time. Thirty years later, in his book-length interview with Arcadio Díaz Quiñones, González explained his fundamental problem with these rural representations: "En principio el ruralismo sigue siendo un refugio derrotista y en principio los temas capitales de la literatura puertorriqueña deben ser los temas urbanos, *no por desprecio al mundo rural sino porque ese mundo es cada vez menos rural y más urbano*. Lo que yo propongo . . .

no es desatender al campesino sino atestiguar su transformación social" (In principle, ruralism continues to be a defeatist refuge and in principle the main themes of Puerto Rican literature should be urban themes, *not for disdain against the rural world, but because that world is less and less rural and more and more urban*. What I propose . . . is not to neglect the peasant but to give evidence of their social transformation) (*Conversación* 18; original emphasis). This is exactly what González's early stories achieve.

ESPOUSING THE COUNTRYSIDE

There is another gaze from the city that constructs a slightly different reading of the countryside, one that does not appear in literature or in film—not even in graphic arts: I am talking about popular dance music. Cortijo y su combo seemed to propose a rural space not without idealization, but conscious of the modernizing machinations of the tumultuous 1950s and of that decade's momentous migration.

As I discussed in the introduction, the repertoire of Cortijo y su combo mostly resided in the urban space, but there are a few songs in which the countryside makes a brief yet intriguing appearance. Even though these songs are perhaps participating in a nostalgic gesture toward the rural—something very common in the 1950s and, as mentioned above, integral to the constructions of national culture at this time—the band's positioning does recall its urban formation, and it does break away from that landscaping sheltered by the distance of social class.

"Pa' tumbar la caña" (To cut the cane), a bomba from *Bueno, ¿y qué?* (1960), hilariously suggests an alternative to the human-powered sugarcane harvest:

Coro:	Chorus:
Pa' tumbar la caña	If you're cutting cane
Pa' tumbar la caña	If you're cutting cane
Pa' tumbar la caña	If you're cutting cane
Tú te buscas un alacrán.	Go find yourself a scorpion.

Que lo buscas de cuatro patas	You must find one that's got four legs
Con boca como machete	And a mouth that's like a machete
El corte—de la raíz	It cuts the cane to the ground
Y la despacha en paquete.	And spits it out packaged already.
Cuando dan las doce y media	When it gets to be half past twelve
El punto para comer	The time for food in your bowl
El "ala" transportador	This scorpion conveyor belt
No se puede contener.	Completely loses control.
Que qué buena está la comida	"Look how wonderful all this food is"
dice el alacrán contento	It says with a happy toss
tengo pan, tengo yautía	"There's bread, there's sweet potato
malanga y mojito isleño	and taro in garlic sauce."
Le echa mano a la palomita	Then it grabs for the pigeon stew,
suelta el machete pa'l lao	Machete dropped somewhere about,
agarra la cucharita	And it takes up the spoon,
y agúcese Manolao.	Manolao, you better watch out!

If, superficially, the song appears to be escapist—this is undeniably the fantasy of a worker—"Pa' tumbar la caña" does not forget, cannot forget, the arduous labor conditions of the surgarcane plantation. Like in Tufiño's linocut *Cortador de caña*, this is not a bucolic countryside but instead a space, literally, of labor. The song never revels in scenes of sugarcanes in bloom blowing in the wind or gorgeous fields of rich greens—in fact, the landscape is entirely absent here. Its focus, and subtext, is hard work: machetes and sweat. If indeed the recording was referring to the livelihood of many jíbaros who were coastal rural laborers in the 1940s and 1950s (though these were rapidly decreasing), it was also alluding to a historical reality of African and African-descendant slaves on the island and their lives on the sugarcane plantation. The fact that the song is a bomba heightens the reference, since this musical genre had its roots in the plantation culture of the island. "Pa' tumbar la caña" was a song about a present that refused to forget the historical, agricultural context of Puerto Rico.

Be that as it may, the song is also about industrialization. "Pa' tumbar la caña" is animalizing mechanized agriculture: this scorpion is, to all intents and purposes, a machine. The creature, however, is not merely an automated contraption. Like the humans who have done this work for centuries, in the last two stanzas the scorpion is excited at the prospect of lunch and can't contain itself at the sight of the delicious food that is being served. While Cortijo's song melds the industrialized human with the modern, efficient apparatus in this energizing scorpion, it also refuses to erase the enthusiastic, bodily cravings of the worker, in a sort of internalized humanity. The super-creature is human and animal and machine without denying any of their inherent elements.

Even songs in which Cortijo participates in a possible nostalgic gesture toward the countryside, the band's positioning recalls its urban formation. "Yo soy del campo" (I'm from the country) distinguishes itself in Cortijo y su combo's repertoire because it moves pleasure away from San Juan and its neighborhoods to locate it in the mountains of the island. The song exalts the country folk over the urbanites.

Coro:	Chorus:
Yo no soy de la ciudad	I am not from the city—
Yo soy del campo	I'm from the country,
Y no sé porque será	And I don't know why it is
Que gozo tanto.	I have such fun, see.
Que tú dices que soy del campo	If you say that I'm from the country
No te lo voy a negar;	I won't deny it at all.
Oye, tú eres de la ciudad	Okay, you may be from the city
Pero yo gozo más.	But I have much more fun.
Que de la montaña venimos	You all know we come from the mountains
Para ponerte a gozar,	So you can come have a ball.

Oye, tú bailas en el casino	Okay, you're dancing at the casino
Pero yo gozo más.	But I have much more fun.
Es que en casa 'e siñá María	At the house of old Miz Maria
La fiesta se va a formar;	There'll be a bash, I recall.
Oye que yo me llevo a Sofía	Okay, you bet I'm taking Sofia
Para que goce más.	So she has much more fun.
¡Eh! cuando oigo sonar el güiro	Hey! When I hear the scraping *güiro*
Yo no me puedo aguantar.	My feet must follow its call!
Oye, tú eres de la ciudad	Okay, you may be from the city
Pero yo gozo más.	But I have much more fun.

The standpoint presented here is much more typical of traditional jíbaro music (a decade or so later, it will also appear in some salsa music), but it is not characteristic of the 1950s dance music of the island. Why this displacement of pleasure, away from the exciting world of the city? The song even goes so far as to have the singers claim that they come from the mountains, an origin that is clearly not the case with this band.

In a very important way, "Yo soy del campo" insists on a series of marked distinctions between the rural subject and the urban citizen.[18] But crucially, the song is fundamentally about the recognition that many of the inhabitants of San Juan were originally rural subjects, pointing in Cortijo's repertoire to the phenomenon of urban migration: the ones who truly have fun in the song are from the countryside, though they do not reside there anymore.

It is true that the song takes part in the idealized construction of the countryside—where pleasure supposedly comes from—but its lyrics and bomba rhythms are also a reaction against the hegemonic stance in the 1950s of the urban space: the city might have been thought of as the space of economic development and progress, but the notion of pleasure—at least for the recently arrived new urbanites—is not found there. Arguably, "Yo soy del campo" is a noteworthy document of the countryside internalized into the urban environment. The song could be conceived as the return of the rural in Cortijo's repertoire, but unlike other manifestations of the period, the song's gesture positions itself as a redefinition of the countryside in order to question both the commonwealth's overwrought notion of the rural (the one so prevalent in DIVEDCO films and in some literature) and the euphoric rhetoric of the urban—especially because its gesture is one informed by that essential experience of migration. Moreover, it's quite important that this critique came from the city itself and, more importantly, from its margins.

FOLKLORIZATION AND THE RURAL

En verdad que es hermoso este campo. . . . Contemplando así, de lejos. Porque cuando uno se le acerca, es puro trabajo y sudor. Y cuidado que el sudor hiede. Pero de lejos, el campo siempre invita.

Truly, this countryside is beautiful. . . . Looking at it like this, from far away. Because when you get close to it, it's pure work and sweat. And, let's face it, sweat stinks. But from far away, the countryside is always inviting.

Pepe, in César Andreu Iglesias's *El inciso hache*

Cuando lo rural se vuelve arcaico tiende a convertirse en patrimonio común y deseable desde el punto de vista simbólico.

When the rural becomes archaic, it tends to turn into a shared and desirable heritage, from a symbolic point of view.

Graciela Montaldo, *De pronto, el campo*

How we tell stories about landscape, whether through words, pictures or maps, ends up having an effect on landscape itself, as we try to fit the material world into our ideas of what it should be.

E. Melanie DuPuis, "Landscapes of Desire?"

Listening to the radio in my car on a trip to Puerto Rico during the early years of the twenty-first century, a minor reggaetón artist who was being interviewed—I honestly don't remember who he was—used the magic word to confirm and establish his Puerto Ricanness: the young man identified himself, after thinking about it for a moment, as a jíbaro. Tego Calderón, one of the most important and intriguing music performers of the first decade of the 2000s, declared matter-of-factly in a song from 2007, "Soy campesino" (I'm from the countryside) ("Tradicional a lo bravo"). When, today, music artists of such an urban musical genre as reggaetón still locate their identity on a subject as evidently rural as the jíbaro, it may be because a certain cultural project has gelled, a cultural relationship has been consummated, internalized, and naturalized about what it means to be a jíbaro, what it means to want to be a jíbaro. And the cultural machinations of the commonwealth in the midcentury were an important part of that process. It seems that Luis Lloréns Torres's charge from 1916 at the funeral of the political leader Luis Muñoz Rivera—"But let us all be, before anything, pure and simple, Puerto Ricans, pure and simple jíbaros" (qtd. in Díaz Quiñones, "La isla" 57)—has been taken to heart by generations of Puerto Ricans.[19]

Without a doubt, the jíbaro today is not a national subject in the way it was in the middle of the twentieth century; it is, rather, an image, an icon, a sign charged with meaning. Similarly, stating "I am a jíbaro" today implies neither a desire to return to rural spaces nor a nostalgic gesture for a life away from the apparent dissonances of the city; instead, the statement is part of the desire to identify oneself with what has been the national Puerto Rican subject par excellence of the twentieth century.[20] In a way, this contemporary attachment to the jíbaro subject conveys not only how the rural remains an originary space for Puerto Rican culture but also how the supposed shift from rural to urban is actually never complete: a predominantly rural society does not cease to be one absolutely. I would argue that perhaps since the 1960s we could speak of Puerto Rico and Puerto Ricans as postrural; even the urban space has been persistently haunted by the countryside.

But the issue that I have been trying to raise in this chapter is not simply the fundamental identification with the rural in a predominantly urban society. What is fascinating here are the ways in which the rural—the various spaces and their subjects, along with the economic, social, and cultural history—has been processed and refracted in its artistic and cultural production of Puerto Ricans at the transformational moment of modernization. The scholar Graciela Montaldo, in her thought-provoking book *De pronto, el campo* (Suddenly, the countryside)—a study of the rural image in 1920s Argentina—explains this phenomenon: "Mientras que, por un lado, se degradan en la percepción de la mayoría los rasgos de la vida rural—¡ya no se quiere vivir en el campo!—, por otro, se concibe lo rural como un espacio en el que perduran ciertos valores necesarios a los que, simbólicamente, se puede recurrir. Y la 'añoranza' o 'nostalgia' de lo rural que la cultura letrada comienza no a experimentar sino a construir, se alimentará de aquí en más de los discursos de esa cultura" (While on the one hand, the traits of rural life are debased in the view of the majority of people—no one wants to live in the country!—on the other hand, the rural is conceived as a space in which certain necessary values remain, values that, symbolically, one can resort to. And the yearning or nostalgia for the rural that the lettered culture begins not to experience but rather to construct, will feed off the discourses of that culture) (23). Montaldo points to a paradox that applies perfectly to Puerto Rico in the midcentury: the rural was not desired as an actual place but as a symbolic space that represented a certain notion of the national. But more than that, it seems to me that her observations are keenly implying what I would call the distorting process of folklorization: the urban cultural configurations of the countryside ultimately dehistoricized the rural, substituting the historical subject and the social space for symbolic avatars of authenticity. That is exactly what was attempted with the bucolic landscaping of a rural geography and its subjects in literature and the visual arts; that is exactly what occurred as certain examples of rural literature were canonized and made into school textbooks. And that is exactly what the counterpastoral gestures of a writer like José Luis González and the music of Cortijo y su combo were fighting against, as they inserted the phenomena of migration, labor, and industrialization into rural configurations. "[T]he natural innocence, the political dominance: it is all there," said Raymond Williams of the countryside (196). The political/cultural struggle for the rural, in the name of the rural, though almost never from the rural itself, was in Puerto Rico that battle between the wished-for innocence of the rural and the political appropriation of a space that served as a platform for the construction of national culture.

3

THE COUNTRYSIDE IN THE CITIES
Troubling Urban Cultures

*Y ese es el San Juan de mañana, menos épico que el de ayer, menos abigarrado y
egoísta que el de hoy; bello, sereno, gentil.*

*And that is the San Juan of tomorrow, less epic than yesterday's, less motley and self-
ish than today's; beautiful, serene, gentle.*
El libro de Puerto Rico (1923)

*Y así fue como San Juan se descubrió un mal día la fina cintura marinera llagada de
arrabales.*

*And this is how one bad day San Juan discovered its thin maritime waist blistered
with slums.*
José Luis González, "Paisa" (1950)

*The problem with Latin American cities is not the weight of tradition. Rather, it is
the weight of the modern.*
Attributed to Claude Lévi-Strauss

HOLDING A HAT IN his left hand and standing just inside the threshold of a wooden house, the young man in Eduardo Vera Cortés's silkscreen *La llegada* (The arrival) (1953) seems to have just arrived in the city—possibly for the first time. The house he is entering is very humble, with unpainted walls and no visible decoration. His right arm stretches down against his body; though his right hand is off the image's frame at the bottom, the gesture reads as if he is holding a heavy suitcase with his belongings. It is hard to read his almost expressionless face, perhaps because he is not sure what to think of the new surroundings. This sobering piece is printed in earth tones, almost as if the colors of the silkscreen are reminiscent of the countryside he has very probably left behind.

Eduardo Vera Cortés, *La llegada*, silkscreen, 1953.
Courtesy of the Museo de Arte de Puerto Rico.

His arrival is, pointedly, not in the idealized city of modernization but in a simple abode on the outskirts of Old San Juan—literally *extramuros*, outside the Spanish walls of the capital. The cityscape in the background that frames the young man's head is not the skyline of the city's colonial architecture, with old churches and second-floor balconies; rather, it is a conglomeration of zinc-roofed wooden houses, almost on top of each other. Farther out on the right one can see a *garita*, a circular, one-person sentry box from the San Cristóbal Spanish fort on the northeastern edge of the old city. This house, then, is in a clearly identifiable place: La Perla, a long-established poor neighborhood, outside the walls of Old San Juan, that was a frequent stop for men and women of the countryside when they migrated to the capital. For decades, this community had been labeled—and dismissed—as a slum, and by the commonwealth years it had acquired a symbolic resonance, one emblematic of the housing problems of the city and of the type of community that, in the name of progress and modernization, had to be eradicated. This is precisely the area where, a decade after this print was made, the American anthropologist Oscar Lewis would collect the interviews for his controversial book *La Vida*.

The printmaker Vera Cortés was part of the highly influential graphic collective Centro de Arte Puertorriqueño, or CAP (Center for Puerto Rican Art), a group that helped initiate in the visual arts a shift away from a persistence in depicting rural images, focusing instead on urban practices, spaces, and subjects. The interest in graphic arts in Puerto Rico—linocuts, woodcuts, and especially silkscreens—was actually established during the 1950s (Torres Martinó, "Las artes gráficas" 149). The Center for Puerto Rican Art, along with the Cinema and Graphics Workshop of the Public Parks and Recreation Commission, the Division of Community Education, and a few years later the workshop at the Institute of Puerto Rican Culture, spearheaded a veritable tradition of printmaking on the island that continued for decades. But, it seems to me, at least in the visual arts, it was the Center for Puerto Rican Art that inaugurated a deliberate visual intervention, with the new focus being on all things urban.

Inspired by Mexico's Taller de Gráfica Popular (People's Graphic Workshop), a collective founded in the late 1930s with a focus on social and political critique (some members of the collective actually studied there), the short-lived Center for Puerto Rican Art produced two portfolios that are now considered foundational in the art history of the island: the first one, *La estampa puertorriqueña*, was finished in 1951.[1] The second one, *Estampas de San Juan*, was issued in 1953, shortly after the collective had ceased operating.[2]

The word *estampa* in both portfolio titles is a somewhat troublesome word to translate into English. At face value, the word simply means a print, a reproduction, a picture; therefore, it was perfectly appropriate (and quite common) for graphic artists to use this term to describe what they produced. But the word, at least in Spanish, has also been employed for a scene that characteristically depicts folkloric or traditional customs—usually, though not always, in rural settings. In literature, at least since the nineteenth century and especially in the *criollista* or *costumbrista* tradition—a genre that documented and commented on the autochthonous—*estampas* referred to short, semifictional narratives that represented traditions and rituals; in the visual arts, an estampa could have referred to the illustration of those narratives. In the case of the Center for Puerto Rican Art, the portfolio titles seem to employ both meanings of the word, as the collections were indeed printed depictions that portrayed Puerto Rico and Puerto Ricans, their traditional celebrations, and their daily routines. But there was one peculiarity here: both portfolios were incursions into contemporary traditions and locales. Instead of nostalgic or sentimental depictions of past (or disappearing) traditions and scenes, the center's images distanced themselves from the costumbrista literary and visual tradition in the island—where a certain rural image reigned supreme (see chapter 2). CAP's project seemed to have been the assembling of a new autochthony, one that inserted a plethora of urban elements onto the Puerto Rican estampa.

The collections are, to be sure, not devoid of countryside imagery, though only two prints (from the first portfolio) were set away from the urban world: Carlos Marichal's *Paisaje yaucano* (Yauco landscape) and Rafael Tufiño's *Cortador de caña* (Sugarcane cutter). Both of them presented an alternative to the typically picturesque visual production of the time. Tufiño's linocut, as I discussed in the previous chapter, depicts a labor-intensive countryside by focusing on the worker rather than on the charming landscape produced by plantation economics. Marichal's woodcut at first glance seems indeed closer to a typical costumbrista

Carlos Marichal, *Paisaje yaucano*, woodcut, 1950. Courtesy of the Compañía
de Turismo de Puerto Rico and the estate of Carlos Marichal.

image: the woodcut, set in the southern municipality of Yauco, has DIVEDCO
skies and mountains, the humble abodes of the jíbaro, even a large-wheel oxcart
in the foreground. And yet the scene, far from being picturesque, has instead an
ominous feel. On the right, the low sun in the sky produces deep shadows (is
it sunrise? sunset?) that are instensified by the stark black-and-whiteness of the
xylograph; in the background at the top left corner, a cluster of large, dark clouds
and strong rains is pushing over the mountains toward the collection of homes.
There are no men and women to be seen; the cart has no oxen and it seems old,
even abandoned. We are at the opposite end of a pictorial tradition in Puerto
Rico that portrayed the countryside as a bucolic landscape. Here the countryside
is mysterious, unpopulated, eerie.[3] Has everyone perhaps moved to the city?

If undoubtedly these two prints created a fascinating dialogue with the art
production of the time, the rest of the pieces assembled unprecedented and com-

plex depictions that registered the commonwealth years' incipient urban culture. While a few of the prints (e.g., *Saltimbanquis*, *Día de los inocentes*) portrayed traditional street festivals and celebrations, both portfolios mostly paid attention to the ordinary life of urbanites, both within the old colonial city and outside it. Some of them portrayed typical characters of the city—the shoeshiner, the middle-aged lottery vendor, the hollering newspaper boy. Other prints chronicled the poor and migrant communities: workers helping to build a wooden house (*Obreros* [Workers]), a man begging on the street to feed his family (*Pobreza* [Poverty]). Many, like Félix Rodríguez Báez's *La Perla* and Vera Cortés's *La llegada*, set the estampas on the urban, marginal spaces inhabited by the newly arrived to the city.[4]

Something clearly evident from both portfolios is the center's interest in producing an urban visual account disassociated from the picturesque images of Old San Juan that had become so prevalent in these years because of the tourism industry. René Marqués has accurately pointed this out in the introduction he wrote for the second portfolio, with his characteristically indignant tone: "Nada hay en esta colección que recuerde los trucos fáciles de pintoresquismo tropical ni la ramplonería de estampas turísticas" (There is nothing in this collection that recalls the easy tricks of the tropical picturesque nor the vulgarity of touristic prints) (qtd. in Rosso Tridas 18).[5] As a matter of fact, the silkscreens in *Estampas de San Juan* purposefully reimagine the old city to present the complex existence of Puerto Ricans on an island that was increasingly being publicized as a desirable tourist destination, especially for Americans.[6] Lorenzo Homar's *Turistas* (from the second portfolio, though dated 1952) bluntly tackles this attitude.

Rendered with caricaturesque lines, almost resembling a newspaper political cartoon, and surrounded by a design that looks like a gaudy, bejeweled picture frame, the piece shows four obviously American tourists (one of them, camera in hand, wears an "I like Ike" button on his baseball cap) trying to capture the world that surrounds them. The tourists are placed in the foreground of the print, with stylish sunglasses, large earrings and bracelets, and loud shirts and blouses, but the tourists seem unaware of the regular life Puerto Ricans experience in Old San Juan. In the print's background, behind the tourists and quite distant from them, Homar depicts Cristo Street in the heart of Old San Juan, with men crossing the streets, a woman going home with her groceries, and a boy selling news-papers. The print displays what was, and still is today, the juxtaposed worlds of the old city: the picturesque town for the eyes of the tourist, and the town in which Puerto Rican men and women live their lives in the interstices of tourist attractions and spaces.

Other prints totally erase the touristic image of San Juan, subtly portraying the political tension of the time. Carlos Raquel Rivera's *Billetes y flores* (Lottery tickets and flowers) contrasts the foreground of men and women hanging out around a lottery vendor with the police in the background surveilling the public space of the plaza; the print is a sobering reminder of state control of the city after the 1950 nationalists' uprising. This is an image barely registered in the arts—in any arts—of the time.[7]

Looking back at its artistic output, we can see that the Center for Puerto Rican Art represented a remarkable venture into the complexity of the contem-porary changes in an urbanizing Puerto Rico. At the same time, the center iden-tified in these two portfolios a number of paradigmatic urban images that would circulate and persist in political, cultural, and artistic discourses throughout the Muñoz Marín years: the street and the square, the migrant and the urbanite, the tourist and the police, the solid home and the makeshift shack, the old town and the new city. These emblematic representations sometimes served simply as doc-umentation of change, but many times they were enthusiastically appropriated by different sectors of the island to either praise or condemn the modernization project of the commonwealth. This chapter is an examination of the applications and manipulations, the uses and abuses of these images as they depicted and delineated the incipient urban cultures of midcentury Puerto Rico.

REPRODUCING THE CITY

Without a doubt, the urban space has been an intrinsic part of Puerto Rico since colonial times. As Ángel Rama correctly asserted, the city, as an image of order and regulation, as well as a concrete space for control, was among the European powers' preferred colonizing tools in Latin America (2). But it is equally true that

in the modernizing middle years of the twentieth century—principally embodied in the capital city, though no less in large towns and sprawling subdivisions,
even in the network of paved roads and bridges that connected island residents
and communities—the urban undeniably predominated in the social and geopolitical fabric of Puerto Rico.

As fundamental as the city was to the island, however, there were peculiarities
about thinking and imagining the urban space during these years. Urbanization
was considered inevitable for modernization, but the city, as an image, as a construct, as a template, was never quite part of the sociocultural imaginary in the
commonwealth project. As I argued in the previous chapter, it was the rural that
persisted—for certain sectors of the intelligentsia—as part of the national cultural configuration. It was the jíbaro who stood for "authentic" Puerto Rico, not
the urbanites who lived in the newly designed neighborhoods like Puerto Nuevo
and Reparto Metropolitano, who listened to modern popular music on the radio
and on the recently arrived television, who went to the movies and acquired
automobiles to move around a city that was rapidly becoming congested. The
rural was deemed cultural; the city simply was not.

Why was the urban not part of the national matrix? In part, the reluctance
to insert urban cultures and spaces into the national imaginary of the commonwealth had to do with the fact that they irrefutably laid bare the contradictions
of modernization. Some of these contradictions stemmed from the issue of
migration, which profoundly problematized the image of the urban as the space
where modern living could potentially be realized. As a narrative, modernization stimulated an intense human transit toward cities, but the magnitude of that
movement exposed a city unprepared, and sometimes unwilling, to accomodate
its newcomers. In addition, issues like severe housing shortages and insufficient
(and inefficient) development of infrastructures—running water, paved streets,
sewage systems, electricity, and the like—became readily apparent.

Since the 1898 invasion, migration has been a fact of life for many, many
Puerto Ricans. Migration to the islands of Hawai'i began as early as 1900, and
the double migration from the countryside to the city of San Juan, and from
there to the United States—to cities of the northeastern United States and the
Great Lakes area and more recently to Florida—continued throughout the entire

twentieth century. Today, early in the twenty-first, there are in fact more Puerto Ricans living outside the island than on it. But the intense migration of Puerto Ricans that occurred during the middle of the twentieth century—encouraged by the insular government with the convenient support of modernization and development discourses—totally transformed the urban landscapes and the ways of "thinking the city."[8] To be sure, migration seemed to have been what the 1950s were actually about: it was the pulse that kept alive the incessant talks about the urban space. If the city was the new preocupation of politicians and novelists, printmakers and bureaucrats, engineers and playwrights, migration was the crux of that dialogue.

In addition, I would argue that the phenomenon of migration simultaneously organized and dispersed images of the urban. On the one hand, migration fastened defining notions of what was perceived as urban with what was connected to migration, but it also disseminated and incorporated rural practices and social networks into the urbanscape. This was of course because the majority of the newly arrived urbanites were in fact jíbaras and jíbaros migrating to town— jíbaros who wanted to adopt the modern ways of the city and leave the countryside behind for better health services, education, and living conditions, those same jíbaros who were praised by the government as the embodiment of authentic Puerto Rican culture. The countryside was now in the city.

But there was more. The dominant visual, aural, and textual gestures toward the national representation of the rural seemed intent on consolidating a certain depiction—originary, authentic, folkloric, comforting—precisely at a time when the physical space of the countryside was rapidly yielding to a diversity of urban spaces. This consolidation never occurred for the urban, not even for the city itself; if certain sectors defined, organized, and fixed an image of the rural— albeit one that some appropriated and disseminated, while others critiqued and dismantled—the urban became unruly as an image and a topos, a layered, multifarious representation. It was emphatically plural. Perhaps since things urban were not an integral part of the construction of a certain official national cultural framework, there might have been less desire for cohesion, for conceiving a homogeneous depiction.

And yet, amid this proliferation, the Puerto Rican midcentury seemed to have focused quite obssessively on one representation: the complex and heav-ily charged image of the "slums." Because of the many paradoxes contained in them—tradition and modernization, hygiene and social class, citizenship and liminality—these ostensibly undesirable urban spaces became the ideal instru-ment of discourse for both supporters and critics of the government. Of course, the varied appropriations of the slums by politically diverse artistic, media, and cultural sectors would disclose a series of social and cultural assumptions that would define this period and influence future administrations and cultural practices.

MIGRATING TO MODERN

In a speech given in late 1959, Governor Muñoz Marín spoke, in a somewhat perplexing way, about the effects of modernization on the common man: "La industrialización es el urbanismo, y el urbanismo rápido presupone un desar-raigo súbito del hombre de todo aquello que le es familiar. . . . Hablaba en estos días con un hombre que hace veinte años vivía en una choza techada con yagua de palma y que ahora vive en una casa modesta pero moderna, limpia, amplia, con adecuados muebles, con equipo eléctrico para su confort. Me decía, '¡Qué mucho trabajo tuve que pasar para salir de debajo de las yaguas! ¡Y qué mucho trabajo tengo que pasar para vivir rodeado de todo esto!'" (Industrialization is urbanization, and rapid urbanization presupposes a sudden uprooting from any-thing that is familiar to men. . . . I was recently talking to a man who twenty years ago lived in a hut roofed with dry palm leaves and now lives in a modest but modern house, clean, roomy, with suitable furniture, and electric appliances for his comfort. He was telling me, "How difficult it was to get out from under those dry palm leaves! And how difficult it is to live surrounded by all this!") ("Palabras" 7). This is a very peculiar narrative to construct about the paradoxes of modern living. To be sure, Muñoz Marín, here in his Operation Serenity mode, was once again pointing out the difficulties in the transition to a technologically modern society. But his anecdote skipped a crucial step in the experience of the great majority of the rural men and women who migrated to cities on the island:

in most cases they did not move first to "modest," modern houses but to plain, makeshift shacks in the slums on the city's fringes.

There probably was no better issue than the "problem" of the slums to reveal the contradictions and inequalities of modernization in all its disgusting splendor. As the sociologist Ángel Quintero Rivera has stated, slums were, in 1950s Puerto Rico, a source of shame for the new government and its supporters, even for the United States ("La investigación urbana" 69). In his 1946 memoir *The Stricken Land*, Rexford G. Tugwell, an FDR man who would be the last American governor of the island, described the slum conditions of San Juan thus: "El Fanguito, the shack city over the marshes beside the Martín Peña Channel, had, in 1934, consisted of a few hundred squatters' houses; now we saw it stretching up toward Río Piedras miles away in a seemingly endless spread of squalor. It had a kind of order and governance of its own, such as a homunculus or some other low form of life has: the shacks were in rows, that is, which left some open space for filth to accumulate, and the tide lifted the piles of garbage and deposited them again, in the same place, twice daily" (73). Tugwell's perspective of seeing El Fanguito as a separate space, as a city next to the city, with its own organizing principles, fit in every respect with many of the official (both insular and federal) assumptions of the time, as did the tendency to think of this space and its inhabitants with a paternalistic contempt. If there was a city of the commonwealth, the slums were decidedly not part of that image. Not unlike what occurred in the United States at the time, these social spaces were reluctantly recognized; in fact, they were acknowledged by the island's government and its supporters only to be uprooted and eliminated, to be erased without taking into account the many social and community processes that had developed in those areas. Even with the populist pulse of Muñoz Marín's party and administration, these slums, foundational in the history of several neighborhoods of the capital and indispensable for understanding the urban development of places like Cangrejos/Santurce or Puerta de Tierra, were to serve as the example of what the city was not, or should not be. They were also appropriated and used by government offices for the benefit of the urbanization project: their disappearance would be read as a glorious sign of progress and would arguably bring Puerto Rico closer to a successful urban renewal.

To this day, the word *slum* connotes, both in English and in its Spanish equiva-
lent, *arrabal*, images of inappropriate housing and unhealthy conditions, of undesirable living. Using the term, in fact, implies a necessarily dismal and pessimis-
tic representation of these spaces. "This is not Venice," ominously announces the
narrator at the beginning of the short film *Puerto Rico elimina el arrabal* (Puerto
Rico eliminates the slum) (1950) as we view images of makeshift homes built
over water. In this patently propagandistic piece, produced by Viguié Films, the
move from El Fanguito to new housing was literally filmed as a visual transition
from black to white, in black and white: from the black waters of the Martín
Peña Channel to the white buildings of new public housing; from the dark houses
without electricity—in which children smoke!—to community parks paved
with white concrete; from the dark mud of the mangroves in the channel to government milk stations. To be sure, the film rightly emphasized that transition as a
step toward hygiene, but it seemed incapable of escaping a certain moral hygiene,
an urban cleansing of sorts in the name of progress. The narrator summarized
the objectives of this government purge: "Cada casa que se traslade o queme
es una familia más que se arrebata de las garras del arrabal para convertirla en
ciudadanos libres de paz y orden dignos de gozar la verdadera vida democrática.
Y no se olvide que el arrabal es una pústula que amenaza todo nuestro cuerpo
social" (Each house moved or burned is one more family that is taken away from
the claws of the slum, in order to make them into free citizens of peace and order,
worthy of enjoying the true democratic life. And let us not forget that the slums
are the abscess that threatens our entire social body). This metaphor of illness was
not at all unique to the film. It was part of a rhetoric that had permeated social,
literary, and cultural thought in Puerto Rico since at least the last decades of the
nineteenth century, when naturalist writers like Manuel Zeno Gandía appropriated the image to launch a critique against Spain's appallingly slow adoption of a
modernizing project for the island (Gelpí, *Literatura y paternalismo* 7–9). What is
somewhat perverse in the 1950s was that this social and political gesture of heal-
ing—of violent extirpation, really—was now appropriated to erase a community
that by its mere presence threatened the commonwealth's modernization goals.

Although the slums seemed to have been a source of disgust and revulsion,
that geopolitical space was the period's favorite cancer. In a speech delivered in

1955, Ernesto Juan Fonfrías, then the president of the Autoridad sobre Hogares de Puerto Rico (Puerto Rico Housing Authority), described the slums as "casi un mal endémico, como lo fue la uncinariasis, hoy vencida por la férrea voluntad de los hombres de ciencia y del gobierno" (almost a chronic illness, like hookworm disease was, today defeated by the iron will of scientists and government men) (*La eliminación* 3). Elsewhere in the speech he called them a "costra asqueante" (disgusting scab) (7) on the country's cities. The slums were "parásitos que le van chupando belleza, tranquilidad y arcas" (parasites that drain beauty, tranquility, and the treasury) (8). Genuinely offended by the behavior of their inhabitants, Fonfrías declared, "El arrabal le ha faltado el respeto a la civilización, a la ley y a la naturaleza. Las autoridades se encuentran perplejas ante el crecimiento fantástico de estas zonas. En un abrir y cerrar de ojos, clandestinamente, con la superchera cooperación de los habitantes del arrabal que gustan de violar la ley y el orden, y que prefieren vivir entre aguas estancadas y putrefactas, bajo el azote de la lluvia, entre criaderos de mosquitos y miasmas, entre basuras y desperdicios, se levantan por miles las casuchas indeseables" (The slum has no respect for civilization, law, or nature. The authorities are perplexed by the incredible growth of these areas. In the blink of an eye, clandestinely, thousands of objectionable houses are built with the questionable cooperation of the slums' inhabitants, who enjoy breaking the law and disrupting order, and who prefer to live in stagnant and putrefied waters, under the lashing of rain, among mosquitoes and miasma, among garbage and refuse) (7). Viewed as impertinent and unpleasant, filthy and dishonest, lawless, even disgusting, the inhabitants of these urban spaces were considered by this government official as disposable, underserving subjects. Fonfrías, it seems, refused to see these men and women as citizens of the city, as a civic body of the urban landscape. He saw no other alternative: the slum must be "eliminado a todo trance" (eliminated by any means) (6).

Fonfrías's contempt for these urban spaces is best understood when contrasted with another facet of his public life. He was, without a doubt, an engaged bureaucrat of the commonwealth and an avid supporter, but precisely during the period that he was involved with urban renewal Fonfrías dabbled in literature, publishing three books with a definite *criollista* stance. *Cosecha* (1956), *Conversao en el Batey* (1956), and *Guásima* (1957) were, unsurprisingly, idealized and picturesque renditions of the countryside and the jíbaro. It makes some sense, in a somewhat twisted way, that the man who praised the rural as the last remaining space of the Puerto Rican spirit would speak with such hatred toward marginal urban subjects.

This negative and dismissive representation of the slums was indeed common in spaces that were imbued with ideology in modernization discourses. But stepping out of certain government agencies and media, these urban communities, along with the city itself and the phenomenon of migration, were integrated into quite a different social and political project. In the middle years of the twentieth century, literature—especially fiction and drama—was perhaps the artistic space that most decidedly integrated the urban into its stylistic and cultural objectives.

URBAN WORLDS, URBAN WORDS

> *Un ejército de casas*
> *sobre el dolor se acurruca.*
>
> *An army of houses*
> *huddles over pain.*
>
> Julia de Burgos, "Desde el Puente Martín Peña" (From Martín Peña Bridge)

It is a truth almost universally acknowledged that the literary figures who wrote fiction from the late 1940s to the early 1960s inaugurated a definitively urban literature in Puerto Rico. That statement, however, as Malena Rodríguez Castro has pointed out (506), is not quite accurate.

The urban has frequently been present in the fiction published by Puerto Ricans throughout the twentieth century, both on the island and in the United States. José Elías Levis had already published *Estercolero* (Dung heap) in 1899 (with an expanded version in 1901), squarely set in the slums of an unnamed city on the island. Texts like the multiple versions of José de Diego Padró's eccentric novel *En babia* (the first edition was published in the 1930s) inserted New York City as the epicenter of its literary space. Still, it is also true that the publication of José Luis González's *El hombre en la calle* (Man on the street) in 1948 (intriguingly, the same year Luis Muñoz Marín was elected governor of the island) sparked a desire to utilize the urban as an exceptional space for literary social analysis. The brief words at the beginning of the book (which literary history refers to today as a prologue-cum-manifesto, even though it was in fact a short paragraph dedicating the book to his mother!) today seem uncannily prescient: "En Puerto Rico queda por iniciarse una literatura urbana. Doblemente necesaria porque lo rural ha sido demasiadas veces refugio derrotista para los que todavía no saben que los asaltos del imperialismo en el frente cultural hay que resistirlos lo mismo en la calle que en el surco" (An urban literature has yet to be launched in Puerto Rico. It is doubly necessary because the rural has too many times been a fatalistic refuge for those who still don't know that the attacks of imperialism in the cultural front must be resisted on the street as well as in the furrow) (7). Although the writer Edgardo Rodríguez-Juliá has correctly called González's fiction "the city turned into writing" ("José Luis" 242), González wasn't merely advocating for replacing a tradition of rural literature with an allegedly modern literature of the city. He was proposing a writing that would disassociate itself from the rather conservative uses of the countryside that had been prevalent up to that moment, and he called for a literature that would critically look at the problems of the contemporary city, though without forgetting the surrounding rurality and its context.[9]

What remains incontrovertible is that González and several midcentury writers mounted a social and cultural critique of the urban space as part of their literary project. It is important to point out that the city was never appropriated by this group of writers as a modern haven or as an idealized space of progress and prosperity. These authors, from Emilio Díaz Valcárcel to Pedro Juan Soto, from José Luis Vivas Maldonado to René Marqués, even playwrights like Fernando Sierra Berdecía and Francisco Arriví, exposed, albeit in different ways and intensities, the contradictions of the commonwealth and its modernization program and in the process discarded any possibility for the urban space to become a literary symbol of an ecstatic future.

Perhaps René Marqués was trying to distance himself and this group of writers from the urbanization rhetoric of the commonwealth, but in the prologue to the now canonical 1959 anthology *Cuentos puertorriqueños de hoy*, while he momentously declared a shift in fiction to definitive urban landscapes and topics, he barely mentioned the phenomenon of migration as a recurrent subject of these writings. Without a doubt, the fiction of the time was filled with streets and factories, lampposts and neon lights, airports and brothels (Marqués, "El cuento puertorriqueño" 21), but the foundation was, in most cases (though with some exceptions), the portrayal of an urban space as one unmistakably connected to the human influx into the cities of the island and the mainland and the lasting effects on Puerto Ricans and the spaces they inhabited. The urbanscape of *El hombre en la calle* and the powerfully raw stories in Pedro Juan Soto's *Spiks* (1956), two collections that Marqués draws from for his anthology, directly tackle migration to San Juan and New York City.

The urban world of José Luis González's writings was most definitely one of immigrants. The voice of his stories, sometimes with the tone of a traditional omniscient narrator but many times infused with a vivid orality, was one persistently set in the interstices of the city—common bars and walk-up apartments in New York, homes in El Fanguito and Puerta de Tierra, sidewalks and corners everywhere. The urban space in González's works was often a difficult one, even harrowing. The minimalistic and highly anthologized "La carta" (The letter) (from *El hombre en la calle*), for instance, contrasts the idealized social imaginary of the city that immigrants typically construct before actually experiencing it against the dire situation they could face once they arrive there.[10] The narrative in "El pasaje" (The ticket) (from *En este lado* [On this side]) of a man stealing (and dying while doing so), so as to have enough money to go back to the island, almost stubbornly remains in public spaces, as if the private space of the immigrant almost did not matter or, better yet, did not truly exist. Some stories had a layered quality that moved beyond social documentation. An excellent example is "En el fondo del caño hay un negrito" (There is a little black boy in the bottom of the channel), also from *En este lado*. It is an elusive story in which the depiction of the social conditions of slum living recedes to tackle the myth of Narcissus in the waters of El Fanguito, in an attempt to metaphorically cross out that ever-persistent image of an infantilized Puerto Rican identity.[11] And "Paisa" (Fellow countryman), first published as a novella in 1950, critically depicts and unpacks the common threads of the Puerto Rican migration experience as it moves repeatedly in time and space (see below), though the story again and again pauses to expose the crippling effects of an oppressive masculinity.

The depiction of urban life framed by migration, however, was not without troubling undertones among these writers, especially in regard to the precarious experience of Puerto Ricans in the United States, which was continually shown to be wretched and tragic. Even in the case of as careful a writer as José Luis González, the New York experience was smeared with a fatalistic tone, though this would change in his later writings.

One of the most problematic examples can be found in the otherwise wonderfully stark and jarring fiction of Pedro Juan Soto, especially his collection *Spiks*, set almost entirely in New York City; the one story that is not, "La cautiva" (The captive), is set at the airport, on the way to New York. Although stylistically impressive and narratively powerful—and in direct dialogue with González's *El hombre en la calle*—the stories offer an almost pathological portrayal of the Puerto Rican immigrant in the metropolis.[12]

Perhaps the Faulknerian "Los inocentes" (The innocents) best represents this characterization. The central figure, Pipe, is a developmentally disabled adult who is taken care of at home by his elderly mother. At the beginning of the story, he is dressed formally and is ready to go out with his sister, quite unaware that he is leaving to be handed over to a state mental institution. The piece sways between a detailed narration, honestly bordering on the grotesque, of his two conflicted relatives (the mother is reluctant, the sister thinks it's for the best), and several brief first-person, stream-of-consciousness insertions that give the reader access to Pipe's meandering thoughts and desires, going from fantasies about flying and being a pigeon, to repeatedly stating his dislike for the city and all those urbanites who make fun of him, while reminiscing about living back on the island—among roosters and dogs, church bells and town squares, rivers and plenty of sunshine. In a very genuine way, Pipe seems to stand for a certain image of the Puerto Rican immigrant, one who misses the island, the natural world, and the simpler world of neighbors and open doors, one who longs to "fly" back, like a pigeon, to a more innocent space and away from the brutality of the city. Soto's sobering coupling of a mentally challenged adult with the migration experience might have simply been anecdotal, but the title of the story betrays this assumption: the plural noun implies that Pipe is not the only "innocent" here, potentially lumping the Puerto Rican community in New York together with Pipe. His preliminary notes to the story (added in a 1970s edition of *Spiks*) unfortunately confirms it: "intentaba en este cuento dar testimonio de la vida puertorriqueña en Nueva York" (I was trying in this story to give testimony of Puerto Rican life in New York) (41).

But the writer in the 1950s who most emblematically depicted urban life, including migration, is without a doubt the towering figure of René Marqués. It remains remarkably accurate what Arcadio Díaz Quiñones said many years ago in *El almuerzo en la hierba*: "René Marqués descendió a la ciudad como quien desciende a los infiernos" (René Marqués descended to the city the way someone descends to hell) ("Los desastres" 137). The city was the eternal dark night of René Marqués: death, shadows, vomit, urine, hatred, rancor, murder, rape, exploitation; these are just some of the recurrent images that appeared in his work when he was compelled to write his urban space.

As many scholars have pointed out, the fictional, theatrical, and cinematic worlds of René Marqués were politically and culturally problematic: while his anticolonial critique of the commonwealth government and its project of rapid modernization were shared by other figures of the era, his conservative reaction toward modernization made his positions particularly troubling for a society that was more and more urban and unavoidably modernized.

One of the startling features of Marqués's work is that, though he was considered part of the generation of writers who spearheaded an urban literature on the island, his work does not have a substantial corpus that truly investigates the city and its environs. Indeed, many of his short stories published in the 1950s and early 1960s were set in urban spaces, both in San Juan and New York. Of course his second collection of short stories, published in Mexico in 1960, was entitled *En una ciudad llamada San Juan* (In a city named San Juan), and his canonical play *La carreta* (The oxcart), published in 1952, was indeed a chronicle of migration, urbanization, and their devastating effects on poor rural subjects. Setting aside the play, however, the city in a lot of his fiction functioned for the most part as scenery, rather than as a significant element in the plot or in the internal conflicts of the characters, as is the case in the fiction of José Luis González or even in the novels of someone like César Andreu Iglesias. In Marqués's early story "El miedo" (The fear), the urban environment conveniently feeds the existential vantage point of the protagonist, but the city never takes a prominent role; in "La sala" (The living room), the reader becomes aware that the family lives in a dark house in Old San Juan, but the urban setting, spatially or metaphorically, never adds to the characters' sense of marginalization due to the father having been involved in pro-independence activities. There are exceptions, of course: the extramarital affair that occurs in "La hora del dragón" (The hour of the dragon) is possible only thanks to the anonymity and perennial human circulation in the city. In his famous story "Otro día nuestro" (Another day of ours) the urbanscape does participate in the tenor of the protagonist's house arrest: "La red de cables telefónicos y de hilos eléctricos, como telaraña tejida por un insecto torpe o descuidado. Los postes de alumbrado, negros y ásperos, como esclavos eternizados en servicio público" (The web of telephone cables and electric wires, like a spider web woven by a clumsy or careless insect. The lampposts, black and rough, like slaves in eternal public service) (*Cuentos puertorriqueños* 120). But in the bulk of his fiction, the city is mere backdrop.

Where one does find interesting and intriguing representations of urban spaces is in a few of his plays, though not exactly in their performable sections.

STAGE DIRECTIONS TO HELL

There is always something curious about analyzing drama. The published version is not precisely the play itself but rather a manual, a series of notations, and the guide for the director, the props master, the actors, and the set designers as they mount a performance of the text. Because of this, I have always felt hesitant about analyses that rely only on the text in order to read into the play, since the accomplishments of theater are not on the printed page but on the stage. One should not do for the other. Having said that, what I want to do here is not to look at René Marqués's plays as theatrical performances but rather as symptomatic pulses of the author. What I find most intriguing about the plays of Marqués is not the dialogue or even the story line but rather the marginalia: the scenery descriptions, the playwright's instructions to the props master, the way Marqués explains his characters to the actors and director. In these, his ultimately conservative stance against things urban comes out without any filter, in parentheses, but for all to read. They also allow a more complex understanding of his cultural and political positioning toward the midcentury, modernization, and the Commonwealth of Puerto Rico.

La casa sin reloj (The house without a clock) is a piece from 1961 heavily influenced by the theater of the absurd and set against the Cold War panic against revolution. More specifically, it deals with the police persecution of Puerto Rican nationalists in the aftermath of the 1950 uprising. The play's stage set is the interior of a house in the countryside, though interestingly it is neither a rural house nor a peasants' home. This is the house of an urban, middle-class couple living on the outskirts of a smaller town on the island, and the introductory stage directions are indeed a critique of the aspirations and values of that class. Note the choice of fake flowers instead of natural ones; the "foreign" furniture that is totally inappropriate for tropical weather; the tacky paintings with snowy landscapes that decorate the living room; the tea table, filled with overdue bills and old magazines, at which no ones drinks tea, because, as Marqués explains, tea is drunk only when one has indigestion. This is the playwright's "modern" couple.

His critique, however, goes beyond a simple critique against middle-class conformity. It is an attack against the modernization of life. And the object on the stage that best represents this assault is, as the author declares in the stage directions, "el imprescindible teléfono automático, uno de los descubrimientos útiles y decisivos en destruir lo que le quedaba al ser humano de sociabilidad" (the indispensable automatic telephone, a discovery useful and decisive in destroying what remained of sociability in human beings) (*Teatro III* 17). Indeed, the most absurdist moments in the play occur in telephone conversations, as if the apparatus itself embodied the ridiculousness of modern life.

Marqués's attack even extends to the materials in house construction, disclosing a yearning for a traditional country home. In quite an odd moment, the playwright dedicates an entire paragraph to the following "controversy" in vernacular domestic architecture: "Nada hay en la estructura [de la casa] que pudiera llamarse noble, excepto quizá la madera en sí que, por contraste al cemento, adquiere hoy, como material, cierta inesperada dignidad, cierto insospechado abolengo, no importa su procedencia o calidad" (There is nothing in the structure [of the house] that could be described as noble, except perhaps the wood itself, which, as a contrast to cement, today provides, as a material, a certain unexpected dignity, a certain unsuspected lineage, regardless of its origin or quality) (*Teatro III* 16). Commenting on the nobility and dignity of wood is unnecessary for a director or a set designer. But it helps us understand Marqués's relationship with change: for him, the one redeeming virtue of this house, in spite of the material possessions of the couple living in it, is that it is not made out of concrete, that contemporary sign of development. Marqués's sentence projects a definite nostalgic stance and, with it, a reluctance to accept modernization. Efraín Barradas once described René Marqués as, fundamentally, a man afraid of change (75); here is one of those moments in which his writing lets slip that fear.

This practice of using interior architecture in the stage directions as a way of critiquing the urban, modern space also appears in his most famous play: *La carreta*. Written and premiering onstage in the early 1950s, it is still one of the most performed Puerto Rican plays on the island and is read as a text in public and private schools.[13] Because migration is central to the plot, it was one of the first plays performed by the Teatro Rodante in New York. Today, YouTube has quite a few video versions of the play performed by high school students (with swear words included). Ominously the scholar María Teresa Babín called it "el drama que todos llevamos dentro" (the play we all carry inside) ("Prólogo" xxxi), and the theater critic Lowell Fiet has proclaimed *La carreta* to be part of the "backbone" of Puerto Rican drama (*El teatro puertorriqueño* 163).

It is difficult to disagree with Frank Dauster when, back in the 1960s, he described *La carreta* as "an unabashedly naturalistic portrait of the *via crucis* of a rural Puerto Rican family" (36). We are thus at the other end of the spectrum from the terribly idealized world of Pepe el coquí in *La canción verde*, a children's book by Doris Troutman Plenn. It was another favorite textbook about migration, this time for elementary school students (and published just a year after *La carreta*).[14] Marqués's foremost play follows the downward spiral of a family led by a matriarch, Doña Gabriela, whose adopted son, Luis, drives the clan from the small farm they abandon in the first part of the play, to the extramuros community of La Perla in the second part, and then to a walk-up apartment in the Bronx during the third.

The first peculiarity about the printed version is that Marqués structures the play not in acts but in estampas. If indeed the word loosely connects *La carreta* to the graphic artists who were quickly becoming prominent in those years, as well as to their depiction of a new, contemporary autochthony that I discussed above, it also brings the play oddly closer to the costumbrista literary tradition. To be sure, there is nothing picturesque about *La carreta*, but in the context of a series of stage directions that wallow in a positioning against all things urban and modern, the estampa label seems to nudge the play to gravitate toward a tone of irreparable loss in the face of modernization. The spatial structure of the play— first in the countryside, and the rest in urban spaces—gives the playwright plenty of opportunity to do this.

As in *La casa sin reloj*, this sense of loss is clearest in the stage directions for the living quarters in each of the estampas. In the first, identified as *el campo* (the country), the description of the house that the family is about to leave behind is tender and nostalgic, though even here Marqués feels the need to insert his irritation toward the influx of "foreign" construction materials caused by the modernization of the island: "Casita de buenas maderas del país, como restos de una época de mejor situación económica, remendada con pichipén y retazos de madera barata importada" (A small house, made out of good local lumber, as the remains of a period with a better economic situation, patched with pine and scraps of cheap, imported wood) (4). In the second estampa, identified as el arrabal (the slum), the family is now in La Perla, the impoverished community outside the walls of Old San Juan; even though the family lives in a small house, the sympathetic diminutive used for the country house, *casita*, is now replaced by the more pejorative *casucha*. René Marqués spends three entire pages on a detailed description of the abode's interior, pointing out the makeshift quality of the house, "construida con retazos y desperdicios de materiales heterogéneos" (built with remnants and refuse of heterogeneous materials) (54). Sometimes the details provided, while giving the cast and crew the "feel" of the place, are of little use to a props master: "colgando del techo, hay un cordón eléctrico, sucio de excremento de mosca" (hanging from the ceiling, there is an electric wire soiled with fly excrement) (55). There is a fine line in Marqués between the wish for a hyperrealistic portrayal of this casucha and the uncontainable desire to sordidly and moralistically represent these spaces.

When the family moves to New York in the final estampa, labeled *metrópoli* (metropolis), they do not live in a house but in a walk-up apartment, with their table featuring tinned food—including some disconcerting canned Puerto Rican *pasteles*—and plastic tablecloths that resemble lace. The stage directions for this act seem to imply some sort of economic improvement in the family. The living room, for example, includes a brand-new radio; Marqués, however, feels compelled to describe it as "reluciente y agresivo" (gleaming and aggressive) (115), giving the object an antagonistic quality and dismissing it as an unnecessary shiny object. Once again, his distaste for modernity raises its curious head, and to confirm this the stage directions request that the wooden sculpture of an oxcart that they had brought from the island—as a symbol of tradition with fundamentally rural or agricultural significations—be placed on top of the radio.

THE REST IS ALL DEAD

Of course, Marqués's vitriolic stance against the urban was not limited in this case to his stage directions or, for that matter, to the architectural space, since the plot of *La carreta* focuses explicitly on the social phenomenon of urban migration. Although other Puerto Rican plays had dealt with the migrations that are documented in the play, *La carreta* covered the entire span of the experience (Fiet, "René Marqués" 210).[15] But Marqués's drama, I would argue, was ultimately not so much a project documenting the migration experience as it was a moral condemnation of it.

If in the rural obsession of the 1950s the landscape was a protagonist—even making the inhabitants a passive element of that landscape—then in the urban fixation of the same period, at least in the case of Puerto Rico, it was the subject that seemed to be the focus. Cityscapes were rare; what predominated were the new and old urbanites—almost always the migrating subject. This is the case in *La carreta* as well, but the play's characters were also particularly useful to Marqués for embodying several attitudes that helped the playwright in mounting his affront to the modernized urban.

Grandfather Chago, who appears only in the first estampa, is actually quite an important character, because he embodies—quite literally—a conservative voice of tradition. Don Chago is not at all tempted by the possibilities of change and progress that the urban world promises. He is indeed the voice that critiques the rampant materialism of modern society, but he is also an antimodern subject in some problematic ways. In a conversation with his grandson Luis, Don Chago lays out for the younger man the worn-out argument of a slower-paced past, with simpler people who were authentically good and for whom dignity and pride were highly regarded values (33). The speech is not presented in the play as a discarded, anachronistic rhetoric, however, and this is confirmed by the characters' reaction to it; the stage directions request a moment of reflection and quiet anxiety among the persons onstage: "A la evocación del abuelo, algo impalpable, como una sombra de nostalgia, un indefinido temor al futuro, una conciencia de incertidumbre del presente, se ha apoderado de los personajes. Hablan pausadamente; sorbiendo el café, saboreando en cada trago algo del pasado que se les escapa" (34) (At the grandfather's evocation, something impalpable, like a shadow of nostalgia, an undefined fear of the future, an awareness of the uncertainty of the present, has taken hold of those on stage. They speak slowly, sipping their coffee, savoring in each swallow something of the past which is slipping away from them" [Pilditch 35]). The old man is, of course, the one member of the family who refuses to migrate to the city, and all throughout the estampa his rhetoric persistently negates a life outside the rural, always stressing an adherence to the land. In fact, at the end of the act Grandfather Chago recedes, quite literally, into the land itself: as the rest of the family leaves for San Juan, he—unbeknown to his relatives—moves with his few personal belongings into a cave!

In contrast, Luis, the eldest son of Doña Gabriela, drives the family toward the new world of modernization: he is the one who persuades the family to move to the city and the one who at the end of the second estampa (albeit with some coaxing from his sister) decides to transplant the family to the United States. For him, the city is the ultimate promise for success and the industrialization of the island, the clearest sign that the future must necessarily be bright. Even after Luis has moved to San Juan and is struggling to find a job, he declares, "Ehte eh mi paíh. Aquí se están jaciendo cosah nuevah, cosah grandeh. Esta eh una nueva época. La época de lah máquinah. Y yo tengo fe en eso. Lo demáh ehtá muerto" (98) (This is my country. New things are bein' done here, big things. These are new times. The era of machines. And I have faith in that. The rest is all dead [Pilditch 92–93]). If Don Chago can't seem to see beyond a revisionist past grounded in the rural, Luis can't seem to see anything but the utopic version of the modernizing discourses of the time. As he says elsewhere, "El porvenir ehtá en lah maquinah" (99) (The future is in machines [Pilditch 93]).

In a way, Luis could be perceived as a true commonwealth jíbaro—at least the jíbaro the commonwealth hoped for, one who believed in modernization, one who trusted that by becoming an urbanite he could guarantee the eradication of his family's poverty. Thus, it seems René Marqués inserted Luis into the dramatic narrative of *La carreta* to lay siege to the commonwealth's project of industrialization. But in the process of making the attack all the more brutal, the playwright ended up with a one-dimensional construction of that pro-urban jíbaro: all throughout the play Luis invariably thinks of the city and the factory as the only option for his betterment, and he believes this with an almost religious fervor. Any other recourse, as Luis explicitly says, is dead—not because he thinks of those possibilities as unsuitable for him but because he has rendered them obsolete. Luis's death at the end of the play—an accident at the factory where he works, in which he is literally devoured by the machines—is Marqués's not-so-subtle condemnation of Luis's positioning in a modern world.[16]

Clearly, Marqués's ideological position is totally opposed to Luis's worldview; Grandfather Chago's perception, while never discarded, is not exactly embraced by the playwright. It is with the matriarch, Doña Gabriela, that Marqués seems to be closest. Portrayed as the tragic female figure who is strong, wise, and sturdy, she realizes at the end of the play the error in having migrated from the rural space: "Porque ahora me doy cuenta lo que nos pasaba a toh. ¡La mardición de la tierra! La tierra eh sagrá. La tierra no se abandona. Hay que volver a lo que dejamoh pa que no noh persiga máh la mardición de la tierra" (171) (Because now I know what was happening to us all. The curse of the land! The land is sacred. The land cannot be abandoned. We must go back to what we left behind so that the curse of the land won't pursue us anymore [Pilditch 153]). Doña Gabriela's lines have the virtue of clarity: by labeling it a curse, Marqués attaches a deterministic quality to that return, and the double meaning of the word *tierra* (land and nation), deemed sacred by the matriarch (and Marqués), connects it to a return to the island itself.[17] Because what the end of *La carreta* ultimately and explicitly declares is that urban migration—either to the city of San Juan or the mainland, there doesn't seem to be a marked difference for the playwright—is not simply a problem but rather a mistake: a fatal, immoral error. Indeed, Marqués's moralistic pronouncement, unashamedly anachronistic, sublimely fatalistic, and politically reactionary, makes Luis Muñoz Marín's Operation Serenity seem like a truly progressive, innovative project, despite its problematic agenda.

AN OTHER'S MIGRATION

Marqués once described the Puerto Rican in the United States as "tireless in his pathetic quest for an easier material life" (qtd. in Martin 78), a simplistic definition at best, and one that almost seemed to assume an upward mobility of comfort, not the meeting of basic needs in an urban space. This image, however, was not shared by many writers. Among the fiction written on migration during these years, one particular story could function as an effective contrast to lay bare René Marqués's thorny stance on migration: I am referring to José Luis González's "Paisa" (1950). Not as canonical as *La carreta*—it has certainly never been part of school curricula—and published a couple of years before the play by a small press in Mexico (Díaz Quiñones, "José Luis" iv), this long short story also deals with rural subjects who migrate to the slums of San Juan and then move to New York. However, its plot and narrating voice situates migration within a more layered context, and the tone of the story is leagues away from the moralistic stance that seems so pervasive in Marqués's play.

Structurally, they are quite different. While the plot of *La carreta* maintains the chronological order of the relocations, "Paisa" is squarely set in New York, where Andrés, a young Puerto Rican man, is getting ready to rob a corner store in his neighborhood with the help of another man who, curiously, is never named but is also Puerto Rican. It is with a series of flashbacks intercalated throughout the story that we are gradually introduced to Andrés's migration story, with his origins in the countryside, his eventual move with his family to the slums of San Juan, and, after his father's death from an accident while working as a stevedore on the piers, his relocation to New York at the invitation of his godfather. Through these flashbacks, Andrés's precarious situation and upcoming rash act in New York are carefully framed by the circumstances of industrialization, migration, and urbanization. Instead of the melodramatic family saga of *La carreta*, what we have here is a socioeconomic history of Andrés: the rural family forced out of the countryside because of the industrialization of sugarcane plantations; the clan transplanted to the slums because there is no other place to go; the dissolution of Andrés's family, after his father's death, principally due to economic necessities; and Andrés's failed attempts at keeping a job in New York because of racial and ethnic prejudices. In addition, the omniscient narration has filled the story with small, resonant details about the social history of migration and its consequences for rural subjects and urban spaces: young men searching for jobs, young women working as maids; country folk figuring out the pace of the city, sometimes getting it, many times not; new urbanites experiencing the excitement of the new and the urban promise, along with the disappointing daily life that the uneven, unfair, and unequal flows and networks of the city tend to produce. "Paisa" truly feels like fiction that leans toward the document, toward a gesture that tells a story while it chronicles history—microhistory and macrohistory.

Furthermore, *La carreta* seems to be structured in what I would call a series of manipulative mood swings: each act ends with a sense of hope that the next location might be where stability and a basic level of comfort can be achieved—hopes that are utterly crushed in the act that follows. In contrast, "Paisa" bypasses any narrative arc of naïve idealism by focusing on the chronological present of a subject who has already migrated and desperately attempts to solve his economic problems by stealing money. There is a character in *La carreta* who steals as well, though the handling of his behavior is radically different. Toward the beginning of the second estampa, during the family's stay in La Perla, Luis confesses to his mother that, a while back, Chaguito, Doña Gabriela's adolescent son, had been caught stealing from a peddler in San Juan; fortunately, the boy had been pardoned by the judge because it was his first offense. But when, toward the end of that same part, the boy is arrested after selling his mother's Saint Anthony statue to some tourists and running away with their change, Luis and Doña Gabriela realize that this time Chaguito will not be as lucky. The mother is not only distraught; she is humiliated. Thievery in *La carreta* is fundamentally a clear sign of moral decline, especially for Doña Gabriela, and indicative of a loss of dignity. What's more, Chaguito's actions are portrayed as simply delinquency: Marqués describes him at the moment when he appears onstage as someone who carries himself with the "aire inconfundible de pillete urbano" (65) (the unmistakable look of an urban petty thief [Pilditch 67]). In "Paisa," on the other hand, stealing, though definitely not excused, is depicted as a complex, layered act by its framing within Andrés's social and economic situation. There is still the notion of an ethics in González, but without the sense of the authorial, censorious judgment that permeates Marqués's play and is internalized and vocalized by his characters.

That ethical conflict is present from the very first sentence of the short story: "Cuando [Andrés] abrió los ojos se dio cuenta de que lo había despertado la mirada del otro, igual que un ruido o un golpe" (When [Andrés] opened his eyes he realized that the gaze of the other had awakened him, like a noise or a blow) (14). Beginning the story with this somewhat uncanny statement cannot be a mere effect in the work of such a careful writer as González. Narratively, "the other" is the man who is planning the robbery with Andrés; he is the *paisa* from the title, his compatriot, his fellow man, though their relationship is ironically not one of camaraderie or even solidarity. The man's cold detachment, almost stereotypically urban in his blasé attitude, along with an overbearing masculinity that Andrés finds offputting (even slightly disturbing), makes the young immigrant very wary. This is perhaps why the man's gaze startles him so, "like a noise or a blow," a gaze that, throughout the story, questions Andrés's determination, doubts his courage, even scrutinizes his masculinity. But Andrés is dependent on him if he wants to go through with the holdup, since this man is the one who has meticulously planned the operation. This other remains nameless throughout the entire story; he is always referred to as "el otro" (the other), with no further hints at who he is. The refusal to name this character, in fact, allows for the possibility of reading that label in other ways. On the one hand, this other becomes an Other, a figure of authority (of masculine authority) that Andrés will have to struggle with in "Paisa"; on the other hand, this figure of abject power also turns into his double, a veritable doppelganger, and so "el otro" is in many instances, emblematically, no other than Andrés himself. This is how "Paisa" turns into a tale of Andrés's moral dilemma in regard to questions of money and mobility, migration and success without ever becoming a dismissive moral condemnation—even when Andrés is shot dead by the New York police at the end of the story.

González, like Marqués and a large portion of the literature written in these years, deliberately used migration and the urban space as part of a literary project to denounce the trappings of modernization. Concerned with the human and social consequences (and rightly so), these two writers saw the phenomenon of migration and the urban experience in the 1950s and early 1960s as inherently transformational, cataclysmic for Marqués, a game-changer for González, though both perceived it as fundamentally unfortunate.[18] But while González conveyed migration as a complex and layered phenomenon better understood with a historical-materialist analysis in the context of the political economy of the time, in Marqués migration was depicted as a social failure, even quite literally as a curse. I don't think I am incorrect in thinking of his writing as a gesture of moral condemnation, but it is crucial that his positioning is located in the proper context.

Marqués seemed to have equated modernization and the effects of urbanization with the Americanization of Puerto Rico and therefore as a transformation that would undermine a national project for Puerto Ricans. Migration was the social event that would guarantee the loss of a certain identity—Hispanic, rural, island-bound, patriarchal—one that he thought was inherent in Puerto Ricans. In short, what was at stake for Marqués in the midcentury was a loss of authenticity, in the way that term was used in existentialism, an intellectual discourse that was quite influential for this writer. The singularity of the self, in existentialism, is constantly bombarded by what one ought to do, what "the crowd" or "the public" expects one to do morally and socially. Authenticity is the gesture in which the self builds a project of identity that is chosen by that self; it is a moment of self-making and autonomy. "To be truly authentic," notes one scholar of existentialism, "is to have realized one's individuality and vice versa" (Flynn 74). For Marqués, the modernization of the island, in the way it was conducted, led to the end of individuality and therefore to the end of authenticity. For him, the United States and its culture, in the context of Puerto Rican identity, were the hallmark of inauthenticity. And the city and its culture represented the first step away from an authentic Puerto Rican spirit. I still find this position problematic, because it is fundamentally assuming an essentialist notion of cultural identity, but it helps us make some sense of the literary project of René Marqués.

SINGING THE CITY

¡canción dezcalza no vale!

¡verso sufrido no gusta!

A shoeless song doesn't count!

A suffering poem doesn't please!

Julia de Burgos, "Desde el Puente Martín Peña" (From the Martín Peña Bridge)

La carreta had an urban soundtrack of commercial music, and Doña Gabriela absolutely detested it: "Y apehta esa condenasión que ñaman música" (62) (And that damn stuff they call music stinks" [Pilditch 65]). The second act in La Perla is full of frenzied mambos blasting out of a jukebox from a nearby establishment.[19] In New York the family owns a radio, and here it's African American blues coming out of the modern contraption. It makes some sense that Doña Gabriela would feel invaded by this music. For her it could be both a generational issue and another instance of the urban as foreign to certain rural subjects—but her over-the-top reaction seems to be another instance of the matriarch channeling Marqués's affront with the urban, in this case with popular music, which the playwright describes as "savage" in his stage directions (56, 112).

When it comes to considering the musical production of Cortijo y su combo, however, and particularly in a discussion of the incipient urban culture of the island, dismissing the commercial music of the time would be a gross error. Totally different from pro-commonwealth newsreels and official speeches, and unlike the fatalistic view of much literature and drama, Cortijo's songs are a unique and fascinating record of the urban poor and working-class communities, of migration and the experience of new urbanites, and of an urban, Afro–Puerto Rican existence.

As I discussed at the beginning of this chapter, during the early years of the commonwealth mainstream media and government offices depicted many poor and working-class communities as remnant spaces of the city, indeed as slums, almost never recognizing them as legitimate spaces of the modernizing city. When they were acknowledged, it was done to single them out as spaces to be eradicated, without truly taking into account the social and cultural processes that existed in these spaces. This is, I want to argue, exactly what Cortijo y su combo combats in their songs. It should come as no surprise that in Cortijo these communities are never portrayed as slums: that is, not as pitiful, pathetic, depressing places to live and survive in but rather, quite simply, as communities. In fact, the word *arrabal* (slum) never appears in any of their songs, perhaps because Cortijo refuses to participate in the commonwealth's spectacular melodrama of poverty. This makes their music even more valuable: the notion of slums here is not an "issue"; they are not a problem to be solved. These spaces were portrayed as living spaces, filled with social histories and experiences. While government offices, newsreels, and newspapers continually praised the construction of concrete houses in new areas of San Juan, lauded the elimination of slums and poor neighborhoods, and considered its inhabitants as citizens-in-erasure, Cortijo y su combo offered one of the strongest refusals of all those gestures.

In the context of 1950s Puerto Rico, one of the most important contributions of Cortijo y su combo was documenting—literally recording—the existence of working-class life in the neighborhoods of the capital. Especially in the first albums the songs made frequent reference to the urban geography of the area. On the very first recording of the band, the smash hit "El bombón de Elena" (Elena's candy) (from the album *Cortijo y su Combo Invites You to Dance*), the lyrics of this plena mention Calma Street in the coastal neighborhood of Villa Palmeras (where lead singer Ismael Rivera grew up) and their tradition of dancing plena. Another plena from the same album, "Pa' lo que tú le das" (In spite of all you give her) makes remarks about a man looking for his wife in the community of Tras Talleres, located in the southwest part of Santurce. The numbered bus stops in the community of Santurce (still used today by the capital's inhabitants, though not officially), especially the ones close to poorer neighborhoods, were also a frequent reference in their songs. In short, Cortijo's songs tended not to be set in a generic urban space but in very particular places: in the San Juan inhabited by the working-class men and women of the capital.

Beyond simple geographic allusions, however, what the songs do best is to register the life of the inhabitants of these neighborhoods. Typical of their songs is the joy in music. "Báilala bien" (Dance it well) (from *Baile con Cortijo*), "Mañana es domingo" (Tomorrow's Sunday) (from *Bueno, ¿y qué?*), "Alegría y bomba" (Happiness and bomba) (from *Baile con Cortijo*)—song after song, the titles and lyrics allude to singing, dancing, and having a ball: these are, let us not forget, dance tunes. But, interestingly, the repertoire is not simply fun and games. In the song mentioned above, "Pa' lo que tú le das," the listener eventually realizes that the song is actually about domestic abuse: the wife has left because of the terrible mistreatment by her husband. The title is actually a play on words: "pa[ra] lo que tú le das" (considering what you give her) can also phonetically signify "palo que tú le das" (the stick that you give her). The lyrics of the song confirm this double entendre during the call-and-response section of the song, as the community accuses the man of abuse:

Para lo que tú le das	In spite of all you give her
Pa'lo que tú le das	Seems like spite is all you give her
Para lo que tú le das	*In spite of all you give her*
Arroz y habichuelas colorá	Rice and beans that you deliver
Para lo que tú le das	*In spite of all you give her*
Bacalao con funche nada más	Cod with plantain you deliver
Para lo que tú le das	*In spite of all you give her*
Palo, puño y bofetá	Blows and beatings you deliver

Other songs are not afraid to criticize the behavior of these neighborhoods' inhabitants: "La hija de la vecina" (The neighbor's daughter) (from *Fiesta boricua*) and "La crítica" (Criticism) (from *Cortijo en New York*) focus, for instance, on the damaging effects of gossip in these spaces.

To be sure, work creeps up frequently in Cortijo's repertoire. In a unique musical moment of fatherly tenderness, "Lo dejé llorando" (I left him crying) (from *Baile con Cortijo*), written by Sammy Ayala, one of the combo's backup singers, conveys the utter sadness of a father leaving his son at home; the son is crying because the father has to go off to work.

Como yo me iba a trabajar	Because I had to go to work
se quedó llorando;	I left him behind, crying.
lo sentí mucho en el corazón	I felt it deep in my heart,
pero seguí andando.	But I kept on walking.

In the last verses of the song, the whistle of the factory that marks the end of the work day announces to the father that he can now rush home to be with his son again. This detail about factory work is compositionally interesting: in an interview, Ayala confessed the song was inspired by an autobiographical moment—his needing to leave San Juan to perform with the band and the son disconsolately sad that his dad had to go—but the song's narrative is inserted into a more general notion of labor: the world of the factory and the strict management of time and leisure—time and family—these spaces require.

At the core of that documentation of working-class life in San Juan, the band persistently chronicled Afro–Puerto Rican life, something several scholars have drawn attention to in recent years (see chapter 1). Unlike other bands of the decade, Cortijo y su combo was one of the first bands from the island's commercial music scene that was composed predominantly of black Puerto Ricans. In addition, most of the characters in the song narratives are dark-skinned Puerto Ricans, with names like "la negra Marcola," "el negrito Culembo," "la negra Mariana," "la negrita Fela," "el negro bembón," and "el mulato Cachón." If in other bands these terms might have implied a dismissive or demeaning tone, here they work first simply as identifiers and second as a way to record that the characters in these songs were unquestionably Afro–Puerto Rican subjects.

The other important element of urbanization that these songs incorporate is the massive migration to cities, a phenomenon that directly affected the neighborhoods in which these songs are set. Cortijo y su combo, from the very first album, is aware that their music has an audience not only on the island but on the mainland as well, and the lyrics frequently recognize the Puerto Rican community in the United States. Their fifth album is, in fact, titled *Cortijo en New York*.

One song directly addresses and documents migration to the urban space. Organized by a series of short tales, "Te lo voy a contar" (I'm going to tell you) (from *Baile con Cortijo*) relates various narratives of the migration experience. The first line of each story paraphrases the traditional Christmas song "De la montaña venimos" (From the mountains we come), as if to assure the listener of the rural origins of all the immigrants mentioned in the song; this is reinforced by the frequent refrains of *le lo lai* sung throughout, a typical *lalala*-ing in jíbaro music. The newcomers' specific destination, however, remains unclear—in some of them the reference to cold weather suggests a North American location, while in others it is impossible to tell; what is certain is that they all arrive in a city.

It is intriguing that the song balances hardships with more lighthearted experiences. In one story, someone gets arrested—for apparently walking around the city without pants on—while in another one a newly arrived man is a hit at a dance marathon with his talent at bomba and plena. One man's toes freeze after walking two miles with inappropriate shoes in yet another story, while in another a man seems to finally eat to his heart's content. There is a certain hilarity in the stories (humor is a constant in the band's repertoire), but the song is not afraid to include the arduous conditions of the recent immigrant. Although it's very probable that these stories are not exactly fact-based renditions of specific individuals, the title of the song, "Te lo voy a contar" points to the documentary aspirations of the song: Cortijo y su combo wants to tell their audience about the human circulation from the country to the city, including the difficult as well as the heartening experiences of migration, perhaps to act as a form of recognition for those who lived through migration, or simply as a chronicle of the phenomenon.

In addition to placing Cortijo y su combo as an important musical response to the social inconsistencies inherent in the modernizing social venture of 1950s Puerto Rico (see chapter 1), I would argue that the cultural maneuverings in their musical output fit precisely within the manifestations that Ángel Rama discussed as he considered the cultural contradictions of twentieth-century Latin American national culture in his magnum opus, *The Lettered City*: "The living popular culture of the moment was not the conservative, declining folk heritage of the countryside that urban intellectuals admired for its picturesque local color. It was the vital, vulgar culture of the urban masses, who drew on rural folk traditions as the natural matrix of their own creativity but did so without a nostalgic urge to conserve. The exuberant popular culture of Latin America's great cities testified instead to the present—to the experience of rapid urbanization and to the emergence of a working class as a major historical protagonist" (103). That impulse to draw from the rural tradition while refusing the urge to conserve, it seems to me, is precisely what I find so valuable about this ensemble: the "veritable revolution" of Cortijo y su combo, as Juan Flores called it ("Introduction" 1), lies in the insertion of an urbanizing culture that does not forget the rural roots of many of the city's inhabitants but does so without idealizing the countryside. This is why commercial music needs to be integrated into the discussion of the national culture of the time—because it is a glimpse into an incipient urban culture that government offices and some newspapers were simply not seeing as such. The commercial nature of this music—music to sell, music as diversion—is not, of course, absent in Cortijo, but while it sold quite well, while it was insanely popular, it also managed to record spaces and subjects that other arts were simply not documenting in the complex and layered living of the city.

CINEMATIC URBANITES

Things urban were quickly becoming a common image for island Puerto Ricans, with newsreels boasting of the latest factory opening and newspapers advertising new housing construction; it would have been hard, however, to notice this modernizing euphoria from the filmic output of the Division of Community Education. DIVEDCO's cinematic production had quite a timid relationship with the city, and the incipient urban culture barely appeared in the images generated by that office—at least in the films from the 1950s and early 1960s. It is indeed true that some of the film production of the Cinema and Graphics Workshop, the office that would become the Division of Community Education, did focus on documenting the modernization of the island—the 1948 short film *Informe al pueblo No. 1* (Report to the people no. 1) is a prime example—and in those films the urban space was unavoidably included. But the division itself filmed the city infrequently and, I would dare say, almost reluctantly.

Of the completed film productions in the first fifteen years of the division, one film dealt with the city, though it did so in passing. Produced in 1957 to accompany the film *Modesta* in community screenings (Marqués, "Plan y libreto"), *¿Qué opina la mujer?* (What do women think?) was an eighteen-minute documentary about the contemporary role of female subjects in Puerto Rican society, mostly comprising interviews with three well-known women: Inés Mendoza de Muñoz Marín, the governor's wife; Margot Arce de Vázquez, a renowned university professor of literature; and the medical doctor Rebeca Kolberg (who was also known as a successful athlete). Written by René Marqués and directed by Dominican-born Oscar Torres, the short film aimed to give evidence of the integration of women as active and fully rendered citizens in the modernizing process. The objectives of *¿Qué opina la mujer?* were not only commendable but necessary: DIVEDCO's group leaders had pointed out in memos and meetings that women were not treated as equals by several men in the postscreening discussions, and chauvinist, sexist behavior was quite common. In addition, these were also the years when the radio was cheerfully playing misogynous songs like "La mujer de palo" (The wooden woman), recorded by jíbaro music performers but popularized by the Orquesta Panamericana, with the following chorus: "Ni de palo son buenas" (Not even wood ones are good ones).[20]

The interviews in *¿Qué opina la mujer?* were bracketed by a series of brief, dramatized situations about the treatment of women in the countryside and in the city, in one of the few moments when the division evenhandedly recognized the relevance of both spaces in 1950s Puerto Rico. It included some humorous additions done in graphic illustrations: a caveman dragging his woman by her hair and an urban, nineteenth-century middle-class man first courting a woman to marry him and later making her a slave of the kitchen and a mother of many children. The rest of the framing device was filmed and identifiably set in Puerto Rico: a little boy in the countryside who hits a girl because he doesn't want her to play with the boys; a jíbaro who does not allow his wife to go to a community meeting; and a man in a street of Old San Juan who doesn't help a woman with her fallen packages, when it was he who, by accidentally bumping into her, caused the packages to fall. At the beginning of the film, the situations were presented to point out the mistreatment and prejudice against women; at the end, most of the situations are presented again and are either dismissed as a thing of the past—the caveman and the nineteenth-century man—or the voice-over narrator speaks directly to the filmed characters and persuades them to behave differently toward the women.

The establishing shots that preceded each of the interviews undeniably located the living and working experience of the three women within urban spaces— Doña Inés Mendoza in La Fortaleza, the official house of the governor; Professor Arce de Vázquez in her urban home; and Dr. Kolberg at a hospital in Río Piedras, a neighborhood of San Juan. But the documentary never deals directly with the urban itself as a space of opportunity, a place where women already participated as full citizens. The urban in *¿Qué opina la mujer?* is purely cosmetic in nature.

What's more, the first interview of the film, with the wife of governor Luis Muñoz Marín, practically erases the urban: not only is the entire scene filmed in the lush gardens of La Fortaleza, where Doña Inés Mendoza is depicted as a master gardener instructing and educating the male gardeners in the details of growing and pruning plants, but her words focus on what she described as the woman's mission in life: "to make things grow" (in Spanish, *hacer crecer*). At the beginning of her speech, the phrase almost seemed to be her own way of calling for economic development and modernization, the need for making the island "grow." But very quickly her words reveal the real meaning of the phrase. On the one hand, it implicitly refers to an essentialist connection of women to motherhood in the act of gardening itself; on the other hand, and more importantly here, the phrase *hacer crecer* explicitly introduces an exhortation from Doña Inés Mendoza to have women, at the side of their men, return to the land to till it and, in this way, contribute to the development of the island. In a gesture that resembles the objectives of her husband's Operation Serenity, though with a slightly antimodern twist, the governor's wife even adds that women should desire this agricultural vocation with the same intensity women today desire a car or a piece of furniture. Even in the city, in the house of a governor who is dedicated to industrialization and urbanization, the paradoxical message to women is to consider the possibilty of a traditional rural existence in order to aid in national progress.

This first interview also managed to reveal a very specific anxiety toward women, something that becomes even clearer with the filming of Arce de Vázquez and Kolberg. The interviewees were clear examples of women in social and economic positions of power: government, higher education, medicine.[21] However, the documentary ends up undermining the position of these urban women by framing them within traditional spaces and practices and by stressing stereotypical feminine traits connected to nurturing, gardening, and motherhood. Almost as if in the city of DIVEDCO women who fully participated as citizens required a good measure of domesticity and submissiveness, the second interview, with Professor Arce de Vázquez, is interestingly enough not filmed in her office at the university, nor even in a classroom, but rather at home, in her living room, where she is sitting on a sofa while her daughter plays with a doll next to her; after the interview is finished, the last shot is the professor and scholar playing with the doll and her daughter.

Dr. Kolberg is the only woman interviewed in her workspace. She is filmed finishing a surgical procedure and is interviewed in her office as she signs some paperwork. Setting aside the fact that she focuses on the importance of women as mothers and teachers—something that had already been stressed by the other two women—and only briefly mentions engineering, science, and medicine as possible professions for women, her body language, her demeanor, even the way she is asked to sit behind her desk, make her seem quite masculine, especially if we compare her to the filming of Doña Inés in her garden and Professor Arce de Vázquez playing with dolls. I find it quite intriguing that the one woman in the film who is actually set in her professional space is the most masculine of the three, as if the creators of the film could not accept (or allow) the possibility of femininity in traditionally masculine professions. The original script doesn't recommend Dr. Kolberg as the ideal person for the interview—it merely says "any female doctor from the Municipal Hospital"—so it is not inconceivable that choosing Rebeca Kolberg was not randomly done. I recognize this is simply a hunch, but it is one that I believe fits the stance of the division toward women.

This anxiety of the film creators—all of whom were men as far as I have been able to discern from production notes, the script, and the credit sequence in the finished film—is ultimately and definitively disclosed in a copy of the script preserved at the Archive of Motion Pictures in San Juan, Puerto Rico. An unsigned handwritten note on the last page suggested the addition of one more interview: a housewife, pure and simple; a "Model Mother," in order to "attenuate the emphasis" of the film on the "mujer extramuros" (Marqués, "Plan y libreto"), that is, on the woman outside of the home. *¿Qué opina la mujer?* celebrated women in the city as important participants in the development of Puerto Rico, as long as they do not wander too far away from their naturalized domestic space and the realm of the feminine.

In addition to this anxiety, something else is glaringly manifest in the documentary's image of the urban: it concealed working-class subjects. In the situations that frame the interviews, the woman in the Old San Juan scene is clearly middle class, with her plethora of shopping bags and boxes as proof; any sign of a lower-class social standing is relegated to the rural space, with the children playing and the jíbaro couple. Of course, the interviews themselves are definitely outside any working-class subjectivity. This was not, it must be said, the original intent of the documentary. René Marqués's script in fact tried to keep a balance by structuring the film around four or five different women, including a jíbara and a woman working at a factory, but the finished film completely left out the voices of rural female subjects and working-class women. To be sure, the fact that this film was shown along with *Modesta*, which is squarely set in the countryside, allowed a more urban focus to prevail in the documentary. But *Modesta* was filmed as a story of long ago, and thus the absence of contemporary rural, lower-class female subjects in *¿Qué opina la mujer?* reads as a silencing of that sector of society. In addition, by excising them, the film avoided dealing with what perhaps was one of the defining elements of the urban landscape: the migrating subject.

A DAY IN THE LIFE

Nowhere in the law that created the Division of Community Education does it state that its adult education program should have been limited to the countryside; it actually emphasized that urban zones as well as rural ones would be part of their charge.[22] As a few scholars have noted, even though the division focused its energies on rural communities, there actually was an attempt to bring the community education project to urban areas, more specifically to several slums in the San Juan metropolitan area. In fact, Catherine Marsh Kennerly has discovered that since the first years of the division, director Fred Wale had expressed the need to include urban communities in the assignments of the office (*Negociaciones* 188–89). In the mid-1950s, the Analysis Section of DIVEDCO conducted research on low-income communities of San Juan.[23] Even a booklet and a film about urban migration were in the works. Although several members of the division, including the writer Pedro Juan Soto, were actively pushing for some involvement in the city, the attempt never really took off; it also did not help that the mayor of San Juan, Felisa Rincón de Gautier, had major disagreements with the office (Vázquez Hernández 114). Although she was a passionate supporter of the commonwealth, Doña Fela, as she was endearingly called, was most definitely not a supporter of DIVEDCO; she thought of the division as somehow too radical, full of "nationalists" and pro-independence artists and writers. By 1958 all activities of the division in the city had ceased (Vázquez Hernández 122).

The film that was being produced to tackle the issues of urban migration, *Un día cualquiera* (A day like any other), is unique in the corpus of the division, even stylistically. With a plot treatment by Pedro Juan Soto and a script written by Ángel F. Rivera, who also directed the film, this forty-five-minute drama inserts the audience not simply into the city but into the world of the slums. It thus displayed the one urban image that the commonwealth was trying so desperately to erase.

The film is structured as a day in the life of a family who had recently moved from the countryside to El Fanguito, a community that grew next to and even into the waters of the channel. This area had become infamous among government officials, literary figures, and photojournalists. *Un día cualquiera* manages to portray the slum not as the abominable place that Ernesto Juan Fonfrías was determined to depict in his speeches, nor as the disgusting place René Marqués forced us to picture in *La carreta*, but rather as an authentically social space, a difficult one, no doubt, and a perplexing one for a recently arrived family, though definitely not a place where the inhabitants have "no respect for civilization, law or nature," as Fonfrías had put it (*La eliminación* 7).

Joaquín and Pascuala do live a precarious life with their two children—Raulito and Martita—in a small house on the channel. Joaquín, still unemployed after two weeks in the city, gets up in the early morning to catch a bus that would take him to the business district of Santurce, where he tries to sell his handmade baskets; unsuccessful, he walks around the city trying to get any kind of work. He eventually lands a few hours' work taking horses to the racetrack, but the job is not permanent. Pascuala has to deal with making ends meet and buying food with the very little money they have, besides dealing with the cold reception of the women in El Fanguito as she goes to fetch water at the communal tap with her daughter. But the film is also filled with moments of compassion, understanding, and even friendly connection. A Santurce barman offers lunch and a cigarette to Joaquín, as he goes around looking for a job. In an errand to get food at the store, a middle-aged woman overhears Martita wishing for a pet dog; the woman tells the kids that she knows someone who is giving puppies away and kindly offers to take them to the house to pick one up—the face of Martita holding her new pet is priceless. A woman who at the beginning of the film had treated Joaquín coldly as he left his house, greets him back with neighborly affection when he comes home at the end of the day. This is not a pleasant place to live, but neither is it a dystopic urban hellhole.

The film was shot around 1954, but it was never finished under the division; in fact, it was canned. It was apparently quite common that the governor would screen the films before they were finished and distributed; the film did not please Muñoz Marín at all (Marsh Kennerly, *Negociaciones* 198). It also was quite different from other division films in that narratively and structurally there were no clear morals or messages, no "bad" characters that audiences could easily criticize or censure during the postscreening discussions. This was no "problem" film with an optimistic outlook in the way *El puente* (The bridge) or *El yugo* (The yoke) were (see chapter 1). There were several attempts throughout the 1950s and 1960s to finish the film, but all were unsuccessful.[24] It was not until the early 1990s, with the aid of the Archive of Motion Pictures and the Puerto Rican Foundation for the Humanities that the film was finally completed.

Perhaps because *Un día cualquiera* was unlike the rest of DIVEDCO's filmic output, it feels refreshing and remarkable today. Stylistically, the pacing of the film is slow, with editing and camera work that are not afraid of pauses and silences, creating an almost meditative mood. There is no omniscient voice-over narrator that would take the spectators by the hand in order to educate and enlighten them about urban migration, sparing us those know-it-all voices, as Félix Jiménez describes them (7), that were so typical in DIVEDCO films. There is a voice-over, but it is the voice of Joaquín, who is allowing the audience to have access to his thoughts and fears, to his anxiety about making it in the city. This is a rarity in the filmic output of the division.

An exceptional aspect of *Un día cualquiera* is the depiction of Puerto Rican urban space and urban culture, something almost totally nonexistent in the division's filmography. While Joaquín wanders looking for any job, the film allows the viewer to enter into and circulate in different geographies of the city: the crowded streets and avenues teeming with buses and heavy traffic, sidewalks full of men and women hurrying through, flashy marquees and electric posts, impressive commercial buildings and quiet residential neighborhoods, all in stark contrast to the meager living of the family in the liminal space of El Fanguito, with makeshift homes made out of anything, wood planks above the water functioning as sidewalks, and an overall impermanence to the whole neighborhood. In the entire corpus of the division, this is the one instance where audiences truly get to wander through and wonder about the city, both the modernized city of progress and the marginal sectors of the city that felt the impact of modernization; in *Un día cualquiera* a complex urban landscape is cinematically exposed.

This urban landscape is visible as much as it is audible—traffic noise and vendors hawking their stuff, music coming out of jukeboxes, though the one sound source that is practically omnipresent in the film is the radio. While most DIVEDCO films are accompanied either by classical music, classically inspired contemporary music (done by Puerto Rican composers), or traditional genres like jíbaro music or quaint *danzas*, *Un día cualquiera*'s principal soundtrack is almost always the radio.[25] It is there from the very beginning of the film (with the station identification, first in English, then in Spanish), and it is what threads the entire film-day, with advertisements, songs (mostly boleros and guarachas), jokes, science news, and general information; it lingers until the very last shot, when the station signs off the air. Even though there is an intradiegetic explanation for it—Joaquín and Pascuala's neighbors own a radio and they play it all day—the aural presence of this form of mass communication extends beyond where they live and meanders through the city, becoming almost extradiegetical. The sounds of the radio, in fact, accompany the lives of the urbanites; it is indeed the urban soundtrack of San Juan in the film.

In the last scene of the film, as the family is closing up the house and getting ready to sleep, the last thing we hear on the radio before the station signs off is a man reciting "El valle de Collores" (The valley of Collores) by the poet Luis Lloréns Torres:

Ay, si estuviera en mis manos . . .	If I could only, by some charm,
a mi bohío de Collores	Reclaim my hut in Collores
volver en la jaca baya	And on my little bay ride there
por el sendero entre mayas	Along the path where daisies stir
arropás de cundiamores.	And flow'ring vines line the roadways.

At a certain level, the placement of this poem at the end of the film would seem to bring back in full force DIVEDCO's bucolic relation with the countryside. But at another level, perhaps, these lines may be trying to address the genuine, conflicted feelings of jíbaros and jíbaras as they adapted to a new environment. Yes, there is more than a touch of nostalgia in Lloréns Torres, but in the context of Joaquín and Pascuala the poem could also point to their uncertainty about having left behind familiar surroundings.

Several times in the film, Pascuala questions their decision to move to the city, but Joaquín insists on staying and trying it out. At one point, in an economically and beautifully edited flashback from Joaquín's point of view, the family's move from the countryside to the city is photographed with the classic narrative of urban migration in mind: to abandon a locale that had ceased to be a feasible place to prosper and to adopt another place that claims to provide the opportunity to improve living conditions. The sequence goes from the empty sugarcane fields where Joaquín makes his decision to leave, to his packing a truck with the family's belongings, leaving el campo behind, and entering at night the promising city, which is decked with electric lights. That somewhat optimistic flashback is bluntly dismantled in the rest of the film, which shows migration proving to be quite a difficult experience. Migration many times is downright dislocation, and making a home in a new space, feeling at home in a new community, requires a drastic uprooting that not everyone is capable of doing swiftly. At the same time, the film makes sure that the margins of the city are not portrayed as simply uninhabitable, and this day in El Fanguito is actually not like any other because it visualizes the family's realization that there is indeed a community in this utterly precarious space.

Why did Governor Muñoz Marín react so violently to the film? Why didn't he see all the moments in it where community and solidarity, where affection and human compassion were depicted? Possibly because *Un día cualquiera* unequivocably presented an urban space that the commonwealth was very reluctuant to admit existed in the new Puerto Rico. Places like El Fanguito, La Perla, and Tokío were never thought of as spaces with a potential for urban, or even community, development; they couldn't be conceived as communities, as legitimate social spaces by the government; they were places, as I mentioned before, to be eradicated in order to relocate those inhabitants to the clean, well-lit public housing that was being constructed in cities and towns all over the island.

Un día cualquiera was the lone attempt at trying to rethink this space in the DIVEDCO oeuvre, and a pretty astonishing one at that.

CONCLUSION

¡Qué va, nena! Este país entero es una gran ciudad.

No way, baby! This whole country is a big city.

Pepe, in César Andreu Iglesias's *El inciso hache* (The H clause)

It is undeniable that Puerto Rican culture today is inherently urban, both on the island and throughout the United States. As early as 1963, in a little-known play by the fiction writer and journalist César Andreu Iglesias, *El inciso hache* (The H clause), the cynical, urbanite character Pepe claimed that the island was already one gigantic urban sprawl—a bit of an exaggeration then, though difficult to dismiss today. But in the midcentury there was a troubling tension, cultural and otherwise, in the way Puerto Ricans faced the diverse configurations of the city: troubling because they disturbed the official rhetoric of the commonwealth by exposing the contradictions of the era, troubling because they permanently transformed the layout and the location of culture.

The trouble with the city and its environs had mostly to do with the fact that the urban was still culturally elusive. The government was reluctant to absorb it as part of the national cultural project, and an office like the Division of Community Education felt out of touch with the incipient urban culture. The literary figures of the time tended to make symbolic use of the urban in a frontal attack on the establishment, and only in a few instances would they delve into the complexity of the urban. Cortijo y su combo, precisely because the group didn't have a self-conscious project of cultural construction, was able to document the city as the musicians saw it and experienced it, though of course this created a partial view of things urban. Add to this the fundamental paradox of the 1950s—the disconnect between the rural as the core of the national cultural imaginary and the modernizing urban as the lived experience of a large portion of the historical subjects of that time—and the messy, paradoxical, thorny preoccupation with the urban starts to come into focus.

In one of the essays from *The Book of Puerto Rico*, a 1923 bilingual volume that registered the achievements of the island after twenty-five years of American occupation, the San Juan of the future is envisioned as "beautiful, serene, gentle" (qtd. in Sepúlveda Rivera 9). This is an unbelievably unattainable image of the city, though in a way it uncannily foreshadowed the harmonious cultural wishes of Operation Serenity. Not surprisingly, the fast-paced changes that came with modernization, industrialization, and urbanization would make this "future" city an utter impossibility. Indeed, the urban in the midcentury, under the realm of the commonwealth, was paradoxical and problematic, triggering a series of fascinating responses in the arts that uncovered both the anxieties and desires of the time: in the hellish world of René Marqués and the dynamic, socially aware milieu of José Luis González; in the precarious, yet livable space of *Un día cualquiera* and the hopeless New York of Pedro Juan Soto's "Los inocentes"; in the construction of a new autochthon in the prints of the Center of Puerto Rican Art and in the persistent documentation of class and race in the danceable city of Cortijo y su combo. At a time when the urban was becoming inevitable, it also became an apparatus for exposure and discovery, as well as the palpable location in the arts of the transformational nature of modernization.

Epilogue and Conclusions

CONCRETE WITH COUNTRYSIDE

Ningún proyecto de futuro se construye sin una reapropriación del pasado, sin una reconsideración de las raíces que lo alimentan.

No project of the future is constructed without a reappropriation of the past, without a reconsideration of the roots that feed it.

Ariel Jiménez, *Utopías americanas*

It may well turn out that those who most glory in the past are spared the necessity of living it; while those who must live it are indeed most disposed to change.

Sidney W. Mintz, "Puerto Rico:
An Essay in the Definition of a National Culture"

AROUND THE TIME THAT Luis Muñoz Marín was ending the last of his sixteen years as governor, an American anthropologist was in Puerto Rico collecting data for a book on poverty and migration. His cadre of Mexican, American, and Puerto Rican social scientists had been recording interviews with the extended members of a family living between the community of La Perla in San Juan and several large cities in the northeastern part of the United States. The social scientist was none other than Oscar Lewis, and the interviews became the core of his 1966 book *La Vida: A Puerto Rican Family in the Culture of Poverty—San Juan and New York*. The publication created a furor on the island, due to its blunt and unvarnished description of the poor Puerto Rican family presented in its pages. Some condemned the book for smudging the new image that Puerto Rico had fought so hard to create and for reinforcing that stereotypical image of Puerto Rico as a backward, overpopulated, poverty-infested Caribbean island. Others, however, admired it for laying bare the contradictions of the commonwealth's modernizing project.

I do not wish to deal here with the problematic assumptions around Lewis's idea of a culture of poverty that he presented in this book—which was, it must be admitted, a weak theoretical ground for his project and a concept that he would eventually abandon as too simplistic in its interpretation of social interaction, economic status, and citizenship among low-income subjects across the globe. Nor am I interested in *La Vida* as an anthropological text per se.[1] I am intrigued by this massive tome, first, as a document that gives us partial access to the daily lives of a sector of Puerto Rican men and women who had a very limited voice at the time, even though the rhetoric of modernization frequently spoke in their name. But more importantly here, I feel that the "scandal" of *La Vida* deserves a closer look because the reactions to the book by Puerto Ricans, on both the island and the mainland, though mild in comparison with what occurred in Mexico after the publication of Lewis's *The Children of Sánchez* in the 1950s (Rigdon, *The Culture Façade*), capture the series of preoccupations that I have been exploring in the context of the paradoxical configurations of the urban and the rural. Wrapping up this study with *La Vida*, then, gives us access to the series of gestures in the cultural politics of Puerto Rico that by the mid-1960s had become widespread in the cultural spaces of the island.

The "fireworks" (a term the sociologist Manuel Maldonado Denis used in a letter to Lewis to describe the reaction on the island) began in late November 1966, immediately after the publication of the book. The president of the Puerto Rican Senate, Samuel R. Quiñones, called the book not only an insult to

Puerto Rico but an insult to poor people all over the world ("Presidente"). There were letters from angry readers printed in all of the major newspapers on the island and of course dozens of letters sent directly to Oscar Lewis—from Puerto Ricans on the island and in New York—bashing *La Vida* as perpetuating stereotypes about Puerto Ricans in the eyes of the American public.[2]

The most recurrent complaint—bordering on obsession—centered on the issue that several of the women interviewed repeatedly resorted to prostitution as a way of earning money, some of them even after becoming mothers and wives. This fact was read by many as an attempt by Lewis himself to generalize that most poor Puerto Rican women were prostitutes—something he never implied in *La Vida* or in any subsequent text.[3] Joseph Monserrat, then the director of the migration division of the commonwealth's Department of Labor, made the (in my view, wildly inaccurate) claim that the book was actually "a study of a Puerto Rican family *in the culture of prostitution*" (18; emphasis added). If, indeed, *La Vida* seemed to have established a problematic and unflattering image of Puerto Ricanness in American popular culture (the prostitute who hides a Gem blade in her mouth in the 1981 Hollywood film *Fort Apache, The Bronx* might have been inspired by the interviews of Fernanda in the first section of the book), the attacks against *La Vida* and prostitution delivered a profound shock to many middle-class Puerto Rican readers, senators, journalists, and writers, in terms of decency and morality among Puerto Ricans. The middle-class public could not think of these women as ordinary people trying to make ends meet—they could only view them as sinful, unethical citizens. Rather than attempting to understand the context that would make a woman resort to prostitution, the offended readers attacked Lewis for generalizing about the behavior of poor Puerto Rican women.

Not all reactions to the book were negative. There were a few published articles and reviews that ardently supported *La Vida* as an important document of the contradictions of the commonwealth, of modernization, and of the colonial status of the island. In his review for the newspaper *El Mundo*, Manuel Maldonado Denis stated, "Al apuntar hacia áreas de nuestra vida colectiva que permanecerán piadosamente ocultas bajo el manto de una imagen prefabricada de lo que es nuestra isla, el doctor Lewis ha incurrido en el imperdonable pecado de emapañar 'la vitrina,' aunque haya sido para cumplir con su responsabilidad como sociólogo [*sic*] que se atreve a explorar las zonas neurálgicas del cuerpo social, no empece ello pueda granjearle la irreductible enemistad de los ideólogos del sistema" (By pointing to areas of our collective life that remain piously hidden under the mantle of a prefabricated image of our island, Dr. Lewis has fallen into the unpardonable sin of smearing "the showcase," even though he has done so to fulfill his responsibility as a sociologist [*sic*] who dares to explore the weak spots of the social body, even though this may result in the unyielding enmity of the system's ideologues) (*"La Vida"* 37). Strategically referring to the image so prevalent during the first years of the Commonwealth of Puerto Rico as a "showcase" (*la vitrina*), that is, as a model of economic development practices, Maldonado Denis squarely positioned *La Vida* against the hegemonic image-making of the 1950s and early 1960s.

The journalist, fiction writer, and political thinker César Andreu Iglesias, in his column Cosas de aquí (from the newspaper *El Imparcial*) dedicated several days in late 1966 and early 1967 to Lewis's *La Vida*. He even predicted—as the book came out—that the volume was sure to scandalize certain sectors of Puerto Rico ("La cultura"). Andreu Iglesias, unlike many readers, was fascinated by the female figures in the book—he thought them strong and independent ("La familia Ríos")—and by the many tender moments that the interviewees described throughout the text, tender moments that almost no one pointed out in the published commentaries. This is an important point about the book: indeed, the volume depicted these characters with warts and all, but it also included many, many moments of familial affection, conjugal love, and steadfast friendship. The matriarch Fernanda was quick to beat the children and clearly had her favorites, but she expressed her utter distress when unfortunate things happened to her progeny; she candidly and openly talked about sex, but she also followed a strict set of morals.

The last paragraph in Andreu Iglesias's final column dedicated to *La Vida* expressed the importance and gravity of what Lewis's book ultimately achieved:

> Asómbrense los que . . . han ayudado a formar (o a deformar) a Fernanda, Amparo, Erasmo, Soledad y demás personajes de *La Vida*, en tanto son representativos de la

sociedad puertorriqueña. Escandalícense, y envíenle sus trabajadores sociales, que no son nada más que una forma de tranquilizar la conciencia de los responsables de esa situación. Y sigan con sus fallidos intentos de remendar lo que ya no tiene espacio para un remiendo más. . . . Nosotros, por nuestra parte, diremos: lo que reviste de importancia a *La Vida*, como estudio de la vida, es decidirse a cambiarla. [Let them be appalled, those who . . . have helped to form (or deform) Fernanda, Amparo, Erasmo, Soledad, and the other characters of *La Vida*, insofar as they are representative of Puerto Rican society. Let them be scandalized, and let them send their social workers, who are nothing more than a way of calming the conscience of those who are responsible for this situation. Let them keep at it with their failed attempts to mend what cannot be mended anymore. . . . We, for our part, will say: what grants *La Vida* importance, as a study of life, is the decision to change that life.] ("La clave")

Andreu Iglesias, like Maldonado Denis, points out that the book presented an image of Puerto Rico that the government and other official sectors were not interested in disseminating during these years; it was an image that complicated matters for the commonwealth.

Another ardent supporter was the novelist Piri Thomas, an important figure in English-language Puerto Rican literature. He wrote a brief letter to Oscar Lewis in the spring of 1967 and to it attached a manifesto of support in which he described *La Vida* as a source of pride for Puerto Ricans. "We must understand that in our zeal for our people to rise," writes Piri Thomas toward the end of the document, "we must also recognize the presence of the ugly conditions and the reality of these mean streets" ("My Own Thoughts" 1–2). In his letter, Thomas even addressed Lewis as "mi hermanito" (my little brother), a term of endearment commonly used among Puerto Rican men.

FOR A NEW LIFE

But perhaps the most intriguing response to *La Vida* was the publication of a slim hard-cover volume called *Puerto Rico: La Nueva Vida / The New Life*. The book comprised brief selections of canonical and contemporary Puerto Rican literature, presented bilingually and accompanied by color illustrations of recent Puerto Rican art, though with a smattering of paintings by José Campeche from the eighteenth century and by Francisco Oller from the nineteenth century, two figures widely revered as the fathers of visual arts on the island. The publication was in conjunction with a touring art exhibition by the Housing Investment Corporation, a San Juan–based mortgage banking institution that owned most of the art included in the book. *La Nueva Vida / The New Life* was edited by two Americans and one Puerto Rican. The Americans were Nina Kaiden, a staunch supporter of corporate acquisition of art (she wrote a whole book about it), and Andrew Vladimir, a writer and marketing consultant working in Puerto Rico for WAPA-TV. The Puerto Rican editor was the writer Pedro Juan Soto. Although not credited in the book, the visual artist Domingo García served as artistic advisor ("Puerto Rico—La Nueva Vida" 16).[4]

La Nueva Vida was published in November 1965, almost a year before *La Vida*. It is quite unlikely that the book was developed from the beginning as a response to Lewis's project. However, many in the intellectual and media circles of Puerto Rico had been aware long before the publication of *La Vida* that Lewis was working on a book about socially marginalized sectors, and as early as November 1964 sections of the book had appeared in several American magazines (*Harper's*, the *New Yorker*, *Commentary*). Moreover, in March 1965 the English-language monthly magazine *San Juan Review* (whose associate editor was none other than Pedro Juan Soto) published a small excerpt from *La Vida*. The title of Lewis's book had changed a few times; one of the early titles, as Nilita Vientós Gastón reported in the *San Juan Star* newspaper in early 1967, was an English translation of a Puerto Rican phrase: "No se puede tapar el cielo con la mano!" (You can't cover the sky with your hand!). But the phrase *la vida* (the life) was already being mentioned as part of the title of Lewis's book in the March 1965 excerpt in *San Juan Review*, eight months before the release of *La Nueva Vida*. Thus, it is conceivable that even if *La Nueva Vida* had not originally been intended as a response to the image of Puerto Rico in Lewis's work, in the process of putting the book together the project might have become a response to *La Vida*. Its title seems to corroborate this idea. Its contents, I believe, leave very little doubt.

First of all, the book positioned itself as diammetrically opposed to *La Vida*'s purported view of Puerto Rican poverty. Almost as a slap in the face to Lewis's book, *La Nueva Vida* included a disproportionate number of visual and literary renditions of tender parents and innocent children in delightful settings: at a carousel or a circus, in the arms of a mother, or about to get a *piragua*, a traditional shaved ice treat sold in the streets of cities and towns. But beyond this mere thematic attack, *La Nueva Vida* also portrayed a Puerto Rico that saw itself as modern and proud of its culture, as if to counteract the ostensible backwardness of the island in *La Vida*. Much of the art is visibly influenced by high modernism (even abstract expressionism): a stunning collage by newcomer Rafael Ferrer, some striking pieces by Luis Hernández Cruz and Julio Rosado del Valle, and a couple of abstract landscapes by Domingo García. The prints in the volume are a remarkable collection; pieces by Rafael Tufiño, Antonio Martorell, Myrna Báez, and Lorenzo Homar pointed to a genuine school of printmaking in Puerto Rico of the highest quality that had already been established by the mid-1960s. This was a country, *La Nueva Vida* seemed to clamor, with outstanding "high" art.

The literary selections—chosen by Pedro Juan Soto himself—gave the reader a sense of intense national and cultural pride. Poems and prose excerpts from throughout the twentieth century, by José de Diego, Ramón Julia Marín, Edwin Figueroa, Luis Muñoz Rivera, and René Marqués, among many others, were openly patriotic and even anti-American.

As if to offset *La Vida*'s dreary urban hell, the city is quite present in *La Nueva Vida*, both its urban landscape and its inhabitants, though in some cases the literary and artistic images either remained safely in touristy depictions of Old San Juan or were eerily close to the picturesque. The work of Luis Germán Cajiga, for example, is included, depicting a charming small town in bright, cheerful colors. There are indeed images of the poor sectors of San Juan, as well as literary renditions of urban migration, plus a fantastic print of a dark and smoky jazz bar by Tufiño. But in the process of "defending" Puerto Rico, its culture, and its people, the book was not capable of avoiding that naturalized, ruralized national culture that the commonwealth and its allies had been sponsoring and disseminating. While the book tries to construct a modern, urban Puerto Rico, it still seems to be haunted by the countryside. Thus, Luis Lloréns Torres's "Vida criolla" (see chapter 2) makes its embarrassingly odd appearance; a sonnet by Guillermo Atiles García idealizes the *jíbaro*'s rustic hut:

Yo soy rico, muy rico en el momento,	I am rich, very rich at the moment
y el temor de ser pobre no me espanta.	And the fear of being poor does not scare me.
Monumental palacio que me encanta	Monumental palace that enchants me
la choza es, en que feliz me siento.	is the shack in which I feel so happy.[5]

Even María Teresa Babín's *Fantasía boricua* (see chapter 2) paternalistically presents a view of the countryside as a space of pure leisure for the landowning class. And one of Tufiño's prints, portraying a mother tenderly embracing her baby, is clearly set *en el campo*. (In a November 1966 letter to Nilita Vientós Gastón, Oscar Lewis confesses, not without irony, "It is too bad that my first book on Puerto Rico did not deal with a class jibaro type. That would have made everybody happy.")

La Nueva Vida thus comes across as a text that attempted to inoculate the perceived negative stereotypes of *La Vida* with a series of "positive" stereotypes about Puerto Rico and Puerto Ricans, many of them imbued with the commonwealth's notions of modernization and of a national culture with decidedly rural origins. It is curious and somewhat startling to have a writer like Pedro Juan Soto, who helped ignite an urban literature in Puerto Rico, resort to the rural machinations of the establishment, but it seems that in this case his distaste for the commonwealth was trumped by his disdain for *La Vida*.

LA VIDA, EN ESPAÑOL

Oscar Lewis went ahead with a Spanish version of *La Vida*, which was published in Mexico in February 1969 by the renowned Joaquín Mortiz. This version went back to the original Spanish transcriptions and therefore is not quite a translation, since the original book presented the Spanish interviews translated into English. If indeed the Random House version did quite a good job of capturing

the colloquial and creative way in which these Puerto Ricans expressed themselves linguistically, the phonetic and lexical transformations of Puerto Rican
Spanish were lost in English. It is the Spanish version of *La Vida* that presents the
reader with a fascinating transcribed oral document. This is the version of the
book that, as Arcadio Díaz Quiñones has pointed out, was a crucial influence for
the composition of Luis Rafael Sánchez's magnum opus, *La guaracha del Macho
Camacho* (Díaz Quiñones, Introduction 50–52).

The book did require some translation—the first-person sections from the
transcriptions were prefaced by a series of chapters in the third person that had
been written in English for the original edition. Each of these chapters was constructed as a day in the life of each one of the main characters of *La Vida*. The
translation was assigned to the writer José Luis González, who during his exile in
Mexico had already done quite a few translations for several publishers. The project must have seemed a fascinating opportunity to him: here was a Puerto Rican
writer who had focused his work on the inconsistencies of modernization and the
urban space, who had managed a literary frontal attack against the stratagems of
the commonwealth, and who was now being asked to help in the publication of
a book that some key Puerto Rican scholars and writers had supported as urgent
and valuable. *La Vida*, as a text that maintained the human character of its subjects
while looking at the paradoxes of the city, the lasting effects of migration, and
the marginalization of the poor, in some way carried on the political and literary
project of González.

The book had a lasting influence on him. In interviews, he repeatedly pointed
to his work on the Spanish version of *La Vida* as the linguistic and narrative inspi-
ration for his early 1970s short story "La noche que volvimos a ser gente" (The
night we became people again) (González, "El arte del cuento" 30–31), which is
one of the first literary creations that deliberately moved away from the typically
fatalistic rendition of the New York Puerto Rican community. It is quite revealing that a book that was criticized for presenting such a bleak picture of Puerto
Ricans would inspire such a sympathetic short story.

There seems to be some evidence that González helped as well in the editing of the interview transcriptions (Rigdon, "Correspondence"). Although Lewis
had a small battery of helpers for this task, the scant correspondence between

the anthropologist and the writer points to a certain involvement of González in the Spanish transcriptions as they were turned into "chapters" of the book. A sentence-by-sentence comparison between the two versions clearly indicates that there was quite a bit of deleting and inserting of material for the Spanish-language edition. In addition, González created a glossary for the Mexican publication of *La Vida*. Without a doubt, most non–Puerto Rican Spanish-speaking readers would have trouble with *dron*, *límber*, *mapo*, *ponchar*, *títere*, *troc*, *feca*, and *crica*, plus the numerous English words that the family members sprinkled through their speech (which were also included in a separate section of the glossary). At least in a Latin American literary context, this glossary nudges the book toward *la novela de la tierra*—in this case, *la novela de la ciudad*—in which the local flavor of the novel's world required a translation for those who live outside the space depicted.

All of these elements—the translations of the introductory chapters, the possible editing of the transcriptions, the glossaries—make me want to suggest a radical notion: to think of *La Vida* in its Spanish incarnation as part of the works of José Luis González. What's more, placing González's appropriation of Lewis's book against Pedro Juan Soto's reactions to the same text articulates an important contrast. The act of Pedro Juan Soto taking on *La Vida* in *La Nueva Vida / The New Life* exposes the ambivalent stance of depicting a modernized Puerto Rican reality within the cultural paradox of a constructed urban rurality. As José Luis González takes *La Vida* and makes it his own, this author incorporates what seems to be a negative rendition of an urbanized nation to expose and dismantle a certain modernized reality.

CONCRETE *WITH* COUNTRYSIDE

Placed in the larger context of this book, what Oscar Lewis's *La Vida* achieved was to document the practices and spaces of certain subjects who were not recognized as truly integrable citizens of the commonwealth. They were those "potentially disruptive outsides" (6) that Gareth Williams talks about in the context of Latin American nation-building under the populist mechanisms that were so prevalent throughout the twentieth century: "The formation of the modern nation-state in Latin America . . . was for the most part predicated on the active integration and institutionalization of the notion of the people—of the common populace, or the popular/subaltern aspects of society—as the originary ground from which to consider the contours of national history, national identity formations, and national modernization" (4). If we set aside Puerto Rico's not being a sovereign state, this fits perfectly with the island's four administrations of Luis Muñoz Marín. Williams goes on to describe the gestures of populism aimed at a useful consolidation: the production of "common geographies, histories, identities, and destinies" (5) for the forging of a national community that could serve as a stepping-stone to embark on a project of economic development (in most instances, capitalist development). But, as he accurately points out, certain sectors of the population were "integrated into the nation *as exceptions, as exam*ples of forms of membership in the nation that are *included without inclusion*" (6; emphasis added). These exceptions were repudiated by the state, while at the same time they conveniently served to define the limits and boundaries of what the nation was not. And yet, their condition within the national configuration ultimately became potentially disruptive, because in their positionality as "outsides," they interrupted the naturalized constitution of the social and cultural formation of the nation-in-progress. Hence the strongly negative reaction by some (including several political leaders) to *La Vida* and the praise of the text by others who recognized the power of Fernanda and her family as "disruptive outsides" of a modernized Puerto Rico.

It has been my argument in this book that the populist narrative of national construction outlined by Williams, as it unfolded in the Puerto Rican midcentury, is better understood framed by the complex articulations of urban and rural geographies and subjectivities that were appropriated and reconfigured during those years. Rural subjects were integrated as core citizens of the new commonwealth, and the countryside—a very specific place, mountainous and bucolic—was adopted as an autochthonous site of national culture. The films of the Division of Community Education consolidated this visually and aurally, and a lot of the literature that was adopted in school curricula and canonized by scholars solidified that claim, even when those same jíbaras and jíbaros were migrating away from this supposed authentic space of Puerto Ricanness and into the burgeoning urban spaces of the island and the mainland, where modernization was being promised in newsreels and other media. As newly minted urbanites, who for the most part had to settle in the margins of the city in precarious living conditions, they ceased to be those core citizens; dismissed as "slum" dwellers, they were reluctantly acknowledged by the government and its intelligentsia and perceived as veritable outsiders in the commonwealth's vision of a newly fashioned Puerto Rico. These men and women are the ones whom Cortijo y su combo inserted into the popular dance culture of the time and integrated into the urban space where others had been living for decades; they are the ones whom DIVEDCO courageously depicted in *Un día cualquiera*, complicating its filmic output; they are the ones who were made protagonists in the new urban literature, to attack the silence of the government and the media about the contradictions of modernization. What defined the 1950s, in my view, was the persistent consolidation of a rural cultural imaginary at odds with an unstoppable urban culture that would end up predominating in subsequent decades. The transnational development of salsa music, perhaps the musical form that most definitively established Puerto Rican culture as unquestionably urban; the explosive fiction of the 1970s and 1980s by writers like Ana Lydia Vega and Luis Rafael Sánchez squarely set in the sidewalk and the automobile, the traffic jam and the sex motel; the unruly, ever-shifting visual work of someone like Rafael Ferrer, especially those early collages of metal junk and garbage that scandalized the art scene in the 1960s— all of these artistic manifestations owe a great deal to the contradictions and tensions of the cultural debates in the Puerto Rican midcentury as they were connected to the rural and the urban.

Of course, it is actually more complicated than that. Puerto Rican culture cannot be explained away with the simplistic dichotomy of the city and el campo, of concrete and countryside; the binary inaccurately assumes a separation, a dividing line. Rather, it might be more precise to talk about concrete *with* countryside: an assemblage of assemblages in which the rural and the urban appropriate each other, absorb each other, dissipate each other, redefine each other. In the 1950s and early 1960s, because of the tension that modernization brought, this fusion had not congealed yet, but it would soon appear, for example, in the momentous and gigantic explosion of poetry that surfaced in the 1970s with the Nuyorican movement. Víctor Hernández Cruz, in "Los New Yorks" from the collection *Maraca*, invites us into a new space: "I present you the tall skyscrapers / As merely huge palm trees with lights" (51). And in "Mountain Building," his city is hallucinatorily rural:

> The mountains have changed into buildings
> Is this hallway the inside of a stem
> That has a rattling flower for a head,
> Immense tree bark with roots made out of
> Mailboxes? (120)

This is indeed a transnational rural, as Daniel Bell might have identified it (154), but it is also an urban ruralized, a countryside that pervades as a cultural phantom, as an apparition that refuses to go away. This is, after all, the country that calls bus terminals *un corral de guaguas*, a buses corral.

Looking today at photographs on Facebook of my friends' children dressed up as jíbaros for school events, it is evident that those appropriations, as a sign of nation and culture, as a sign of authenticity à la the 1950s, are still with us. But there are other uses that do not constitute a simple construction: one clear example is the *nuevos jíbaros* ecological movement, in which urban, mostly middle-class young families are moving out of the city and establishing small organic farms around the island to service restaurants in San Juan (Rivas). This is by no means a return to the countryside in the way René Marqués had wished it at the end of *La carreta*; it is indeed a migration back to the rural space, but one very aware of the urban quality of the island.

It is quite true that the realms of the urban and the rural in midcentury Puerto Rico were already a fused network of flows, but the social and cultural imaginary still read them as separate, as opposites. Part of the reason for this separation is that, in a way, this period could be defined as an epoch of an anachronistic construction of tradition, not unique in the processes of modernization in Latin America but absolutely fundamental to understanding the machinations of culture in Puerto Rico, then and now. The scholar Graciela Montaldo has asked us to think about the idea of tradition as that which activates the past in the present and deliberately stops the flow of meanings, not purely for nostalgic reasons, but to establish a dominant cultural narrative that might serve the purposes of the present time (25). Conceived this way, the building blocks of tradition in Puerto Rico were indeed made out of noncontemporary elements—the jíbaro is at the top of that list—but their selection, as we have seen in this book, was totally propelled by the contemporary conflicts of nation and culture, of modernity, of sovereignty, and of coloniality. But what remains remarkable about this moment, this conjunctural moment, is the launching of a plural countertradition in literature and film, in music and the visual arts, that persistently gnawed at the cemented tradition based on that anachronistic gesture, transforming the image of both urban and rural, of ruralized urban and urbanized rural, in the entire spectrum of Puerto Rican cultural spheres.

NOTES

INTRODUCTION

1. "Cuba has turned to the Communist world for help, used violence and murder, confiscated property and launched a vicious propaganda war against those it regards as its enemies. Puerto Rico, guided and supported by the U.S., has used the ballot, preserved civil rights and private property and, with imagination and self-discipline, created the beginnings of a modern economy" ("Surprising Puerto Rico" 33).

2. Using the word *revolution* for what was occurring in Puerto Rico during these years was not unique to *Look* and its editors. A pro-commonwealth book published in 1963 by the American photojournalist Homer Page was in fact called *Puerto Rico: The Quiet Revolution*, a title that not only highlighted the typical Cold War contrast of the island with revolutionary Cuba but also encapsulated the perception of Puerto Rico's development as measured and, curiously, as agreeable.

3. Muñoz Marín was not blind to this tumultuous transformation. Already in late 1960, realizing how quickly Puerto Rico was changing and the series of problems those changes were creating, the governor recorded in his Dictaphone, "Más lentitud en

el desarrollo, más hondo para mejora social" (Slower development, deeper development for social improvement) ("Operación Sócrates" 1).

4. Biron eloquently and succinctly posits this: "On the one hand, images of shiny urban magnificence and futurism highlight by contrast the backwardness and primitivism of so-called pre-modern, or anti-modern, rural traditions; on the other hand, images of urban decadence, cultural imitation, and social alienation emphasize the purity, autochthony, and sense of community to be found in idealized rural landscapes" ("Marvel" 119).

5. My approach is very much in line with (and inspired by) a group of scholars—most of them based in Australia—that have been advocating for a certain rural cultural studies. See Gorman-Murray for a good introduction to their approach.

6. As the geographer Michael Wood accurately affirms, "agriculture is one of the most potent and enduring emblems of rurality" (qtd. in Gorman-Murray).

7. Ayala and Bernabe's *Puerto Rico in the American Century: A History since 1898*, published in 2007, is an excellent reference, with extensive cultural and economic history. In Spanish, Francisco Scarano's *Puerto Rico: Cinco siglos de historia* has a larger historical scope and is also first rate.

8. As Ayala and Bernabe summarized Supreme Court justice Edward Douglass White's explanation of the term "unincorporated territories," all "[i]ncorporated territories were part of the Union, and its inhabitants were fully protected by the Constitution; unincorporated territories were possessions but not part of the United States. They were not foreign in an international sense, since they were under U.S. sovereignty, but they were 'foreign in a domestic sense,' since they had not been incorporated into the United States" (27). This is, as Pedro Cabán has stated, inherent to the nature of colonialism: "incorporated into the empire, but not part of the empire" (10).

9. "The colonial relation took on the appearance of a compact, giving greater participation to the colonized in the running of internal affairs while maintaining intact the key structural features of the colonial relation" (Pantojas-García 67).

10. Cultural nationalism was also a way of discarding the Albizu Campos slogan "either Yankees or Puerto Ricans" and allowing the possibility of being Yankees and Puerto Ricans simultaneously: American citizens who possessed an autonomous culture separate from North American traditions.

11. These entities were the Autoridad de Fuentes Fluviales (AFF) in 1941, the Autoridad Metropolitana de Autobuses (AMA) in 1942, the Autoridad de Acueductos y Alcantarillados (AAA) in 1945, and the Autoridad de Comunicaciones de Puerto Rico (ACPR) in 1946 (Sepúlveda Rivera 58).

12. Although Córdova correctly points out that the party's emblem was solid red (the color of the party), partially erasing the possibility of a racialized jíbaro (179), there had already been quite a bit of whitening of the jíbaro on the part of the cultural elite—in essays, poems, and the visual arts. The minuscule nose in the PPD's emblem (let us not forget, it is a profile) sides with the elite's whitened iconography of the jíbaro, and it becomes another invitation for the elite to ally with the party.

13. Álvarez Curbelo's essay is required reading for a political-economic understanding of the genealogy of populism in Puerto Rico.

14. In Edgardo Rodríguez Juliá's literary chronicle on Luis Muñoz Marín, *Las tribulaciones de Jonás* (The tribulations of Jonah), the Puerto Rican writer also stresses the politician's linguistic and performative transformation of political rhetoric: "Ya pronto descubrirá que mejor será descender de la tribuna, hablar con el pueblo, convertir el discurso en tertulia, transformar la oratoria en conversación atenta. Muñoz Marín bajó la política puertorriqueña de la tribuna custodiada por 'los picos de oro'" (He will soon discover that it is better to get down from the platform, to talk to the people, to turn the speech into a chat, to turn oratory into attentive conversation. Muñoz Marín pushed Puerto Rican politics down from the platform guarded by "the silver-tongued") (104).

15. In his memoirs, the political analyst Juan Manuel García Passalacqua points out another important factor in Muñoz Marín's jíbaro turn. After universal suffrage was established in 1935, people were no longer required to prove they could read and write in order to vote. Thus, thousands of Puerto Ricans were added to the electorate beginning in 1936, and the appropriation of the jíbaro as a visual icon, along with Muñoz Marín's direct, simple language, would win over a substantial number of those new voters (24).

16. The *zapatista* connection of the slogan comes from Álvarez Curbelo (35).

17. The rhetorical appropriation of the land was not exclusive to Luis Muñoz Marín. Álvarez Curbelo points out that in the discourse of the pro-independence Nationalist Party, Pedro Albizu Campos had also used the land as part of its party's imagi-

nary, but in his case it was linked to a Catholic and Hispanic affinity, something that Muñoz abandoned in the 1940s as he approached more seriously a tweaked relation with the United States (28).

18. The logo has changed several times since the 1940s, eventually becoming a silhouette (not unlike the pava) during the 1970s. The Fomento man has since disappeared from the logo, leaving the cogwheel in a stylized design and in eco-friendly green.

19. It was also a thoroughly Cold War move. In the words of Conrad Hilton, "Our Hilton house flag is one small flag of freedom which is being waved defiantly against Communism exactly as Lenin predicted. With humility we submit this international effort of ours as a contribution to world peace" (qtd. in Merrill 196).

20. Jorge Duany's *Puerto Rican Nation on the Move* and Arlene Dávila's *Sponsored Identities* remain invaluable scholarly contributions to the complexities of cultural nationalism on the island.

CHAPTER 1. FABRICATIONS, CONFABULATIONS, CONTESTATIONS

1. It is important to point out here that I am using the term "the arts" as a most inclusive denomination, the way the humanities has historically thought of it: not only visual arts but also performing arts, media arts, and literary endeavors.

2. I appropriate the notion of the spectacularity of cinema from the writings of the Cuban filmmaker Tomás Gutiérrez Alea, as discussed by the scholar Astrid Santana Fernández de Castro in her monograph on the filmmaker. Gutiérrez Alea explains: "In times of social convulsion, reality loses its everyday character, and everything which happens is extraordinary, new, unique. . . . The dynamics of change, the trends of development, the essence are manifested more directly and clearly than in moments of relative calm. For that reason, it attracts our attention and in that sense we can say it is spectacular" (qtd. in Santana Fernández de Castro 129). Although the case of revolutionary Cuba is politically quite different from the Puerto Rico of the 1950s, their transformations share a sense of the momentous.

3. For more information on film production during the first half of the twentieth century, see the essay José Artemio Torres published bilingually, "'Apaga Misiú': Los primeros pasos del cine puertorriqueño"/ "'Lights Out, M'sieur': The Beginnings of Puerto Rican Cinema."

4. The Archivo de Imágenes en Movimiento (Archive of Motion Pictures), which is part of the Archivo General de Puerto Rico, has the largest collection of DIVEDCO films, along with very valuable documentation on the office. There are other films at the Fundación Luis Muñoz Marín and the Ateneo Puertorriqueño. The *Catalogo de colecciones del Archivo de la Imagen en Movimiento*, published in 2001, lists fifty films from DIVEDCO, but the film output was much larger. Several films are currently lost; there are also several films that never reached postproduction.

5. Mariam Colón Pizarro's dissertation studies these so-called "field workers" (in Spanish, *organizador comunal*) and provides a detailed description of their training process. Many of these group organizers were persons (men, in fact) selected from the communities themselves, in an attempt to emphasize the agency's desire to educate, as it were, from the inside.

6. The films were shown all over the island. From the 1960s on, they were also shown in stateside Puerto Rican communities, although I have found no evidence that post-screening discussions were held there. There is some evidence that the films traveled not only to New York but to cities like Cleveland and Philadelphia, places where there already was a sizable Puerto Rican population.

7. Besides *Una gota de agua* and *Jesús T. Piñero*, the Cinema and Graphics Workshop produced three other films: *Informe al pueblo No. 1*, *La voz del pueblo*, and *La caña*. All of these films were finished between 1947 and 1948. A film called *Desde las nubes* (From the clouds) was shot under the auspices of this office, perhaps in 1947 (García Morales 52), but it was not finished until 1950, under DIVEDCO.

8. DIVEDCO became a film school of sorts, one in which many Puerto Ricans trained to become filmmakers and screenwriters. The 1950s, thanks to the division, became the decade in which cinema was taken seriously as an art and an industry on the island, and the films produced during the era undoubtedly influenced subsequent directors and writers.

9. A large collection of Viguié's newsreel series, La industria en marcha (Industry on the march), is housed at the Archive of Motion Pictures in San Juan.

10. Backup vocalist Sammy Ayala, in an interview by the author, made several references to performing in La Riviera, a well-known brothel at the time.

11. The first three albums were recorded by Seeco Records, a renowned US label that specialized in Latin music. After their contract expired, the band signed with

Gema Records, a label founded by the Álvarez Guedes brothers, and recorded their remaining albums with them. Sammy Ayala pointed out in my interview with him that the attraction to record with Gema was that this label had much better distribution throughout Latin America. The Gema albums were later picked up by Rumba Records.

12. "What all *bombero* [*sic*] drummers can agree upon is that dancing is an indispensable part of the lead drummer's improvisations. Whether the dancer is present or imagined, without a dancer there is no real bomba" (Cartagena 17). As the anthropologist Halbert Barton has noted, "[B]omba is one genre where dance is central to the performance of the music" (qtd. in Quintero Rivera, "El tambor camuflado" 207).

13. Although Orquesta Panamericana did record some bombas, the sheer volume of bombas in Cortijo's output was unmatched.

14. Frances R. Aparicio has stated it succinctly: "Rafael Cortijo's historical significance lies in the *visual* presence of blacks on television . . . and in their musical prominence in radio; in other words, they 'occupied' the social space of media and entertainment that threatened and contested the 'whiteness' . . . of social clubs and dance halls" (35; original emphasis). See also Rodríguez Juliá, *El entierro* 33; and J. Flores, "Introduction" 5.

15. It is important to point out that during the early years of television in Puerto Rico, metropolitan San Juan and other towns around the island installed television sets in squares for public viewing. Therefore, even if a lot of the population might not have been able to afford a TV set for their homes, there were indeed alternative ways of "becoming" a television audience without owning the appliance.

16. The indigenous element was vigorously reincorporated during these years, especially through archeological excavations and historical research on Taíno culture. Alegría was particularly involved in these projects.

17. Much of the scholarship on Cortijo y su combo has focused on the band's musical and cultural significance. In the early 1980s, the Puerto Rican writer Edgardo Rodríguez Juliá, albeit from a gaze imbued in social distance, published the chronicle *El entierro de Cortijo / Cortijo's Wake*, recounting the funeral and burial of the bandleader and drawing attention to the importance of the band to understanding contemporary Puerto Rican culture. But there has also been a series of outstanding academic studies on the ensemble. The work of the sociologist Ángel G. Quin-

tero Rivera is paramount for anyone who wants to delve into Cortijo's music. Juan Flores's essay "Cortijo's Revenge" and his introduction to the bilingual edition of *El entierro de Cortijo / Cortijo's Wake* also merit careful study, as do the works by Rafael Figueroa Hernández and Aurora Flores on Ismael Rivera, which have substantial sections on Cortijo y su combo. Frances Aparicio has a short but truly valuable section on Cortijo y su combo in *Listening to Salsa*. What follows here owes a great deal to these writers and scholars.

18. Roberto Roena, who would later become a renowned salsa performer in his own right, was hired not only to play bongos but also to sing and dance with Ismael Rivera and the backup singers.

19. Quintero Rivera also notes that Cortijo was one of the first bandleaders to require that his percussionists (who had no academic training) be paid the same rate as the rest of his musicians (who did have it). This was not common practice.

20. The group's impact was not only on Puerto Rican salsa. For an account of the influence of Cortijo y su combo and Ismael Rivera on Venezuelan salsa, see the essay by Marisol Berríos-Miranda.

21. As a way of continuing the legacy across musical genres, Tego Calderón, one of the most important reggaetón performers in Puerto Rico, has often expressed his debt to Ismael Rivera in his lyrics.

22. The word *máquina* in Puerto Rico can refer to a locomotive. In addition, the sound that a train makes in Puerto Rican Spanish, *chu chu*, is the first syllable in *chúmalacatera*.

23. As if this was not clear enough from skimming through the book and reading the prologue (written by Marqués), *Cuentos puertorriqueños de hoy* is prefaced by a revealing quote from the British literary critic Herbert Read: "It is merely a lack of intelligence to refuse the experience emobodied in the past; but it shows an even greater lack of intelligence to refuse the experience embodied in the present" (7).

24. The writers, in the order presented in the book, are Abelardo Díaz Alfaro, José Luis González, René Marqués, Pedro Juan Soto, Edwin Figueroa, José Luis Vivas Maldonado, Emilio Díaz Valcárcel, and Salvador M. de Jesús.

25. The anthology was, in fact, dedicated to José Luis González, as well as to the influential literary critic Concha Meléndez.

26. Pedro Juan Soto wrote the one-act *El huésped* (The guest) in 1955 and *Las más-*

caras (Masks) in 1958. *El huésped* was staged in 1956; *Las máscaras* was never staged, though it did receive an award from the Ateneo Puertorriqueño.

27. A similar issue occurred in the visual arts: artists like Carlos Raquel Rivera, Rafael Tufiño, and Lorenzo Homar worked "for the government" at the division and at the Institute of Puerto Rican Culture, while producing outside of these entities work that critiqued the government's policies in venues like the graphic collective Centro de Arte Puertorriqueño (see chapters 2 and 3).

28. See particularly Marsh Kennerly, *Negociaciones* 77–99.

29. The thoughts of the Italian theorist Antonio Gramsci on intellectuals and the rise of a new hegemonic block are eerily insightful in regard to the case of René Marqués and the Division of Community Education: "One of the most important characteristics of any group that is developing towards dominance is its struggle to assimilate and to conquer 'ideologically' the traditional intellectuals, but this assimilation and conquest is made quicker and more efficacious the more the group in question succeeds in simultaneously elaborating its own organic intellectuals" (304–5).

CHAPTER 2. UNSUSTAINABLE EDENS

1. The anthology was coedited with the American author Stan Steiner, who in the 1960s and 1970s published mostly on minorities in the United States. The book was released by a major American press, Random House, in 1974.

2. She was, in fact, in New York City. It was first published there by Las Americas Publishing Company, in a series named Colección Símbolo that published works written by Puerto Ricans who resided in New York. Clemente Soto Vélez, Emilio Delgado, and Pedro Carrasquillo were some of the authors published under the banner of this series during the 1950s.

3. "The social elites create the rural idyll either through excluding others from rural communities or by making them invisible" (DuPuis 126).

4. The connections among these authors go beyond mere literary influence. Babín studied at the University of Puerto Rico and Pedreira, Arce de Vázquez, and other figures, such as Concha Meléndez—all of them important figures in the 1930s— were her teachers while she was pursuing a Hispanic studies degree there (Doncel et al.).

5. There is an inescapable case of *ruralis extremis* in the career trajectory of the realist

artist Luis Germán Cajiga, who in the twentieth century became the Puerto Rican master of the countryside picturesque. Like many of the artists who began work in the 1950s, he was trained in the printmaking tradition of the island at DIVEDCO's graphics workshop, where he worked for six years. It is true that his output during the 1950s, with a number of exceptions, dealt more directly with quaint representations of small-town Puerto Rico and Old San Juan. But from the 1970s on, when most artists had completely abandoned the rural (and, for the most part, realism), his brightly colored noncommissioned work—in painting and print—focused obsessively on the mountainous countryside: green hills, flamboyan trees, the rural house, and oxen plowing a field, all framed by impossibly blue skies. His works today—turned into placemats, posters, and postcards—are ubiquitous items that sell well in the island's tourist shops.

6. During the first decade of the commonwealth, the work of Lloréns Torres appeared in the most unlikely of places. To give just one example, his poem "Song of the Antilles," written in 1913, is the epigraph for the *Regional Plan for the San Juan Metropolitan Area*, prepared by the architect Eduardo Barañano for the Puerto Rico Planning Board and published in 1956. The poem has little to do with urban planning and city development; it is instead a sweet evocation of Puerto Rico as one of the islands of the Caribbean.

7. Juan Otero Garabís rightly tackles this issue when he says, "La folclorización de las décimas de Lloréns y Virgilio Dávila ('La tierruca') es el signo más claro del triunfo de una estrategia de hegemonía cultural y política. Mediante su enseñanza en las escuelas, su divulgación en los periódicos y su iconización en las academias y la legislatura . . . estos poetas han pasado a ocupar el espacio de la tradición oral y han sustituido la voz campesina por la voz letrada" (The folklorization of Lloréns's décimas and Virgilio Dávila ["The tender land"] is the clearest sign of the triumph of a cultural and political hegemonic strategy. By teaching them in schools, disseminating them in newspapers, and turning them into icons in the academy and the legislature . . . these poets have come to occupy the space of oral tradition and have substituted the peasant's voice for the lettered voice) (37).

8. Lloréns Torres also seemed to be, politically speaking, connected to the populist strategies of the commonwealth. In his 1914 play *El grito de Lares*, which centered on the famous nineteenth-century attempt to forge independence from Spain, a

character's speech seems to anticipate—in a truly uncanny moment in Puerto Rican letters—the ideological designs of Luis Muñoz Marín:

Me acerqué a los campesinos,	I approached the men of the country,
hablándoles en su jerga.	Addressing them in their own speech—
Fui de bohío en bohío,	Going from homestead to homestead
Por toda la cordillera,	Along the whole chain of mountains
Despertando el patriotismo	To awaken patriotism
De esa gente noble y buena.	In this good and noble people.

(qtd. in Díaz Quiñones, "La isla" 51)

9. The rural as an actual space of labor is an image that was, interestingly enough, pretty much absent in DIVEDCO's cinematic output of the 1950s and early 1960s. One remarkable exception was *El yugo* (The yoke), directed by the Dominican-born filmmaker Oscar Torres and finished in 1959. In it, a group of fisher folk are trying to join forces to resist the local boss. The film is also remarkable because it is set away from the mountains, on the coast of the municipality of Fajardo.

10. It is interesting to note that Antonio S. Pedreira, fundamental in the 1930s for positioning the jíbaro as a paramount figure in the national culture of the island, was himself critical of this romantic notion toward the jíbaro's abode and favored its modernization: "[C]uando ese campesino pueda poner su casa a la altura de las que poseemos en la zona urbana, nadie debe lamentar que cambie su pocilga y desaparezca de nuestro paisaje esa nota pintoresca tan llamada a desaparecer" ("[W]hen that peasant can place his home at the level of those we possess in urban zones, no one ought to lament his changing his pigsty and the disappearance of that picturesque bit of local color from our landscape" [trans. in Babín and Steiner 134–35]) (*Insularismo* 169).

11. The film was originally going to be called *Modesta, or The Rebellion of Women* (Rojas Daporta 35), but that title didn't last very long.

12. As Marsh Kennerly points out, *Modesta* was indeed inspired by a situation that arose at a meeting with the members of a community, in which a woman who was expressing her opinion was told to shut up by a man (*Negociaciones* 239).

13. The essays in Spanish by Efraín Barradas and Agnes Lugo-Ortiz, as well as Juan Gelpí's book *Literatura y paternalismo en Puerto Rico*, are required reading on the subject.

14. Although none of the typed screenplays included production credits, Marqués confirmed in a 1965 memorandum that he had written it ("Película de dibujos animados").

15. Díaz Valcárcel's bringing together of a literature that critiques the urban images of the countryside and contemporary graphic arts production couldn't be more appropriate. The print was part of *La estampa puertorriqueña*, the first portfolio created by the Centro de Arte Puertorriqueño (CAP), a collective interested since its inception in the neocolonial conditions of Puerto Rico and the incipient urban culture of the island (see chapter 3).

16. This maneuvering was not exclusive of literary figures; the graphic artists who worked at the division and at the Institute of Puerto Rican Culture faced a similar dilemma. Needless to say, the artists were well aware that the work they did in government spaces participated in an idealized notion of the rural. One example suffices here: the highly political artist Carlos Raquel Rivera created a print that was used as the cover art for a DIVEDCO Book for the People called *La Familia* (*Carlos Raquel Rivera* 45). In the foreground, the heads of a husband and wife in profile contemplate the countryside in the background, trees waving in the wind, gorgeous clouds, jíbaros working the land, and the couple's children—clearly on their way to school, with books in hand—waving goodbye. This piece was untitled in the booklet, but when he titled it later (presumably for an exhibition), he gave it the revealing title *Bucoliquerías*. The made-up word says it all: it is a blend of the word *bucólico* (bucolic) with a suffix that recalls words like *boberías* (silly things) or even *porquerías* (worthless things).

17. See especially Acosta Cruz, "From the Lush Land to the Traffic Jam," chapter 3 in her book *Dream Nation*.

18. The distinction is further articulated in the song. In the second stanza, where Ismael Rivera directly addresses the urbanite, the singer asserts that he or she might dance at a casino, but Ismael (impersonating the rural man) has more fun; this reference to the casino clearly points out a class difference. Furthermore, in the third stanza there is also a pretty definite racial difference as well: casino dancing is contrasted with dancing at the house of someone addressed as "siñá María" (Miz María).

19. Luis Muñoz Rivera was a leading figure in politics at the turn of the century and one of the designers of the autonomous government that had been created in concert with Spain in 1897, months before the American invasion. For his patriotic spirit, he was called "the jíbaro of Barranquitas" (his hometown). He was also, quite famously, Gov. Luis Muñoz Marín's father.

20. The one exception is the recent coinage of *nuevos jíbaros* in Puerto Rican media to talk about young islanders who have moved back to the countryside to develop organic farms. See the final chapter, "Epilogue and Conclusions."

CHAPTER 3. THE COUNTRYSIDE IN THE CITIES

1. *La estampa puertorriqueña* consisted of the following prints: Lorenzo Homar's *Saltimbanquis* (linocut), Carlos Marichal's *Paisaje yaucano* (woodcut), Carlos Raquel Rivera's *Pobreza* (linocut), Rubén Rivera Aponte's *Obreros* (linocut), Féliz Rodríguez Báez's *La Perla* (linocut), Samuel Sánchez's *Día de los inocentes* (linocut), José A. Torres Martinó's *Cangrejos* (silkscreen), and Rafael Tufiño's *Cortador de caña* (linocut) (Tió, "Carlos Raquel Rivera" 34).

2. This all-silkscreen portfolio included Juan Díaz's *La lancha de Cataño*, Lorenzo Homar's *Turistas*, José Manuel Figueroa's *El limpiabotas*, Manuel Hernández Acevedo's *Esquina de la plaza*, an untitled piece by Luis Muñoz Lee, Francisco Palacios's *Calle Virtud*, Carlos Raquel Rivera's *Billetes y flores*, Rafael Tufiño's *Niños jugando*, and Eduardo Vera Cortés's *La llegada* (Tió, "Carlos Raquel Rivera" 35). See Tió's "El portafolios gráfico o la hoja liberada" for a complete description of these two portfolios.

3. One other print from the first portfolio could possibly portray the countryside, but it is difficult to determine. The activity of catching crabs at night in José Antonio Torres Martinó's silkscreen *Cangrejeros* (Crab catchers) was an activity that could occur around rivers in the countryside but also in certain waterways of the city. As is well known, *cangrejeros* was also a term used for someone from the metropolitan area of Santurce—originally called Cangrejos—so the print could be directly referrring to urbanites. I have always wondered if this print was inspired by José Luis González's minuscule and powerful short story of the same name from 1944.

4. Compare, for example, the work of the center's artists with the attempts of other artists to represent the city in graphic arts. Once again Luis G. Cajiga, who later on would become famous for his idyllic countryside landscapes, is quite revealing here.

His 1961 woodcut *El Fanguito* resembles more a charming small town of wooden houses than the impoverished "slum" in the waterways of San Juan that he is trying to depict. There is even a touch of utopian modernization: government-installed electric utility poles appear at the top of the image. Although he was trained at the workshops of the Division of Community Education and at the Institute of Puerto Rican Culture (*La xilografía* 46), where the artists of the center worked for many years, Cajiga didn't seem to have internalized the complexity of his colleagues' visual relation to the city.

5. Teresa Tió has noted the same objectives when talking about the center, although her statement—"no aparece una sola garita de tarjeta postal" (not even one postcard sentry box appears) (Tió, "Carlos Raquel Rivera" 17)—is not totally accurate: Vera Cortés's silkscreen does contain one. To her credit, this sentry box is not, as I discussed above, part of a picturesque image of Old San Juan.

6. The feature story in *Look* magazine (discussed in the introduction), published eight years after this collection was issued, confirms this trend—a trend that has persisted to this day.

7. Some might argue that some of the short stories by René Marqués do allude to the aftermath of the nationalists' uprising, such as the famous "Otro día nuestro" (Another day of ours) from his first collection of stories, in addition to "La sala" (The living room) and to some extent "El delator" (The informer), from his second collection. I would argue that in Marqués, however, the uprising and the government reactions primarily motivated the tales' plots; Carlos Raquel Rivera's print seems more about re-creating the tension and anxiety of the times.

8. Listen to the words of a leader in the Migration Bureau talking about Puerto Ricans and development: "Every country has something to export. If some have petroleum, others nitrate and others sugar, we [Puerto Rico] are the only country in America that besides sugar, has an incalculable wealth that should be exported and should be used for the benefit of all. We have men, intelligence and working hands" (qtd. in Pantojas-García 92).

9. Literary historians have usually labeled González's fiction as urban literature; a closer look at his oeuvre reveals, however, that there was a constant recognition of not only rural presences within the phenomenon of urbanization but also a documentation of the effect of the urban space on the rapidly diminishing rural areas

(see chapter 2). Curiously enough, González wrote the thoroughly urban stories of *El hombre en la calle* while working in the countryside (Díaz Quiñones, *Conversación* 149). This collection is one of the few works that González wrote while actually living in Puerto Rico.

10. The story is barely a page long, consisting of the letter a man writes to his mother out in the countryside, and a short paragraph where a third-person narrator recounts the man's actions to ensure that the letter is mailed. What he writes to his mother in the letter is that narrative of the city as the site of opportunity: he has quickly found work and earns a decent amount, enough to promise gifts to a friend's child and even clothing for his own mother. His excuse for not sending those things yet is because he wants to get them in an expensive store. The paragraph that follows the letter swiftly dismantles that image: the man feigns to be missing a hand and begs on the street for the four pennies he needs to buy the envelope and stamp for mailing the missive to his mother.

11. I have yet to find a more seductive analysis of this story than Rubén Ríos Ávila's in the essay "Melodía," from his book *La raza cómica*.

12. Soto confessed the influence of González's *El hombre en la calle* in the prologue he wrote for the 1973 annotated edition of *Spiks* (10).

13. The play was first published in three successive numbers of the important literary journal *Asomante* between 1951 and 1952 (each of the three parts appearing in an issue). It was later released as a book in 1952. In 2008, it was already in its twenty-fifth printing. Charles Pilditch translated the book into English as *The Oxcart* in 1969, but in the process he deleted all swear words from the text; the swearing of the characters would have brought problems with curricular censorship if it had been used as a text in its original form. The first performance was in New York City, in 1953 (Fiet, "René Marqués" 206); the first performance on the island was produced at the Ateneo Puertorriqueño in 1954 (Philips 93; "Primer Festival" 10). There was a revival of the play at the Fourth Annual Puerto Rican Theater Festival in May 1961; the critic Frank Dauster stated that "its reception [was] nothing short of apotheosic" (36). The actors Míriam Colón and Raúl Juliá performed the play throughout the 1960s.

14. The book was published in English as *The Green Song* in 1954 and translated into Spanish two years later. *The Green Song / La canción verde* narrates the adventures of

Pepe, a *coquí*—the term for a small toad indigenous to the island—who travels to New York in order to learn about the world. But his experience is unbelievably painless, one in which all Americans are considerate and welcoming, even accommodating—the airline builds a small plane chair for him so that he may travel in comfort, and he is even awarded the keys to the city by the mayor of New York for his charming singing. The book was taught in elementary schools across Puerto Rico for several decades.

15. Gonzalo Arocho del Toro's *El desmonte* (The clearing) (1938) is set in the countryside and the slums; *Encrucijada* (Crossroads) (1958), by Manuel Méndez Ballester, and Fernando Sierra Berdecía's *Esta noche juega el jóker* (The joker plays tonight) (1938) both focus on Puerto Ricans in Spanish Harlem. Pedro Juan Soto's rare incursion into theater, *El huésped* (The guest), is also set in New York City.

16. What's more, Luis is an adopted son of Doña Gabriela, as if Marqués could not conceive of the young man as a biological part of this family that will get it "right" at the end of the play—a family that unequivocally stood for the image of the Great Puerto Rican Family.

17. Jordan Philips has encapsulated this "theme" in *The Oxcart* as the "salvation of the national soul by adherence to the land" (95). José Luis González, in his book-length interview with Arcadio Díaz Quiñones, talks about this literary convention of the return; although he is speaking about Puerto Rican literature in general, I can't imagine him not including *La carreta* in this accurate observation: "El famoso 'regreso a la tierra' o 'regreso a la montaña' que postulan las obras más representativas de nuestra literatura del siglo veinte no es más que un imposible regreso al pasado" (The famous "return to the land" or "return to the mountain" that the most representative works of our twentieth-century literature posit is nothing more than an impossible return to the past) (Díaz Quiñones, "Conversación" 68). It is a past, it is important to add, that never actually existed.

18. González would "tweak" this attitude years later, with the publication in 1970 of the short story "La noche que volvimos a ser gente" (The night we became people again), in which Puerto Ricans in New York City ceased to be portrayed as a sad, pitiful community.

19. Marqués calls the music "una rumba salvaje" (*La carreta* 56), but he is not referring to the traditional Cuban rumba; rather, the term was used at the time to generically

describe danceable, fast-paced Cuban nightclub music. This is why I am describing it as a mambo. Traditional rumba was simply not played on Puerto Rican radio in the 1940s and 1950s.

20. The song has several titles, including "El carpintero Narciso" and "Ni de madera son buenas," but the lyrics are equally troubling:

Al carpintero Narciso	Old carpenter Narciso
se le murió la mujer	Lost his wife, out of the blue,
y como no halló que hacer	And not knowing what to do,
una de madera hizo	Made a new one out of wood.
porque la encontró muy buena	Happy with how good he made her,
la metió en una alacena	In a cupboard he displayed her.
la alacena se le abrió	But the cupboard wasn't stout,
la mujer se le salió	And the woman, she fell out.
encima se le cayó	She landed right on his head
y al carpintero mató.	And killed the carpenter dead.
Y por eso . . .	And that's why.. . . .
ni de madera son buenas.	Not even wood ones are good ones.

21. Doña Inés Mendoza's scene is quite puzzling because DIVEDCO seemed to have chosen her as a "political" figure, yet her words are far removed from any discourse connected to women's participation in politics. Marqués's original script suggested a very different woman for this sequence—Felisa Rincón de Gautier, the mayor of San Juan. I have not found any specific reference in documents as to why she did not do the interview, but I suspect that she categorically refused: she was never friendly to DIVEDCO (see below). Interviewing the governor's wife, I suppose, was the division's "next best thing," though hardly a substitute for a female political figure like the mayor of the capital city of the island.

22. "The Division shall be in charge . . . of the development of an ample program of promotion and extension of adult education in the *rural and urban districts* of Puerto Rico" (Law 372 1; emphasis added).

23. The 1957 sociological report *San Juan: La ciudad que rebasó sus murallas* was a result of this attempt.

24. For a detailed account of the adversities encountered while trying to get *Un día cualquiera* finished, see Marsh Kennerly, *Negociaciones* 186–98.

25. The completed version of the film from the 1990s added some unfortunate extradiegetic music to it. But the radio still dominates the soundtrack of the film. The idea of the radio as the overall soundtrack of the film was explicitly stated in Soto's plot treatment and actually developed further in Rivera's screenplay (Soto, "Un día cualquiera").

EPILOGUE AND CONCLUSIONS

1. My intentions here should not be read as a dismissal. The book was intensely debated in academic spaces on the island, and in many ways *La Vida* helped spark important debates about social sciences research.

2. These letters are in the Oscar and Ruth Lewis Papers, archived at the library of the University of Illinois at Urbana-Champaign.

3. The self-righteous anger of some of the letter writers was undermined by their blatantly anti-Semitic tone and their call for Lewis to interview Jewish prostitutes first before daring to study other ethnicities.

4. An advertisement for the book in the *San Juan Review* claimed that *Puerto Rico: La Nueva Vida / The New Life* had an introduction by René Marqués ("Puerto Rico La Nueva Vida" 16), but the final edition of the book does not include it.

5. This translation comes from the book itself and was done by Georgina Pando.

WORKS CITED

Acevedo, Rafael. "Quién." *Moneda de sal*, Fragmento Imán, 2006, p. 5.

Acosta Cruz, María. *Dream Nation: Puerto Rican Culture and the Fictions of Independence.* Rutgers UP, 2014.

Álvarez, Luis Manuel, and Ángel G. Quintero Rivera. *Raíces*, liner notes, Banco Popular, 2001.

Álvarez Curbelo, Silvia. "El discurso populista de Luis Muñoz Marín: Condiciones de posibilidad y mitos fundacionales en el paríodo 1932–1936." *Del nacionalismo al populismo: Cultura y política en Puerto Rico*, edited by Silvia Álvarez Curbelo and Maria Elena Rodríguez Castro, Ediciones Huracán/Decanato de Estudios Graduados e Investigación (UPR–Río Piedras), 1993, pp. 13–35.

AmericaSalsa.com. "Biografía de Ismael 'Maelo' Rivera." 2001–2, www.americasalsa.com/biografias/ismael_rivera.html. Accessed 2 November 2015.

Andreu Iglesias, César. "Cosas de aquí: La clave del acertijo." *El Imparcial* [San Juan, PR], 15 February 1967.

Andreu Iglesias, César. "Cosas de aquí: La cultura de la pobreza." *El Imparcial* [San Juan, PR], 8 November 1966.

Andreu Iglesias, César. "Cosas de aquí: La familia Ríos." *El Imparcial* [San Juan, PR], 9 November 1966.

Andreu Iglesias, César. *El inciso hache, comedia en dos actos y un epílogo.* In *Teatro puertorriqueño: Quinto festival*, Instituto de cultura puertorriqueña, 1963, pp. 277–392.

Andrews, Malcolm. *Landscape and Western Art.* Oxford UP, 1999.

Aparicio, Frances R. *Listening to Salsa: Gender, Latin Popular Music, and Puerto Rican Cultures.* Wesleyan UP, 1998.

Arce de Vázquez, Margot. "El paisaje de Puerto Rico." López-Baralt, pp. 68–75.

Arce de Vázquez, Margot. "Las décimas de Llorens Torres." *Asomante*, vol. 21, 1965, pp. 37–46.

Arriví, Francisco. "Medusas en la Bahía." *Bolero y Plena*, Editorial Cultural, 1971.

Arriví, Francisco. *Vejigantes.* 1958. Editorial Cultural, 2007.

Ayala, César J., and Rafael Bernabe. *Puerto Rico in the American Century: A History since 1898.* U of North Carolina P, 2007.

Ayala, Sammy. Interview by author. New York, 7 December 2007.

Babín, María Teresa. *Fantasía boricua: Estampas de mi tierra.* Las Américas Publishing, 1956; Instituto de cultura puertorriqueña, 1973.

Babín, María Teresa. *Panorama de la cultura puertorriqueña.* Las Americas Publishing, 1958.

Babín, María Teresa. "Prólogo." Marqués, *La carreta*, pp. v–xxxi.

Babín, María Teresa, and Stan Steiner, eds. *Borinquen: An Anthology of Puerto Rican Literature.* Random House, 1974.

Barradas, Efraín. "El machismo existencialista de René Marqués." *Sin nombre*, vol. 8, no. 3, 1977, pp. 69–81.

Bell, Daniel. "Variations on the Rural Idyll." Cloke et al., pp. 149–60.

Berríos-Miranda, Marisol. "'Con sabor a Puerto Rico': The Reception and Influence of Puerto Rican Salsa in Venezuela." *Musical Migrations: Transnationalism and Cultural Hybridity in Latin/o America*, edited by Frances R. Aparicio and Cándida F. Jáquez, Palgrave Macmillan, 2003, pp. 47–67.

Biron, Rebecca, ed. *City/Art: The Urban Scene in Latin America.* Duke UP, 2009.

Biron, Rebecca. "Introduction: City/Art; Setting the Scene." Biron, *City/Art*, pp. 1–34.

Biron, Rebecca E. "Marvel, Monster, Myth: The Modern City in Latin American Literature." *Cruelty and Utopia: Cities and Landscapes of Latin America*, edited by Jean-François Lejeune, Princeton Architectural Press, 2003, pp. 119–32.

Bolívar Fresneda, José L. *Guerra, banca y desarrollo: El Banco de Fomento y la industrialización de Puerto Rico*. Fundación Luis Muñoz Marín and Editorial del Instituto de cultura puertorriqueña, 2011.

Braschi, Wilfredo. *Nuevas tendencias en la literatura puertorriqueña*. Instituto de cultura puertorriqueña, 1960.

"Braulio Dueño Colón." *Wikipedia*, 11 November 2012, en.wikipedia.org/wiki/Braulio_ Dueño_Colón. Accessed 11 April 2013.

Burgos, Julia de. "Desde el Puente Martín Peña/From Martín Peña Bridge." *Song of the Simple Truth: The Complete Poems*, edited and translated by Jack Agüeros, Curbstone Press, 1997, pp. 38–39.

Cabán, Pedro. "The Puerto Rican Colonial Matrix: The Etiology of Citizenship—An Introduction." *CENTRO Journal*, vol. 25, no. 1, 2013, pp. 4–21.

Cadilla, Carmen Alicia. "La puertorriqueñidad de José Luis González." Introduction, *En la sombra*, by José Luis González, pp. 5–7.

Calderón, Tego. "Loíza." *El Aballarde*, White Lion Music, 2002.

Calderón, Tego. "Tradicional a lo bravo." *El abayarde contra-ataca*, Warner Music, 2007.

Calle 13. "Latinoamérica." *Entren los que quieran*, Sony Latin, 2010.

Carlos Raquel Rivera: Obra gráfica 1951–1990. Décima Bienal de San Juan del Grabado Latinoamericano y del Caribe, 1993.

Cartagena, Juan. "When Bomba Becomes the National Music of the Puerto Rican Nation. . . ." *CENTRO Journal*, vol. 16, no. 1, 2004, pp. 15–35.

Catálogo de colecciones del Archivo de Imágenes en Movimiento. Insituto de Cultura Puertorriqueña/Archivo General de Puerto Rico, 2001.

Clark, Donald. "Cortijo, Rafael." *Donald's Encyclopedia of Popular Music*, 30 November 2011, www.donaldclarkemusicbox.com/encyclopedia/detail.php?s=763.

Cloke, Paul, Terry Marsden, and Patrick Mooney, eds. *Handbook of Rural Studies*. SAGE Publications, 2006.

Colón Pizarro, Mariam. "Poetic Pragmatism: The Puerto Rican Division of Community Education (DIVEDCO) and the Politics of Cultural Production, 1949–1968." Dissertation, University of Michigan, 2011.

Community Education Program in Puerto Rico / Un programa de Educación de la Comunidad en Puerto Rico. Booklet, RCA Corp., n.d.

Córdova, Nathaniel I. "In His Image and Likeness: The Puerto Rican Jíbaro as Political Icon." *CENTRO: Journal of the Center for Puerto Rican Studies*, vol. 17, no. 2, 2005, pp. 170–91.

Dauster, Frank. "The Theater of René Marqués." *Symposium*, vol. 18, no. 1, 1964, pp. 35–45.

Dávila, Arlene M. *Sponsored Identities: Cultural Politics in Puerto Rico*. Temple UP, 1997.

Dávila, Virgilio. "La tierruca." *Aromas del terruño*, Editorial Cordillera, 1991, pp. 19–20.

De Diego Padró, José. *En babia*. Biblioteca de Autores Puertorriqueños, 1940.

Delano, Jack. "Entrevista a Jack Delano." *Investigación en acción: Revista del Consejo General de Educación*, vol. 1, no. 1, 1992–93, pp. 16–31.

Deleuze, Gilles, and Félix Guattari. *A Thousand Plateaus*. Translated by Brian Massumi, Continuum, 2004.

Díaz Alfaro, Abelardo. *Terrazo*. 1947. Editorial Plaza Mayor, 1999.

Díaz Quiñones, Arcadio. *Conversación con José Luis González*. 1976. Ediciones Huracán, 1977.

Díaz Quiñones, Arcadio. Introduction. *La guaracha del macho camacho*, by Luis Rafael Sánchez, Cátedra, 2000, pp. 9–95.

Díaz Quiñones, Arcadio. "José Luis González: La luz de la memoria." Introduction, González, *Cuentos completos*, pp. iii–ix.

Díaz Quiñones, Arcadio. "La isla afortunada: Sueños libertadores y utópicos de Luis Lloréns Torres." Introduction, Lloréns Torres, *Luis Lloréns Torres: Antología verso y prosa*, pp. 13–72.

Díaz Quiñones, Arcadio. "La vida inclemente." *La memoria rota*, Ediciones Huracán, 1993, pp. 17–66.

Díaz Quiñones, Arcadio. "Los desastres de la guerra: Para leer a René Marqués." *El almuerzo en la hierba (Lloréns Torres, Palés Matos, René Marqués)*, Huracán, 1982, pp. 133–68.

Díaz Valcárcel, Emilio. "El asedio." *Cuentos completos*, Alfaguara/Ediciones Santillana, 2002, pp. 35–43.

Doncel, Margarita, María Silvestrini, and Walberto Rodríguez. "María Teresa Babín, Biografía." Centro de Acceso a la Información, Universidad Interamericana de Puerto Rico—Recinto de Ponce, 2006, ponce.inter.edu/cai/MariaTeresaBabin/inicio.html. Accessed 11 January 2006.

Duany, Jorge. *The Puerto Rican Nation on the Move: Identities on the Island and in the United States*. U of North Carolina P, 2002.

Dueño Colón, Braulio, and Manuel Fernández Juncos. *Nuestras canciones*. Revised by María Luisa Muñoz, Silver Burdett, 1954.

DuPuis, E. Melanie. "Landscapes of Desires?" Cloke et al., pp. 124–32.

Fernández, José B. "Entrevista con José Luis González." *Revista Chicano-Riqueña*, vol. 9, no. 1, 1981, pp. 47–57.

Fiet, Lowell. *El teatro puertorriqueño reimaginado: Notas críticas sobre la creación dramática y el performance*. Ediciones Callejón, 2004.

Fiet, Lowell. "René Marqués." *Latin American Dramatists: First Series*, Thomson Gale, 2005, pp. 206–19.

Figueroa Hernández, Rafael. *Ismael Rivera: El sonero mayor*. 2nd ed., Instituto de Cultura Puertorriqueña, 2002.

Flores, Aurora. "¡Ecua Jei! Ismael Rivera, el Sonero Mayor (A Personal Recollection)." *CENTRO Journal*, vol. 16, no. 2, 2004, pp. 63–77.

Flores, Juan. "Cortijo's Revenge: New Mappings of Puerto Rican Culture." *Divided Borders: Essays on Puerto Rican Identity*, Arte Público Press, 1993, pp. 92–107.

Flores, Juan. "Introduction." Rodríguez Juliá, *El entierro*, pp. 1–14.

Flynn, Thomas R. *Existentialism: A Very Short Introduction*. Oxford UP, 2006.

Fonfrías, Ernesto Juan. *Conversao en el Batey: Historia de un jíbaro bragao*. 1956. Editorial Club de la Prensa, 1958.

Fonfrías, Ernesto Juan. *Cosecha*. 1956.

Fonfrías, Ernesto Juan. *Guásima: Cuadros jíbaros*. Editorial Club de la Prensa, 1957.

Fonfrías, Ernesto Juan. *La eliminación del arrabal: Problema multifacético*. Autoridad sobre Hogares de Puerto Rico, 1955.

Fort Apache, The Bronx. Directed by Daniel Pietre. Performances by Paul Newman and Edward Asner. 20th Century Fox, 1981.

García Canclini, Néstor. "What Is a City?" *City / Art: The Urban Scene in Latin America*, edited by Rebecca Biron, Duke UP, 2009, pp. 37–60.

García Morales, Joaquín (Kino). *Breve historia del cine puertorriqueño*. 1984. Taller de cine La Red, 1989.

García Passalacqua, Juan Manuel. *Casa sin hogar: Memoria de mis tiempos. Puerto Rico, 1937–1987*. Edil, 1990.

Gelpí, Juan. "Literatura puertorriqueña." González Vales and Luque, pp. 475–89.

Gelpí, Juan. *Literatura y paternalismo en Puerto Rico*. Editorial de la Universidad de Puerto Rico, 1993.

González, José Luis. *Cuentos completos*. Alfaguara, 1997.

González, José Luis. "El arte del cuento." Interview, *La experiencia literaria*, vol. 2, 1976, pp. 7–35.

González, José Luis. *El hombre en la calle*. Editorial Bohique, 1948.

González, José Luis. "El país de cuatro pisos." *El país de cuatro pisos y otros ensayos*. 1980. Ediciones Huracán, 2001, pp. 11–42.

González, José Luis. *En la sombra*. Imprenta Venezuela, 1943.

González, José Luis. "Paisa (un relato de la emigración)." González, *Cuentos completos*, pp. 11–36.

González Vales, Luis E., and María Dolores Luque, eds. *Historia de Puerto Rico*. Vol. 4 of *Historia de las Antillas*, Consejo Superior de Investigaciones Científicas/Ediciones Doce Calles, 2012.

Gorman-Murray, Andrew, Kate Darian-Smith, and Chris Gibon. "Scaling the Rural: Reflections on Rural Cultural Studies." *Australian Humanities Review*, vol. 45, November 2008, www.australianhumanitiesreview.org/archive/Issue-November-2008/gormanmurray.html. Accessed 25 February 2013.

Gramsci, Antonio. *The Antonio Gramsci Reader: Selected Writings, 1916–1935*. Edited by David Forgacs, New York UP, 2000.

Grosfoguel, Ramón, "Developmentalism, Modernity and Dependency Theory in Latin America." *Coloniality at Large: Latin America and the Postcolonial Debate*, edited by Mabel Moraña, Enrique Dussel, and Carlos E. Jáuregui, Duke UP, 2008, pp. 307–31.

Grossberg, Lawrence. *Cultural Studies in the Future Tense*. Duke UP, 2010.

Gutiérrez Alea, Tomás. "The Viewer's Dialectic." *New Latin American Cinema: Volume One, Theory, Practices, and Transcontinental Articulations*, edited by Michael T. Martin, Wayne State UP, 1997, pp. 108–31.

Hebdige, Dick. *Subculture: The Meaning of Style*. 1979. Routledge, 2002.

Hermandad de Artes Gráficas de Puerto Rico, ed. *Puerto Rico: Arte e identidad*. Editorial de la Universidad de Puerto Rico, 1998.

Hernández Cruz, Víctor. *Maraca: New and Selected Poems, 1965–2000*. Coffee House Press, 2001.

Idilio tropical: La aventura del cine puertorriqueño. Exhibition catalog, Banco Popular, 1994.

Irizarry, Guillermo B. *José Luis González: El intelectual nómada*. Ediciones Callejón, 2006.

"Ismael Rivera: 'Maquinolandera.'" *YouTube*, 5 June 2008, www.youtube.com/watch?v=hHppcTzqRYU. Accessed 27 July 2012.

Jiménez, Ariel. *Utopías americanas*. Fundación Cisneros, 2000.

Jiménez, Félix. *Las prácticas de la carne: Construcción y representación de las masculinidades puertorriqueñas*. Ediciones Vértigo, 2004.

Kaiden, Nina, Pedro Juan Soto, and Andrew Vladimir, eds. *Puerto Rico: La Nueva Vida/The New Life*. Renaissance Books, 1966.

"La cucarachita Martina." Script by René Marqués, storyboards by Juan Díaz and Paco Palacios. Box 14, DIVEDCO Files, Archivo General de Puerto Rico.

Laguerre, Enrique. *La llamarada*. 1935. 34th ed., Editorial Cultural, 2000.

Lauria-Perricelli, Antonio. "Images and Contradictions: DIVEDCO's Portrayal of Puerto Rican Life." *CENTRO Journal*, vol. 3, no. 1, 1991, pp. 93–97.

Law 372. An Act to Create the Division of Community Education. Approved 14 May 1949, DIVEDCO Files, Archivo General de Puerto Rico.

Levis, José Elías. *Estercolero*. 1899/1901. Edited by Carmen Centeno Añeses, Editorial de la Universidad de Puerto Rico, 2008.

Lewis, Oscar. *La Vida: A Puerto Rican Family in the Culture of Poverty—San Juan and New York*. Random House, 1966.

Lewis, Oscar. *La vida: Una familia puertorriqueña en la cultura de la pobreza; San Juan y Nueva York*. Joaquín Mortiz, 1969.

Lewis, Oscar. Letter to Nilita Vientós Gastón, 22 November 1966, Box 61, Oscar and Ruth Lewis Papers, University of Illinois Archives.

Lloréns Torres, Luis. *Antología: Verso y prosa*. Edited by Arcadio Díaz Quiñones, Huracán, 1986.

Lloréns Torres, Luis. "Por amor al radio." *El Imparcial*, 26 May 1933, reprinted in *Obras completas*, vol. 3, Instituto de Cultura Puertorriqueña, 1969, pp. 106–8.

López-Baralt, Mercedes, ed. *Literatura puertorriqueña del siglo XX*. Editorial de la Universidad de Puerto Rico, 2003.

Lugo-Ortiz, Agnes I. "Sobre el tráfico simbólico de mujeres: Homosocialidad, identidad nacional y modernidad literaria en Puerto Rico (apuntes para una relectura de 'El puertorriqueño dócil' de René Marqués)." *Revista de Crítica Literaria Latinoamericana*, vol. 23, no. 45, 1997, pp. 261–78.

Luna, Noel. "Paisaje, cuerpo e historia: Luis Lloréns Torres." *La Torre*, vol. 4, no. 11, 1999, pp. 53–78.

Maldonado, A. W. *Teodoro Moscoso and Puerto Rico's Operation Bootstrap*. UP of Florida, 1997.

Maldonado Denis, Manuel. "*La Vida* de Oscar Lewis." *El Mundo* [San Juan, PR], 1 April 1967, p. 37.

Maldonado Denis, Manuel. Letter to Oscar Lewis, 16 November 1966, Box 58, Oscar and Ruth Lewis Papers, University of Illinois Archives.

Marqués, René, ed. *Cuentos puertorriqueños de hoy*. 1959. Editorial Cultural, 2002.

Marqués, René. "El cuento puertorriqueño en la promoción del cuarenta." Prologue to Marqués, *Cuentos puertorriqueños de hoy*, pp. 13–36.

Marqués, René. *En una ciudad llamada San Juan*. Editorial Cultural, 1983.

Marqués, René. *La carreta: Drama puertorriqueño*. Editorial Cultural, 2008.

Marqués, René. *Otro día nuestro*. Prologue by Concha Meléndez, 1955.

Marqués, René. "Película de dibujos animados *La cucarachita Martina*." Memorandum to Pedro Oquendo, 16 January 1965, Box 13, DIVEDCO Files, Archivo General de Puerto Rico.

Marqués, René. "Plan y libreto para corto cinematográfico '¿Qué opina la mujer?'" Mimeographed script, Box 19, DIVEDCO Files, Archivo General de Puerto Rico.

Marqués, René. *Teatro III, La casa sin reloj, El apartamiento*. Editorial Cultural, 1971.

Marsh Kennerly, Cati. "Cultural Negotiations: Puerto Rican Intellectuals in a State-Sponsored Community Education Project." *Harvard Educational Review*, vol. 73, no. 3, 2003, pp. 416–48.

Marsh Kennerly, Catherine. *Negociaciones culturales: Los intelectuales y el proyecto pedagógico del estado muñocista*. Ediciones Callejón, 2009.

Martin, Eleanor J. *René Marqués*. Twayne Publishers, 1979.

McClennen, Sophia. "Cultural Studies and 'Latin America': Reframing the Questions." *The Renewal of Cultural Studies*, edited by Paul Smith, Temple UP, 2011, pp. 188–95.

Merrill, Dennis. "Negotiating Cold War Paradise: U.S. Tourism, Economic Planning, and Cultural Modernity in Twentieth-Century Puerto Rico." *Diplomatic History*, vol. 25, no. 2, 2001, pp. 179–214.

Miller, Marilyn. "*Plena* and the Negotiation of 'National' Identity in Puerto Rico." *CENTRO Journal*, vol. 16, no. 1, 2004, pp. 37–59.

Mintz, Sidney W. "Puerto Rico: An Essay in the Definition of a National Culture." *Status of Puerto Rico*, United States–Puerto Rico Commission on the Status of Puerto Rico, Washington, DC, 1966, pp. 339–434.

Mintz, Sidney W. *Worker in the Cane: A Puerto Rican Life History*. 1960. Norton, 1974.

Monserrat, Joseph. "*La Vida*: A Further View." *Congress Bi-Weekly*, 16 October 1967, 18–19.

Montaldo, Graciela. *De pronto, el campo: Literatura argentina y tradición rural*. Beatriz Viterbo Editora, 1993.

Moreno-Velázquez, Juan A. *Maelo . . . Hijo de Borikén, rey de los soneros*. 2010.

Moscoso, Teodoro. "Origen y desarrollo de la 'Operación Manos a la Obra.'" *Cambio y desarrollo en Puerto Rico: La transformación ideológica del Partido Popular Democratico*, edited by Gerardo Navas Dávila, Editorial de la UPR, 1980, pp. 161–69.

Muñoz, Raúl. "Entrevista a Raúl Muñoz." *Investigación en acción: Revista del Consejo General de Educación*, vol. 1, no. 1, 1992–93, pp. 40–49.

Muñoz Marín, Luis. "An America to Serve the World." Speech delivered at the annual convention of the Associated Harvard Clubs, Coral Gables, Florida, 7 April 1956, www.flmm.org/discursos/1956-04-07.pdf. Accessed 24 May 2012.

Muñoz Marín, Luis. Commencement speech delivered at Harvard University, 16 June 1955, manuscript text, Harvard University Archives.

Muñoz Marín, Luis. Letter to Fred Wale, 23 November 1948, DIVEDCO Folder, Fundación Luis Muñoz Marín Archives.

Muñoz Marín, Luis. "Mensaje al pueblo puertorriqueño: 23 de febrero de 1949." *Memorias: Autobiografía publica; 1940–1952*, Fundación Luis Muñoz Marín, 2003, pp. 434–45.

Muñoz Marín, Luis. "Operación Sócrates." Dictaphone notes, 21 November 1960, section V, series 23, Fundación Luis Muñoz Marín Archives.

Muñoz Marín, Luis. "Palabras del gobernador en la sesión inaugural de la tercera reunión del Consejo Interamericano Cultural." Speech delivered in San Juan, Puerto Rico, 22 November 1959, typed MS, Operation Serenity Folder, Fundación Luis Muñoz Marín Archives.

Orquesta Panamericana. "La mujer de palo." *Orquesta Panamericana*, c. 1954. Ansonia Records, 1993.

Otero Garabís, Juan. "'Nuestro lujo campesino': El jíbaro en Llorens Torres." *Revista de estudios hispánicos*, vol. 27, no. 2, 2000, pp. 25–37.

Page, Homer. *Puerto Rico: The Quiet Revolution*. Viking, 1963.

Pantojas-García, Emilio. *Development Strategies as Ideology: Puerto Rico's Export-Led Indus-*

trialization Experience. Lynne Rienner Publishers and Editorial de la Universidad de Puerto Rico, 1990.

Patton, Paul. *Deleuze and the Political*. Routledge, 2000.

Pedreira, Antonio S. *Insularismo*. In *Sobre "Ínsulas extrañas": El clásico de Pedreira anotado por Tomás Blanco*, edited by Mercedes López-Baralt, Editorial de la Universidad de Puerto Rico, 2001, pp. 121–357.

Philips, Jordan B. *Contemporary Puerto Rican Drama*. Editorial Playor, 1973.

Picó, Fernando. *Historia general de Puerto Rico*. 1986. Huracán, 2003.

Pilditch, Charles, translator. *The Oxcart*. By René Marqués, Scribner, 1969.

Plenn, Doris Troutman. *La canción verde*. Translated by Antonio J. Colorado, Troutman Press, 1956.

"Presidente Senado opina libro 'La Vida' es un insulto a isla." *El Mundo* [San Juan, PR], 24 November 1966.

"Primer Festival de Teatro del Instituto de Cultural Puertorriqueña." *Teatro Puertorriqueño. Primer Festival*, Instituto de Cultura Puertorriqueña, 1959, pp. 1–16.

Programa de educación secundaria. Editorial Departamento de Instrucción, 1952.

Puerto Rico elimina el arrabal. Viguié Films, 1950, 27 min., WIPR-TV Film Archives.

"Puerto Rico—La Nueva Vida." *San Juan Review*, vol. 11, no. 2, 1965, p. 16.

"Puerto Rico: Senate Committee Finds It an Unsolvable Problem." *Life*, 8 March 1943, pp. 23–31.

Quiles Rodríguez, Edwin R. "De la IUPI a Río Piedras un paso es." *Escribir la ciudad*, edited by Maribel Ortiz and Vanessa Vilches, Fragmento Imán, 2009, pp. 46–54.

Quintero Rivera, Ángel G. *Cuerpo y cultura: Las músicas "mulatas" y la subversión del baile*. Iberoamericana, 2009.

Quintero Rivera, Ángel G. "El tambor camuflado: La melodización de ritmos y la etnicidad cimarronada." *Salsa, sabor y control: Sociología de la música tropical*, Siglo XXI, 1998, pp. 201–51.

Quintero Rivera, Ángel G. "La investigación urbana en Puerto Rico, breves comentarios sobre su trayectoria." *La investigación urbana en América Latina: Caminos recorridos y por recorrer*, edited by Fernando Carrión, CIUDAD, 1989, pp. 57–83.

Rama, Ángel. *The Lettered City*. Translated by John Charles Chasteen, Duke UP, 1996.

Rigdon, Susan M. "Correspondence Found." Email message to the author, 12 July 2012.

Rigdon, Susan M. *The Culture Façade: Art, Science and Politics in the Work of Oscar Lewis*. U of Illinois P, 1988.

Ríos Ávila, Rubén. "Melodía." *La raza cómica: Del sujeto en Puerto Rico*, Callejón, 2002, pp. 195–210.

Rivas, Yaritza. "La cosecha de Daniella, relato de una nueva jíbara." *El Nuevo Día* [San Juan, PR], 2 July 2014, www.elnuevodia.com/lacosechadedaniellarelatodeunanueva-jibara-1805681.html. Accessed 12 July 2014.

Rivero, Yeidi M. *Tuning Out Blackness: Race and Nation in the History of Puerto Rican Television*. Duke UP, 2005.

Rizzo, Teresa. *Deleuze and Film: A Feminist Introduction*. Continuum, 2012.

Rodríguez Castro, Malena. "Piedra y palabra: Los debates culturales en Puerto Rico." González Vales and Luque, pp. 491–539.

Rodríguez Juliá, Edgardo. *El entierro de Cortijo / Cortijo's Wake*. Bilingual edition, translated by Juan Flores, Duke UP, 2004.

Rodríguez Juliá, Edgardo. "José Luis González, o el camino a la calle niuyorkina." *Antología personal*, edited by José Luis Gonzalez, 1990. Rev. ed., Editorial Universidad de Puerto Rico, 2009, pp. 241–44.

Rodríguez Juliá, Edgardo. *Las tribulaciones de Jonás*. Huracán, 1981.

Rojas Daporta, Malen. "Filman dos películas largo metraje en PR." *El Mundo* [San Juan, PR], 5 May 1955, p. 35.

Rosa Nieves, Cesáreo. "Guillermo Sureda y las islas." *Boletín de la Academia de Artes y Ciencias de Puerto Rico*, vol. 5, no. 2, 1969, pp. 251–53.

Rosso Tridas, Norma. "La estampa serigráfica en Puerto Rico: Cuatro décadas." *La estampa serigráfica en Puerto Rico: Cuatro décadas*. Art catalog, Museo de la Universidad de Puerto Rico, 1987, pp. 13–32.

San Juan: La ciudad que rebasó sus murallas; Estudio sociológico de algunos aspectos de la vida en el área de San Juan-Santurce-Río Piedras, Puerto Rico. DIVEDCO, 1957.

Santana Fernández de Castro, Astrid. *Literatura y cine: Lecturas cruzadas sobre las Memorias del subdesarrollo*. Universidade de Santiago de Compostela, 2010.

Sarlo, Beatriz. "Raymond Williams: Del campo a la ciudad." *El campo y la ciudad*, by Raymond Williams, translated by Alcira Bixio, Paidós, 2001, pp. 11–22.

Scarano, Francisco. "The Jibaro Masquerade and the Subaltern Politics of Creole Identity

Formation in Puerto Rico, 1745–1823." *American Historical Review*, vol. 101, no. 5, 1996, pp. 1398–431.

Scarano, Francisco. *Puerto Rico: Cinco siglos de historia*. 2nd ed., McGraw-Hill, 2000.

The Schoolhouse on the Screen. Unfinished film from RCA, Archivo de la Imagen en Movimiento, Archivo General de Puerto Rico.

Sepúlveda Rivera, Aníbal. *En clave de gris, 1920s–2000s*. Centro de Investigaciones CARIMAR, 2004.

Soto, Pedro Juan. *A solas con Pedro Juan Soto*. Ediciones Puerto, 1973.

Soto, Pedro Juan. *El huésped: Las máscaras y otros disfraces*. Ediciones Puerto, 1974.

Soto, Pedro Juan. Prologue (1973). Soto, *Spiks*, pp. 9–11.

Soto, Pedro Juan. *Spiks*. 1956. Editorial Cultural, 1989.

Soto, Pedro Juan. "Un día cualquiera." Adapted by Ángel F. Rivera, mimeographed script, Box 22, DIVEDCO Files, Archivo General de Puerto Rico.

Soto, Pedro Juan, Nina Kaiden, and Andrew Vladimir, eds. *Puerto Rico: La Nueva Vida / The New Life*. Renaissance Press, 1966.

Stevens, Camilla. *Family and Identity in Contemporary Cuban and Puerto Rican Drama*. UP of Florida, 2004.

Steward, Sue. *¡Música! Salsa, Rumba, Merengue, and More*. Chronicle Books, 1999.

"Surprising Puerto Rico." *Look*, 17 January 1961, pp. 21–44.

Thomas Montañez, Piri. Letter to Oscar Lewis, 18 April 1967, Box 61, Oscar and Ruth Lewis Papers, University of Illinois Archives.

Thomas Montañez, Piri. "My Own Thoughts in Answer to Criticisms of *La Vida* by Oscar Lewis," 18 April 1967, Box 61, Oscar and Ruth Lewis Papers, University of Illinois Archives.

Tió, Teresa. "Carlos Raquel Rivera o la periferia del misterio." *Carlos Raquel Rivera*, pp. 13–35.

Tió, Teresa. *El cartel en Puerto Rico*. Pearson Educación/Prentice Hall, 2003.

Tió, Teresa. "El portafolios gráfico o la hoja liberada." *La hoja liberada: El portafolios en la gráfica puertorriqueña*. Exhibition catalog, Instituto de cultura puertorriqueña, 1996, pp. 7–46.

Torres, José Artemio. "'Apaga Misiú': Los primeros pasos del cine puertorriqueño"/ "'Lights Out, M'sieur': The Beginnings of Puerto Rican Cinema." *Idilio tropical: La aventura del cine puertorriqueño*, Banco Popular de Puerto Rico, 1994, pp. 11–23.

Torres Martinó, José Antonio. "El arte puertorriqueño de principios del siglo XX." *Puerto Rico: Arte e identidad*, Hermandad de Artes Gráficas de Puerto Rico, pp. 63–81.

Torres Martinó, José Antonio. "Las artes gráficas en Puerto Rico." *Puerto Rico: Arte e identidad*, Hermandad de Artes Gráficas de Puerto Rico, pp. 149–77.

Traba, Marta. *Propuesta polémica sobre arte puertorriqueño*. Ediciones Librería Internacional, 1971.

Tugwell, Rexford G. *The Stricken Land: The Story of Puerto Rico*. 1946. Greenwood Press, 1968.

Vázquez Hernández, Víctor. "El desarrollo de comunidad en Puerto Rico: La División de Educación de la Comunidad (1949–1960)." Dissertation, Universidad de Puerto Rico—Río Piedras, 1986.

Vientós Gastón, Nilita. Interview. *San Juan Star*, 1 January 1967, pp. 4–5.

Wilde, Oscar. *The Picture of Dorian Gray*. 1891. Penguin Classics, 2003.

Williams, Gareth. *The Other Side of the Popular. Neoliberalism and Subalternity in Latin America*. Duke UP, 2002.

Williams, Raymond. *The Country and the City*. Oxford UP, 1973.

DISCOGRAPHY—CORTIJO Y SU COMBO

There is very little documentation on the exact release dates of these albums. Rafael Figueroa Hernández includes a discography in his book on Ismael Rivera, but it docs not provide years, and the albums are definitely not presented in chronological order. The 2010 biography of Ismael Rivera by Moreno-Velázquez proposes a possible chronology, but it curiously misses two important albums in his discography, and he provides no reliable documentation for his chronology. Ángel G. Quintero Rivera's discography in *Cuerpo y cultura* at least provides albums' release numbers so that a chronology of sorts can be reconstructed, but his is not a complete list. The website AmericaSalsa.com provides additional serial numbers for a few albums. Aurora Flores's discography, in an essay on Ismael Rivera, is to date the most comprehensive and complete list, though without release dates. Without a doubt, the group's first album was *Cortijo y su combo Invites You to Dance*—all scholars and biographers agree on this. The CD version of this album actually provides recording dates for each song: all of them were done between October 1955 and April 1957, so it is totally inaccurate to state that this album was released in 1955, as many affirm. That was indeed the year of the recording of "El bombón de Elena," but that was a 78 RPM single release. Donald Clark's online *Encyclopedia of Popular Music* provides years for the albums released under Gema Records; the dates agree at least with the order of the release numbers for those LPs. Their last album, *Los internacionales*, was released in 1962. I have tried to create a chronology based on the release numbers of the albums provided by Flores's and Donald Clark's years. A definitive chronology it is not. (Note: all songs and albums referenced in this book come from the compact discs released decades later.)

Cortijo y su combo Invites You to Dance. Seeco Records, SCLP-9106, c. 1957.

Baile con Cortijo y su combo. Seeco Records, SCLP-9130, c. 1958.

Cortijo y su combo. Seeco Records, SCLP-9160, c. 1958.

Cortijo en New York. Rumba Records, Rumba 55515, 1959 [originally on Gema Records].

Fiesta boricua. Rumba Records, Rumba 55519, 1960 [originally on Gema Records, Gema 1119].

Bueno, y ¿qué? Rumba Records, Rumba 55534, 1960 [originally on Gema Records, Gema 1134].

Quítate de la vía, Perico. Rumba Records, Rumba 55548, 1961 [originally on Gema Records, Gema 1148].

Danger Do Not Trespass. Rumba Records, Rumba 55552, 1961.

Los internacionales. Marvela Records, 1962.

Juntos otra vez. Musical Productions, 1974.

FILMOGRAPHY
CINEMA AND GRAPHICS DIVISION,
PARKS AND RECREATION COMMISSION

Caña. Directed by Jack Delano, c. 1948, 11 min.

Informe al Pueblo No. 1: La obra del gobierno. Directed by Jack Delano, c. 1948, 10 min.

Jesús T. Piñero. Directed by Jack Delano, c. 1948, 25 min.

La voz del pueblo. Directed by Jack Delano, c. 1948, 12 min.

Una gota de agua. Directed by Jack Delano, 1949, 10 min.

DIVISION OF COMMUNITY EDUCATION (DIVEDCO)

Desde las nubes. Directed by Jack Delano, 1950, 37 min.

Doña Julia. Directed by Skip Faust, 1955, 45 min.

El cacique. Directed by Benji Doniger, 1957, 25 min.

El contemplado isla cordillera. Directed by Amílcar Tirado, 1958, 12 min.

El de los cabos blancos. Directed by Willard Van Dyke, script by José L. Vivas Maldonado, 1957, 35 min.

El gallo pelón. Directed by Amílcar Tirado, 1961, 49 min.

El puente. Directed by Amílcar Tirado, 1954, 45 min.

El yugo. Directed by Oscar A. Torres, script by Pedro Juan Soto, 1959, 45 min.

Geña la de Blas. Directed by Luis A. Maisonet, script by José L. Vivas Maldonado, 1964, 45 min.

Ignacio. Directed by Ángel F. Rivera, 1956, 35 min.

Juan sin seso. Directed by Luis Maisonet, script by René Marqués, 1959, 16 min.

La casa de un amigo. Directed by Amílcar Tirado, screenplay by Emilio Díaz Valcárcel, 1963, 38 min.

La guardarraya. Directed by Marcos Betancourt, 1964, 45 min.

Las manos del hombre. Directed by Jack Delano, 1952, 25 min.

Los peloteros. Directed by Jack Delano, assisted by Amílcar Tirado, 1951, 90 min.

Modesta. Directed by Benji Doniger, script by Benjamin Doniger, Luis A. Maisonet, and René Marqués, 1956, 35 min.

¿Qué opina la mujer? Directed by Oscar A. Torres, 1957, 18 min.

Un día cualquiera. Directed by Ángel F. Rivera, script by Pedro Juan Soto, DIVEDCO and Fundacion Puertorriqueña para las Humanidades, 1954/1993.

Un pedacito de tierra. Directed by Benji Doniger, script by Ed Rosskam, 1952, 36 min.

Una voz en la montaña. Directed by Amílcar Tirado, script by René Marqués, 1952, 30 min.

INDEX